ARABIC
AT A GLANCE

PHRASE BOOK & DICTIONARY FOR TRAVELERS

BY HILARY WISE, Ph.D.
Senior Lecturer
Queen Mary College
University of London
Editor, *Palestine News*

Third Edition

BARRON'S

All inquiries should be addressed to:
Barron's Educational Series, Inc.
250 Wireless Boulevard
Hauppauge, New York 11788
www.barronseduc.com

ISBN-13: 978-0-7641-3766-2 (book only)
ISBN-10: 0-7641-3766-2 (book only)
ISBN-13: 978-0-7641-9371-2 (book and CD package)
ISBN-10: 0-7641-9371-6 (book and CD package)

Library of Congress Catalog Card No. 2007043832

Illustrations: Juan Suarez
Typesetting/formatting: ArabScript.com, Tampa, FL.

PRINTED IN CHINA
9 8 7 6 5 4 3 2 1

CONTENTS

PREFACE

So you're taking a trip to a fascinating part of the world. That's exciting! In more ways than one, this new phrase book will prove an invaluable companion that will make your stay far more interesting and truly unforgettable.

This phrase book is part of a comprehensive series from Barron's Educational Series, Inc. In these books we present the phrases and words that a traveler most often needs for a brief visit to a foreign country, where the customs and language are often different. Each of the phrase books highlights the terms particular to that country, in situations that the tourist is most likely to encounter. With a specially developed key to pronunciation, this book will enable you to communicate quickly and confidently in colloquial terms. It is intended not only for beginners with no knowledge of the language, but also for those who have already studied it and have some familiarity with it.

Some of the unique features and highlights of the Barron's series are:

- Easy-to-follow *phonetic pronunciations* for all words and phrases in the book.
- Compact *dictionary* of commonly used words and phrases — built right into this phrase book so there's no need to carry a separate dictionary.
- Useful phrases for the *tourist*, grouped together by subject matter in a logical way so that the appropriate phrase is easy to locate when you need it.
- Special phrases for the *business traveler,* including banking terms, trade and contract negotiations, and secretarial services.
- Thorough section on *food and drink*, with comprehensive food terms you will find on menus; these terms are often difficult or impossible to locate in dictionaries, but our section gives you a description of the preparation as well as a definition of what it is.

■ *Emergency phrases* and terms you hope you won't need: legal complications, medical problems, theft or loss of valuables, replacement or repair of watches, cameras, and the like.

■ *Sightseeing itineraries*, shopping tips, practical travel tips, and regional food specialties to help you get off the beaten path and into the countryside, to the small towns and cities, and to the neighboring areas.

■ A *reference section* providing: expressions of time, days of the week, weather, countries and nationalities, directions, and information on Islamic festivals.

■ A brief *grammar section*, with the basic elements of the language quickly explained.

Enjoy your vacation and travel with confidence. You have a friend by your side.

ACKNOWLEDGMENTS

We would like to thank the following individuals for their assistance on this project: Hala N. Barakat, Hany M. El-Hosseiny, Ashraf Hossein, Ibrahim Gendy, Afaf El-Menoufy, and Eyad Amer; also Dr. Valerie Becker, Anthony Rutgen and Barney Allan of Anthony Rudkin Associates.

INTRODUCTION

There can be few parts of the world where a foreigner's efforts to speak the language are more appreciated than in the Middle East. Even the ability to exchange greetings and express thanks will arouse interest and establish an immediate bond. The wider your knowledge, the warmer your welcome in countries renowned for their hospitality to strangers.

Who Speaks Arabic?

Arabic is spoken by over 200 million people in more than 20 different countries, from Morocco in the west to Iraq in the east, and as far south as Somalia and the Sudan. As the language of the Koran, the holy book of Islam, it is taught as a second language in Muslim states throughout the world. Arabic originated in Saudi Arabia in pre-Islamic times, and spread rapidly in the wake of the Arab conquests from the seventh century. The languages of northern India, Turkey, Iran, Portugal, and Spain are full of words of Arabic origin.

Modern spoken Arabic varies a good deal from country to country, differing as much as, say, Spanish and Italian. The classical, written language has, however, changed little over the centuries, and is the accepted literary language throughout the Arab world.

What Kind of Arabic?

As a visitor to the Middle East you have to decide which kind of Arabic is going to be most useful to you. Although Classical Arabic has a standard form, and carries high prestige, it is primarily a written language, used for all literary purposes; it is only spoken on very formal occasions; for example, when someone is making an official speech. Grammatically it is far more complex than spoken Arabic.

Local dialects are used for all everyday communication, at work and in the home, and will clearly be of more practical use to the average tourist or businessperson. But which of the many dialects should you choose?

Egyptian Arabic

Egypt is at the heart of the Arab world, geographically, historically, and politically. With over 60 million inhabitants, it has by far the highest population of any Arab country, and more than 2 million teachers, doctors, businesspersons, and workers of all kinds are to be found in the wealthier Arab countries. Because Egypt also produces films, songs, and TV series that are immensely popular throughout the Arab world, Egyptian Arabic has acquired a special prestige, and even in remote areas people are familiar with the dialect.

Other Dialects

Egyptian is similar to the dialects of the eastern Mediterranean — Lebanese, Syrian, Palestinian, and Jordanian — and to Sudanese. The dialects of North Africa, from Morocco to Libya, have features in common, as do the dialects of Saudi Arabia and the Gulf. The main differences in pronunciation, and in some key everyday expressions, are outlined on page 211, so that you will have some idea what to expect if you are traveling in the Middle East outside Egypt.

But if you use Egyptian Arabic you will have no problem being understood, and many people will be able to adapt their own accent to help you.

Using the Book

Most of the expressions in the book are given in Egyptian Arabic, using the Western alphabet. Occasionally an alternative is provided, when a different expression is widely used elsewhere. For instance, the Egyptian word for *room* is *'oh-Da*, but **ghur**-*fa* is the usual word in many other Arab countries; both are given, the Egyptian word being listed first: *'oh-Da*/**ghur**-*fa*. If two words are given separated by a comma, they are both equally common in Egyptian.

In addition, a translation is given in literary Arabic, using the Arabic script. This is so you can point to a word or phrase, or circle it in pencil, if you want to make sure you've been understood. Or an Arabic speaker may point to the appropriate phrase if *he* or *she* wants to communicate with *you*. The literary version given here in the Arabic script is not the "high" Classical Arabic of the Koran. It is a simplified variety that should be accessible to speakers who may not have had many years of formal education.

If you are going to point to phrases in the book, it's a good idea to make it clear that you are in fact using Egyptian Arabic (*c**a**-ra-bee* **maS**-*ree*); otherwise it may be assumed that you are learning literary Arabic and people may struggle to use Classical forms in their own speech for your benefit!

You can manage perfectly well *without* learning the Arabic script, though a guide is provided on page 207 for the really ambitious. With a little effort you will be able to decipher simple notices, street names, and the names of shops. The kind of signs you'll encounter most often are given on pages 164–165.

QUICK PRONUNCIATION GUIDE

Most of the sounds of Arabic are similar to sounds used in English; there are just a few that are unfamiliar to English ears. As with any language, a positive approach is much more important than getting the sounds exactly right.

THE VOWELS

SHORT VOWELS		EXAMPLES
a	as in *bat*	**ba**-*lad* (town, country)
e	as in *met*	**ka**-*me-ra* (camera)
i	as in *bit*	*bint* (girl, daughter)
u	as in *book*	**buk**-*ra* (tomorrow)
o	as in *dog*	*do*-**laar** (dollar)

LONG VOWELS		EXAMPLES
aa	as in *father*	**Daa**-*nee* (lamb)
eh	as in *met*, but lengthened	*heht!* (bring!)
ee	as in *feed*	*meen?* (who?)
ey	as in *they*, but lengthened	*feyn?* (where?)
oo	as in *mood*	*shoof!* (look!)
oh	as in *phone*	*yohm* (day)

All these long vowels should be pronounced "pure," with the lips held in the same position throughout (as in Spanish or French).

COMPLEX VOWELS		EXAMPLES
(i.e., where the lips *do* change position)		
ay	as in *try*	*kub*-**bay**-*ya* (glass)
aw	as in *out*	**daw**-*sha* (noise)

THE CONSONANTS

The following consonants are pronounced as in English:
p, b, t, d, f, v, k, g, h, j, l, m, n, s, z, w, y.

Notice that **s** is always as in *see*, never as in *his*, and the **g** is always "hard" as in *good*, never "soft" as in *age*. Also:

■ **l** is the "clear" British English type, rather than the "dark" American sound.

■ **r** is a brief tap of the tongue-tip against the teeth, as in Spanish.

■ **h** may be used in positions in which it doesn't occur in English, such as before consonants. Make it nice and breathy: *ah-lan!* (Hi!). (Exceptions are the sequences **oh** as in *yohm* and **eh** as in *heht!*, which always represent long, pure vowels, not a vowel plus aspirate *h*.)

CONSONANT		EXAMPLES
sh	as in *sheet*	*sheek* (check)
kh	a "soft" **k** sound, as in Scottish *loch*	*kham sa* (five)
gh	a guttural **g** sound, rather like the French *r*	*gha-nee* (rich)
H	a rough, heavily aspirated **h** (as if you've swallowed something hot!)	*Hubb* (love)
q	like **k**, but made further back, so that it has a "darker" quality	*il-quds* (Jerusalem)
' or "	a glottal stop, or catch, found in Cockney and Scottish English, replacing a *t*, as in *bi'er* for "bitter," and *Sco'ish* for "Scottish."*	*ma-"ehs* (size)

* Two symbols are used for this sound because they represent two different sounds in some other dialects; *'a-lam* (pain) and *"a-lam* (pen) sound the same in Egyptian Arabic, but are different in many other varieties. See page 211.

CONSONANT		EXAMPLES
c	made by contracting the muscles at the back of the throat. If you use a glottal stop instead ('), you'll still be understood!	*^cehl!* (great!)

Double Consonants

When the same consonant is written twice, it should be pronounced long. So you should hang on to the *t* in *sit-ta* (six) and the *l* in *"ul-lee* (tell me).

"Heavy" Consonants

There are four "heavy" consonants in Egyptian Arabic, represented in this book by **T**, **D**, **S**, and **Z**. They are like **t**, **d**, **s**, and **z**, except that they are pronounced with loose, lax lip and tongue muscles:

LETTER	EXAMPLES
T	***Tay**-yib* (good, fine)
D	*Deyf* (guest)
S	***Saa**-la* (hall)
Z	*a-**Zunn*** (I think)

These consonants affect the surrounding sounds; as you'll hear from listening to the tape, the whole word will often have a laxer, "heavier" articulation.

Stressed Syllables

The stressed syllables, which are printed in bold type, should be pronounced more loudly and emphatically than the others (think of the difference stress makes in English ***bil**low* versus *be**low***).

It's important to pronounce a long vowel really long (and "pure") in a stressed syllable; for example, *ee* will be longer in *ta-la-teen* (thirty) than in **bin**-*tee* (my daughter).

There is a tendency to drop some unstressed vowels. For example, the first vowel in *khu-**Saa**-ra* (pity) is likely to be dropped in a phrase like *ya kh-**Saa**-ra!* (What a pity!). When one word ends in a vowel and the next begins with one, the second vowel is usually dropped; so **ma**-^c*a is-sa-**leh**-ma* (lit., with peace; good-bye) becomes **ma**-^c*a s-sa-**leh**-ma*.

A "helping" vowel — usually **i** — is often introduced between two words if one word ends in two consonants and the next begins with one:

shuft (I saw) + *mu-**Ham**-mad* (Mohammed) is often pronounced **shuf**-*ti mu-**Ham**-mad*.

Stress usually falls on the penultimate syllable of the word (see *mu-**Ham**-mad* and *is-sa-**leh**-ma*, above). But if the final syllable ends in two consonants, as in *ka-**tabt*** (I wrote), or in a long vowel plus one consonant, as in *ba-**neht*** (girls), or *ta-la-**teen*** (thirty), then this syllable carries the stress.

THE BASICS FOR GETTING BY

The expressions listed below will help you make contact with people, obtain essential information, and express your needs and views. They are the basic building blocks of everyday conversation, which are needed in most situations. Try to learn as many as you can before you leave; you can then combine them freely with words appropriate to each situation as it arises.

Masculine and Feminine

A distinction is often made between the masculine and feminine in Arabic. For instance, to say "How are you?" you'd say *iz-zay-yak?* to a man, but *iz-zay-yik?* to a woman. And if you are a man you'd say *ᶜa-wiz* for "I want," but you'd say *ᶜaw-za* if you're a woman. In this book the feminine forms are given in square brackets.

GREETINGS

Hello!	*ah*-lan!	أهلاً
or	*ah*-lan wa *sah*-lan!	أهلاً وسهلاً
How are you?	*iz-zay-yak? [is-zay-yik]*	ازيك؟
or	*keyf **Heh**-lak?*	كيف حالك؟
	*[keyf **Heh**-lik?]*	
Fine	*kway-yis [kway-yi-sa],*	كويس [كويسة]،
	il-**Ham**-du lil-leh	الحمد لله
or	*bi kheyr*	بخير.
	il-**Ham**-du lil-**leh**	الحمد لله

Pleased to meet you.	*it-shar-raf-na*	تشرّفنا
Good-bye.	*ma-ᶜa s-sa-leh-ma*	مع السلامة

PLEASE AND THANK YOU

Please.	*min faD-lak [minfaD-lik]*	من فضلك
Thank you.	*shuk-ran*	شكراً
Thank you very much.	*'al-fi shukr*	شكراً جزيلاً
You're welcome.	*ᶜaf-wan*	عفواً

COMMON EXPRESSIONS

yes	*'ay-wa*	نعم
no	*la'*	لا
fine, O.K.	*Tay-yib, oh-key*	طيب
There is/are, is/are there?	*fee (?)*	(هل) يوجد/ توجد
There isn't/aren't (any)	*ma feesh*	لا يوجد/توجد
Here you are/do join us/go ahead	*it-faD-Dal [it-faD-Da-lee]*	تفضل/تفضلي
Maybe.	*yim-kin*	يمكن. ربما
Never mind.	*ma-ᶜa-lish*	لا بأس. حصل خير

What a pity!	ya-kh-**Saa**-ra!	يا خسارة!
Honest to God! (protestation)	wal-**laa**-hee! wal-**laah** il ^ca-**Zeem**!	والله العظيم!
Please... (excuse me)	law sa-**maHt**	من فضلك
Sorry.	'**eh**-sif ['**as**-fa]	آسف [آسفة]
Let's go!	**yal**-la	هيا!
Just a minute.	**laH**-Za	لحظة
Wait.	is-**tan**-na	انتظر
That's enough.	kif-**feh**-ya **ki**-da	كفاية
Great! Wonderful!	^c**ehl**! mum-**tehz**!	عال! ممتاز!
Wow! (amazement)	ya s-**lehm**!	شيء عجيب
Look!	shoof! [**shoo**-fee]	انظر [انظري]!
I don't mind, I've no objection.	ma-^can-**deesh** meh-ni^c	ليس عندي مانع
I think (so).	a-**Zun**	أظن
I don't think (so).	ma-**Zun**-nish	لا أظن
I (let's) hope so (God willing).	'in shaa' al-**laah**	إن شاء الله
and	wi	و
but	**leh**-kin	لكن
or	'**aw**	أو

PRONOUNS

I (am) — .	**a**-na — .	أنا —
You (are) — .	**in**-ta [**in**-tee] — .	أنت —
He (is) — .	**huw**-wa — .	هو —
She (is) — .	**hee**-ya — .	هي —
We (are) — .	**iH**-na — .	نحن —
You (pl.) are — .	in-**tum**-ma — .	أنتم —
They (are) — .	**hum**-ma — .	هم —

REQUESTS

Bring me — .	**gib**-lee — .	أحضر لي —
Give me — .	id-**dee**-nee — .	أعطني —
■ this/that one	■ da	هذا
I want — .	^c**a**-wiz [^c**aw**-za]	أريد —
I want to go .	^c**a**-wiz [^c**aw**-za] a-**rooH** — .	أريد أن أذهب —
■ to see — .	■ a-**shoof** — .	أرى —
■ to buy — .	■ ash-**ti**-ree — .	أشتري —
■ to eat — .	■ '**eh**-kul — .	آكل —
■ to drink — .	■ **ash**-rab — .	أشرب —

I don't want — .	*mish **ᶜa**-wiz* [*ᶜawza*] — .	— لا أريد
▪ a lot	▪ *ki-**teer***	كثير
▪ a little	▪ *shway-ya, "a-leel*	قليل
▪ more	▪ *'ak-tar*	أكثر
Is it possible — ? Can you — ?	***mum**-kin* — ?	هل من الممكن —؟
It is possible.	***mum**-kin.*	ممكن
It isn't possible.	*mish **mum**-kin*	مستحيل
Do you know — ?	*ti**ᶜ**-raf* — ? [*ti**ᶜ**-ra-fee* — ?]	هل تعرف —؟
I don't know.	*ma**ᶜ**-rafsh*	لا أعرف

QUESTIONS

Where is/are — ?	*feyn* — ?	أين —؟
Where is the bathroom?	*feyn it-twa-**litt**?*	أين التواليت؟
▪ bus	▪ *il-'u-tu-**bees***	الأوتوبيس
▪ telephone	▪ *it-ti-li-**fohn***	التليفون
What is/are — ?	*'eyh* — ?	ما —؟
What's this/that — ?	*'eyh da?*	ما هذا؟
What's the matter?	*fee 'eyh?*	ماذا جرى؟
When?	*'im-ta?*	متى؟

Why?	*ley?*	لماذا؟
Why not?	*leyh la'?*	لماذا لا؟
Who?	*meen?*	من؟
How?	*iz-zayy, keyf?*	ازي؟ كيف؟
Which — ?	*'an-hee —?*	أي —؟
How much?	*kam? bi kam?*	كم، بكم؟
How many?	*kam?*	كم؟

TIME AND PLACE

here	*hi-na*	هنا
there	*hin-nehk*	هناك
up(stairs)	*foh"*	فوق
down(stairs)	*taHt*	تحت
in(side)	*go-wa*	في الداخل
out(side)	*bar-ra*	في الخارج
near	*"u-ray yib*	قريب
far	*bi-^ceed*	بعيد
now	*dil-wa"-tee*	الآن
later	*ba^c-deyn*	بعد ذلك
soon	*"u-ray-yib*	قريباً
today	*'in-na-har-da/il-yohm*	اليوم

tomorrow	**buk**-ra	غداً
yesterday	'im-**beh**-riH/'ams	أمس
usually	*c*a-**da**-tan	عادةً
never	'**a**-ba-dan	أبداً

COMMUNICATING

Do you speak English?	bi-tit-**kal**-lim [bi-tit-kal-**li**-mee] in-gi-**lee**-zee?	هل تتكلم الانجليزية؟
Does anyone here speak English?	fee-Hadd **hi**-na bi-yit-**kal**-lim in-gi-**lee**-zee?	هل يوجد شخص يتكلم الانجليزية
Do you understand?	fi-**himt** [fi-**him**-tee]?	هل فهمت؟
I don't understand.	mish **feh**-him [**fah**-ma]	لم أفهم
Please speak slowly.	kal-**lim**-nee bir-**raa**-Ha min **faD**-lak	أرجو أن تتكلم على مهلك
I speak a little Arabic.	bat-**kal**-lim *c*a-ra-bee **shway**-ya	أتكلم العربية قليلا
■ Egyptian Arabic	■ *c*a-ra-bee **maS**-ree	اللهجة المصرية
What's — in Arabic?	**tib**-"a 'eyh — bil-*c*a-ra-bee	ما هو — بالعربية؟
Please could you help me?	min-**faD**-lak, **mum**-kin ti-sa-*c***id**-nee?	هل يمكن أن تساعدني؟

Please show me the phrase in the book.	*min faD-lak, war-ree-nee il-gum-la fil-ki-tehb.*	من فضلك أشر إلى الجملة في الكتاب
Please write it down.	*ik-tib-hoo-lee, min faD-lak.*	اكتبه لي، من فضلك

PROBLEMS

Go away!	*im-shee!*	امش!
Leave me alone.	*sib-nee fi Heh-lee.*	اتركني
Behave yourself.	*ᶜeyb, iH-ti-rim naf-sak*	احترم نفسك
Please help me.	*min faD-lak, sa-ᶜid-nee.*	أرجو أن تساعدني
I'm lost.	*a-na tuht.*	ضللت الطريق، تهت
Nonsense.	*ka-lehm feh-righ!*	كلام فارغ!
I'll get the police.	*ha-gib-lak il-bu-leeS.*	سأطلب لك البوليس

SOME USEFUL ADJECTIVES

good, nice	*kway-yis, Tay-yib*	جيد، طيب
beautiful	*Hilw, ga-meel*	حلو، جميل
bad, ugly	*wi-Hish*	سيئ

awful	*fa-Zee*^c	فظيع
expensive	**gheh**-lee	غالي
cheap	ri-**kheeS**	رخيص
old (people)	ki-**beer**	كبير
(things)	"a-**deem**	قديم
new	gi-**deed**	جديد
young, small	Su-**ghay**-yar	صغير
big	ki-**beer**	كبير
noisy	daw-**sha**-gee	صخاب
quiet	**heh**-dee	هادئ
full	mal-**yehn**	مليء
empty	**faa**-Dee, **feh**-righ	فارغ
long, tall	Ta-**weel**	طويل
short	"u-**Say**-yar	قصير
thirsty	^caT-**shaan**	عطشان
hungry	ga-^c**ehn**	جوعان، جائع
tired	ta^c-**behn**	متعب
ill	^cay-**yehn**, ma-**reeD**	مريض
angry, upset	za^c-**lehn**	غاضب
happy, pleased	mab-**SooT**	مبسوط
kind	**Tay**-yib, la-**Teef**	طيب، لطيف
generous	ka-**reem**	كريم
mean	ba-**kheel**	بخيل

easy	*sahl*	سهل
difficult	*Sa^c b*	صعب
correct	*maZ-**booT***	تمام، مضبوط
incorrect	*mish maZ-**booT***	غير مضبوط
early	***bad**-ree*	باكر
late	***wakh**-ree,* *mu-ta-'**akh**-khir*	متأخر

NUMBERS

0	*Sifr*	٠
1	***weh**-Hid*	١
2	*it-**neyn***	٢
3	*ta-**leh**-ta*	٣
4	*ar-**ba**-^c a*	٤
5	***kham**-sa*	٥
6	***sit**-ta*	٦
7	*sub-^c a*	٧
8	*ta-**man**-ya*	٨
9	***tis**-^c a*	٩
10	*^c **a**-sha-ra*	١٠
11	*Hi-**daa**-shar*	١١
12	*it-**naa**-shar*	١٢

13	ta-lat-**taa**-shar	١٣
14	ar-ba^c-**taa**-shar	١٤
15	kha-mas-**taa**-shar	١٥
16	sit-**taa**-shar	١٦
17	sa-ba^c-**taa**-shar	١٧
18	ta-man-**taa**-shar	١٨
19	ti-sa^c-**taa**-shar	١٩
20	^cish-reen	٢٠
21	**weh**-Hid wi ^cish-**reen**	٢١
22	it-**neyn** wi ^cish-**reen**	٢٢
30	ta-la-**teen**	٣٠
40	ar-bi-^c**een**	٤٠
50	kham-**seen**	٥٠
60	sit-**teen**	٦٠
70	sab-^c**een**	٧٠
80	ta-man-**yeen**	٨٠
90	tis-^c**een**	٩٠
100	**mee**-ya	١٠٠
200	mee-**teyn**	٢٠٠
300	tul-tu-**mee**-ya	٣٠٠
400	rub-^cu-**mee**-ya	٤٠٠

500	*khum-su-***mee**-*ya*	٥٠٠
600	*sut-tu-***mee**-*ya*	٦٠٠
700	*sub* ^c*u-***mee**-*ya*	٧٠٠
800	*tum-nu-***mee**-*ya*	٨٠٠
900	*tus-*^c*u-***mee**-*ya*	٩٠٠
1000	*'alf*	١٠٠٠
2000	*'al-***feyn**	٢٠٠٠
3000	***ta**-lat a-***lehf**	٣٠٠٠
4000	***ar**-ba*^c *ta-***lehf**	٤٠٠٠
5000	***kha**-mas ta-***lehf**	٥٠٠٠
6000	*sitt a-***lehf**	٦٠٠٠
7000	*sa-ba*^c *ta-***lehf**	٧٠٠٠
8000	***ta**-man ta-***lehf**	٨٠٠٠
9000	***ti**-sa*^c *ta-***lehf**	٩٠٠٠
10,000	^c***a**-shar ta-***lehf**	١٠٠٠٠
100,000	*meet 'alf*	١٠٠٠٠٠
1,000,000	*mil-***yohn**	١٠٠٠٠٠٠

WHEN YOU ARRIVE

Visitors will need a visa for most Arab countries; these are sometimes obtainable at the point of entry; but it is usually simpler to get them before you leave. If you are touring the Middle East, and expect to come back to the same country, check on the possibility of getting a multiple-entry visa, and also whether you will need an exit visa.

PASSPORT CONTROL

My name is —.	*'is*-mee —.	اسمي —
I'm <u>American</u>	*a-na am-ree-keh-**nee*** [am-ree-keh-**nee**-ya]	أنا أمريكي [أمريكية]
■ British	■ bri-**Taa**-nee [bri-Taa-**nee**-ya]	بريطاني [بريطانية]
■ Canadian	■ **ka**-na-dee [ka-na-**dee**-ya]	كندي [كندية]
■ Australian	■ os-**traa**-lee [os-tra-**lee**-ya]	أسترالي [أسترالية]
My address is —.	ᶜin-weh-nee —.	عنواني —
I'm staying at —.	a-na **neh**-zil [**naz**-la] fi —.	أنا أقيم في —
Here are (is) —.	it-**faD**-Dal —.	تفضل —
■ my documents	■ il-'**aw**-reh"	أوراقي
■ my passport	■ il-bas-**boor**/ ga-**wehz** is-**sa**-far	جواز سفري

■ my identification card	■ *bi-**Ta"**-ti ish-shakh-**see**-ya*	بطاقتي الشخصية
■ my embarkation card	■ *il-bor-ding kard*	بطاقة الصعود
■ my disembarkation card	■ *kart il-wu-**Sool***	بطاقة الوصول
I have (I don't have) a visa.	*ᶜan-de (ma-ᶜan-deesh) **vee**-za*	معي (لا يوجد معي) تأشيرة
I'm (traveling) —.	*da **sa**-far —.*	أنا مسافر [مسافرة]
■ on business	■ *shughl*	في عمل
■ on vacation	■ *'a-**geh**-za*	في عطلة، اجازة
I'll be staying ___.	***ha"**-ᶜud —,*	سأبقى —
■ a few days	■ ***ka**-za yohm*	عدة أيام
■ a week	■ *'is-**boo**ᶜ*	أسبوع
■ a month	■ *shahr*	شهر
I'm traveling <u>alone</u>.	*a-na mi-**seh**-fir [mi-**saf**-ra] li <u>**waH**-dee</u>*	أنا أسافر وحدي
■ with my family	■ *ma-ᶜa ᶜeyl-**teel** 'us-ri-tee*	مع أسرتي
■ with my wife	■ *ma-ᶜa m-**raa**-tee/ **zohg**-tee*	مع زوجتي
■ with my husband.	■ *ma-ᶜa **goh**-zee*	مع زوجي

BAGGAGE AND PORTERS

Where is the baggage claim?	*il-^cafsh **feyn**?*	أين مكان استلام الأمتعة؟
This bag (these bags) are mine.	*ish-**shan**-Ta dee (ish-**shu**-naT dee) bi-**ta**^c-tee*	هذه حقيبتي (حقائبي)
This is mine.	*dee bi-**ta**^c-tee*	هذه لي
Is there a baggage cart?	*fee **trol**-lee?*	هل توجد عربة أمتعة؟
Is there a porter?	*fee shay-**yehl**?*	هل هناك شيال؟
Be careful!	***Heh**-sib!*	احذر!
I'll carry that.	*a-na ha-**sheel** da*	سأحمل هذه الحقيبة
I'm missing one bag.	*fee **shan**-Ta na"-Sa.*	فقدت حقيبة
I have lost my luggage.	*Daa^c **min**-nee il ^cafsh*	فقدت أمتعتي
How much do I owe you?	*^ca-wiz kam?*	كم تريد؟
Thank you.	***shuk**-ran*	شكراً
That's for you.	*da ^ca-la-**sheh**-nak*	تفضل. هذا لك

CUSTOMS

I have nothing to declare.	*a-na fi Hu-**dood** il-mas-**mooH***	أنا في حدود المسموح

I have one carton of cigarettes.	ma-*c*eh-ya khar-Too-shit sa-geh-yir.	معي خرطوشة سجائر
■ two cartons	■ khar-Toosh-*teyn*	خرطوشتـين
I have one bottle <u>of whiskey</u>.	ma-*c*eh-ya "i-*ẓeh*-zit <u>wis-kee</u>	معي زجاجة ويسكي
■ of wine	■ ni-*beet*	نبيد
■ of perfume	■ *c*iTr	عطر
I have nothing else.	ma ma-*c*eesh Ha-ga *tan*-ya	لا يوجد معي شيء آخر
These are gifts.	dee ha-*deh*-ya	هذه هدايا
They are for my personal use.	dee li-'is-ti*c*-meh-lee ish-*shakh*-See	إنها لاستعمالي الشخصي
It isn't new.	dee mish gi-*dee*-da	إنها ليست جديدة
Do I have to pay duty?	leh-ẓim ad fa*c* ga-*meh*-rik?	هل يجب أن أدفع ضريبة؟
Where do I pay?	ad-fa*c* feyn?	أين أدفع؟
Can I pay with dollars?	*mum*-kin ad-fa*c* bid-do-*laar*?	هل يمكن أن أدفع بالدولار؟

Bureaucracy

Dealings with government officials over visas, customs clearance, residence permits, and so on may be slow and frustrating. Showing impatience and irritation usually has an adverse effect, however. Try to get the official(s) on your side by a warm and friendly but courteous approach.

Make use of any contact you have in the office or Ministry, however tenuous. Ideally, go with someone who is familiar with the procedures involved. If a particular bureaucratic process is known to take forever, take along a stack of postcards to write or a book to read.

OTHER AIRPORT INFORMATION

Can I book a hotel room from here?	*mum*-kin *aH*-giz *'oh*-Da/ghur-fa min-*hi*-na?	هل أستطيع حجز غرفة بفندق من هنا؟
Is there a post office in the airport?	fee *mak*-tab ba-*reed* fil-ma-*Taar*?	هل يوجد مكتب بريد في المطار؟
Is there a bank open?	fee bank *feh*-tiH?	هل يوجد بنك مفتوح؟
Can I make a phone call from here?	*mum*-kin a^c -mil ti-li-*fohn* min *hi*-na?	هل أستطيع إجراء مكالمة من هنا؟
Where can I rent a car?	mi-*neyn* a-'ag-gar ^{c}a-ra-*bee*-ya/ say-yaa-*ra*?	من أين أستطيع استئجار سيارة؟

GETTING INTO TOWN

Where can I get a taxi?	a-*leh*-"ee *tak*-see feny?	أين أجد تاكسي؟
Is there a meter?	fee ^{c}ad-*dehd*?	هل يوجد عداد؟
Is there a bus into town?	fee 'u-tu-*bees* li wiST il-*ba*-lad?	هل يوجد أوتوبيس لوسط المدينة؟

Where is the stop?	il-ma-**Hat**-Ta feyn?	أين المحطة؟
When does it leave?	bi-**yiT**-la^c 'im-ta?	متى يرحل؟
How much will it cost?	ha-**yeh**-khud kam?	كم الأجرة؟
How long does it take?	ir-**riH**-la bi-**teh**-khud "ad-di 'eyh?	ما مدة الرحلة؟
I want to go to the — Hotel.	^ca-wiz [^caw-za] a-**rooH** 'u-teel —.	أريد الذهاب إلى فندق —
I want to go to this address.	^ca-wiz [^caw-za] a-**rooH** il-^cin-**wehn** da.	أريد الذهاب إلى هذا العنوان
I'm with a group.	**a**-na ma-^ca mag-**moo**-^ca.	أنا مع مجموعة

PERSONAL SAFETY

Most parts of the Middle East are perfectly safe for foreigners; the major cities have large numbers of foreign residents who have lived there happily for years, and the tourist areas welcome millions of visitors every year.

Countries like Egypt, Morocco, and Tunisia, that depend heavily on the tourist trade, are especially vigilant when it comes to security. (Egypt provides armed escorts in areas that have seen incidents in the past.) You will find the locals in such places all the more anxious to make you feel welcome.

It is, however, a wise precaution to check on the current situation before you leave. The U.S. State Department offers advice to travellers on www.travel.state.gov. The British government provides up-to-date information at www.fco.gov.uk (then) Travel Advice by Country. Common sense rules about not wandering alone at night, or wearing expensive jewelry in the street, apply in this region, as elsewhere.

BANKING AND MONEY MATTERS

The basic currencies in the major Arab countries are as follows:

dinar *(dee-naar)*: Iraq, Algeria, Tunisia, Jordan, Libya, Bahrain, and Kuwait.

riyal *(ree-yehl)*: Saudi Arabia, Yemen, Oman, Qatar.

gineh (gi ney): Egypt and the Sudan.

lira *(lee-ra)*: Syria and Lebanon.

dirham *(dir-ham)*: Morocco and the United Arab Emirates.

These are, of course, all independent currencies. They are all further divided into a hundred units. In Egypt a **gineh** is made up of 100 **piastres** ("irsh), which is also the smaller unit of currency in Lebanon. Sometimes the smaller unit is further divided; in Egypt one piastre is worth 10 **millimes** *(mil-leem)*. In Jordan there are 1,000 **fils** *(fils)* to the dinar.

Sometimes paper money is used for very small denominations, being worth as little as a few cents.

Check on currency regulations before you leave; often there are restrictions on taking local currency out of the country. It may be necessary to prove you have spent a certain amount during your stay, so keep receipts of all exchange transactions.

bank	*bank*	بنك
branch	*far^c*	فرع
exchange	*taH-**weel**, Sarf*	تحويل، صرف
When do you <u>open</u>?	<u>*bi-tif-ta-Hoo* 'im-ta?</u>	متى تفتحون؟

Is that the official rate?	*da is-si^cr ir-ras-mee?*	هل هذا السعر الرسمي؟
Is there a black market rate?	*fee si^cr soo" soo-da?*	هل يوجد سعر سوق سوداء؟
Do I fill out a form?	*leh-zim am-la 'is-ti-maa-ra?*	هل يجب أن أملأ استمارة؟
Where do I sign?	*am-Dee feyn?*	أين أمضي؟
Here's my passport.	*it-faD-Dal il-bas-boor/ ga-wehz is-sa-far.*	تفضل ها هو جواز السفر
I'd like to change <u>100</u> dollars.	^c*a-wiz a-ghay-yar <u>meet</u> do-laar*	أريد تحويل ١٠٠ دولار
■ 200	■ *mee-teyn*	٢٠٠
■ 300	■ *tul-tu-meet*	٣٠٠
■ 400	■ *rub-^cu-meet*	٤٠٠
■ 500	■ *khum-su-meet*	٥٠٠
■ 600	■ *sut-tu-meet*	٦٠٠
■ 700	■ *sub-^cu-meet*	٧٠٠
■ 800	■ *tum-nu-meet*	٨٠٠
■ 900	■ *tus-^cu-meet*	٩٠٠
■ 1000	■ *'alf*	١٠٠٠
■ into local currency	■ *lil-^cum-la l-ma-Hal-lee-ya*	للعملة المحلية

Can you give me small bills? | ***mum**-kin tid-**dee**-nee* *'aw-**reh**" Su-ghay-**ya**-ra* | هل تستطيع أن تعطيني أوراق صغيرة؟

■ large bills? | ■ *'aw-**reh**" ki-**bee**-ra?* | أوراق كبيرة

■ some small change? | ■ ***fak**-ka?* | فكة

(see page 17 for numbers)

AT THE HOTEL

The usual international hotels are to be found in the major cities, at international prices. More interesting places to stay are the few remaining grand hotels of a more leisurely era, such as the Cecil in Alexandria and the Old Cataract in Aswan. But with the help of the local tourist office you can find a room in any price range; generally speaking, you will get what you pay for.

CHECKING IN

Do you have a room?	*^can-du-kum 'oh-Da/ghur-fa?*	هل عندكم غرفة؟
I have a reservation.	*^can-dee Hagz.*	حجزت
I have no reservation.	*ma-^can-deesh Hagz.*	لم أحجز
I'd like a single room.	*^ca-wiz [^caw-za] 'oh-Da/ghur-fa bi si-reer weh-Hid*	أريد غرفة مفردة
I'd like a double room.	*^ca-wiz [^caw-za] 'oh-Da/ghur-fa lit-neyn.*	أريد غرفة مزدوجة
I'd like a room <u>with twin beds</u>.	*^ca-wiz [^caw-za] 'oh-Da bi si-ree-reyn.*	أريد غرفة بسريرين
▪ with a shower	▪ *fee-ha dush*	بها دش
▪ with a bathroom	▪ *bi Ham-mehm*	بحمام
▪ with a TV	▪ *fee-ha ti-li-viz-yohn*	بها تليفزيون

with a refrigerator	*fee*-ha tal-*leh*-ga	بها برادة/ثلاجة
with a balcony	*fee* bal-*koh*-na	لها بلكون/شرفة
with air conditioning	*fee*-ha tak-*yeef ha* wa	بها مكيف هواء
with hot water	*fee*-ha *may*-ya *sukh*-na	بها ماء ساخن
with a good view	*min*-ha *man*-Zar ga-*meel*	مطلة على منظر جميل
(not) facing the street	(mish) ^ca-la-sh-*sheh*-ri^c	(غير) مطلة على الشارع
facing the garden	^ca-la g-gi-*ney*-na	مطلة على الحديقة
on the sea	^ca-la l-*baHr*	على البحر
Can you try another hotel for me?	*mum*-kin ti-*shuf*-lee 'u-*teel* teh-*nee*?	هل تستطيع أن تـبـ لي ندقا آخرا؟
May I see the room?	*mum*-kin a *shoof* il-'oh-Da/il-*ghur*-fa?	أريد أن أرى الغرفة؟
I like it.	^ca-ga-*bit*-nee.	تعجبني
I don't like it.	ma ^ca-ga-bit-*neesh*	لا تعجبني
Can I see another?	*mum*-kin a-*shoof* 'oh-Du tan-ya?	هل أستطيع أن أرى غرفة أخرى؟
larger	'aw-sa^c	أوسع
smaller	'aS-ghar	أصغر
quieter	'ah-da	أهدأ

■ cheaper	■ *'ar-khaS*	أرخص
■ better	■ *'aH-san*	أفضل
This is nice.	*dee kway-yi-sa.*	هذه جيدة
I'll take it.	*ha-khud-ha.*	سآخذها
What floor is it on?	*dee fee an-hee dohr?*	في أي طابق هي؟
Is there an elevator?	*fee 'a-sn-Seer?*	هل يوجد مصعد/أسنسير؟
What's the rate?	*il-'oh-Da bi kam?*	كم السعر؟
Does it include <u>services</u>?	*da bil-khid-ma?*	هل يشمل الخدمة؟
■ taxis	■ *biD-Da-raa-yib*	الضرائب
■ breakfast	■ *bil-fi-Taar*	الإفطار
How much is <u>bed and breakfast</u>?	*bi kam il-'oh-Da bil-fi-Taar*	كم السعر بالإفطار؟
■ full board (3 meals)	■ *bil-'akl*	للإقامة الكاملة
Is there a reduction for children?	*fee takh-feeD lil-'aT-faal?*	هل يوجد تخفيض للأطفال؟
Can you put another bed in the room?	*mum-kin ti-HuTT si-reer teh-nee fil-'oh-Da?*	هل تستطيع وضع سرير آخر في الغرفة؟
I will stay <u>one night</u>.	*ha"-^cud <u>ley-la waH-da</u>*	سأبقى ليلة واحدة
■ two nights	■ *leyl-teyn*	ليلتين

a few days	*ka-za yohm*	عدة أيام
a week	*'is-boo^c*	أسبوع
two weeks	*'is-boo-^c eyn*	أسبوعين

BREAKFAST

I'd like breakfast in the room.	*^c a-wiz [^c aw-za] il-fi-Taar fil-'oh-Da.*	أريد الإفطار بالغرفة
for one	*li weh-Hid*	لشخص واحد
for two	*li 'it-neyn*	لشخصين
Please send up —.	*min faD-lak gib lee —.*	أرجو أن ترسل —
coffee	*"ah wa*	قهوة
tea	*shayy*	شاي
toast	*tust*	خبز محمص. توست
(with jam/ honey)	*(bil-mi-rab-ba/ bil-^c a-sal)*	(بالمربى/ بالعسل)
fruit juice	*^c a-Seer*	عصير الفاكهة
eggs	*beyD*	بيض
(scrambled/ fried/boiled)	*(maD-roob/ ma"-lee/mas-loo")*	(مضروب/مقلي/ مسلوق)
an English language newspaper	*ga-ree-da in-gi-lee-zee*	جريدة باللغة الانجليزية

HOTEL SERVICES

Where is the elevator?	*feyn il-'a-san-Seer?*	أين المصعد/ الأسنسير؟
▪ the bathroom	▪ *it-twa-litt*	التواليت
▪ the restaurant	▪ *il-maT-ᶜam*	المطعم
▪ the phone	▪ *it-ti-li-fohn*	التليفون
▪ the bar	▪ *il-baar*	البار
▪ the swimming pool	▪ *Ham-mehm is-si-beh-Ha*	حمام السباحة
I need a chambermaid.	*ᶜa-wiz [ᶜaw-za] shagh-gheh-la.*	أحتاج لخادمة الغرفة
▪ a bellboy	▪ *far-raash*	لفراش
▪ a hair dryer	▪ *sish-waar*	مجفف الشعر
▪ a reading lamp	▪ *a-ba joo-ra*	مصباح للقراءة
The room is dirty.	*il-'oh-Da wis-kha.*	الغرفة قذرة
There are mosquitoes.	*fee na-moos.*	يوجد ناموس
Please spray the room.	*rush-shi-lee l-'oh-Da min faD-lak*	أرجو أن ترش الغرفة
Please bring me towels.	*min faD-lak gib-lee fo-waT.*	أرجو أن تحضر لي مناشف، فوط
▪ soap	▪ *Sa-boon*	صابون
▪ a pillow	▪ *mi-khad-da*	مخدة

■ a blanket	■ *baT-Ta-nee-ya*	بطانية
■ ice	■ *talg*	ثلج
■ mineral water	■ *may-ya ma^c-da-nee-ya*	مياه معدنية
■ hangers	■ *sham-ma-^ceht*	شماعات
■ toilet paper	■ *wa-ra" twa-litt*	ورق تواليت
■ an adaptor	■ *mu-Haw-wil*	محول
■ a light bulb	■ *lam-ba*	لمبة
■ (bath) plug	■ *sad-deh-da*	سدادة
■ (electric) plug	■ *fee-sha*	فيشة
Just a minute!	*laH-Za waH-da!*	لحظة واحدة!
Come in!	*ud-khul!*	ادخل!
Thank you. Put it here.	*shuk-ran. HuT-Too hi-na*	شكراً ضعها هنا
Please put a board under the mattress.	*min faD-lak HuTT lohH taHt il-mar-ta-ba*	أحتاج للوح تحت المرتبة
There is no <u>hot water</u>.	*fa-feesh may-ya (sukh-na)*	لا يوجد ماء ساخن
■ electricity	■ *kah-ra-ba*	كهرباء
The <u>air conditioning</u> isn't working.	*it-tak-yeef ^caT-laan.*	لا يعمل التكييف
■ toilet	■ *it-twa-litt*	التواليت
■ faucet	■ *il-Ha-na-fee-ya*	الصنبورا الحنفية

■ light	■ in-**noor**	النور
■ radio	■ irr-**ra**-dyo	الراديو
■ TV	■ it-ti-li-viz-**yohn**	التليفزيون
Can you fix it <u>soon</u>?	**mum**-kin ti-Sal-**la**-Hoo <u>bi-**sur**-^ca</u>?	هل تستطيع إصلاحه سريعا؟
Is there <u>satellite TV</u>?	fee ti-li-viz-**yohn** <u>sa-ti-layt</u>?	هل يوجد تليفزيون بالقمر الصناعي؟
■ cable TV?	■ **key**-bil?	كابل؟
Are there English-language channels?	fee qa-na-**weht** bil-'in-gi-**lee**-zee?	هل هناك قنوات بالانجليزية؟
Can you open this?	**mum**-kin tif-**taH**-lee da?	هل تستطيع فتح هذا لي؟
I have lost my key.	il-muf-**tehH** Daa^c **min**-nee.	ضاع المفتاح مني
This is to be <u>laundered</u>.	da <u>lil-gha-**seel**</u>.	هذا للغسيل
■ pressed	■ lil-**mak**-wa	للكي
When will it be ready?	hay-**koon** geh-hiz 'im-ta?	متى سيكون جاهزأ؟
Are there any <u>messages</u> for me?	fee <u>ri-**seh**-la</u> ^ca-sheh-nee?	هل هناك رسائل لي؟
■ letters	■ ga-wa-**beht**	خطابات
■ packages	■ Tu-rood	طرود

Can you make a phone call for me?	*mum*-kin *tuT*-**lub**-lee ti-li-**fohn?**	هل تستطيع أن تطلب مكالمة لي؟
I want to speak <u>to Mr. —</u>.	*ca*-wiz [*c*aw-za-] a-*akal*-lim <u>is-**say**-yid —</u>.	أريد أن أتكلم مع السيد —
▪ to Mrs. —.	▪ *ma*-**dehm** —.	— السيدة
Please give me an outside line.	*id*-**dee**-nee il-**khaTT** min *faD*-lak.	أرجو أن تعطني خطاً خارجياً
Do you have a fax machine?	*c*an-**du**-kum *ma*-ka-nit **faks.**	هل عندكم جهاز فاكس؟
I want to send a fax.	*c*a-wiz[*c*aw-za] *ab*-*c*at faks.	أريد أن أرسل فاكس.
This isn't legible.	*da mish* **waa**-DiH.	هذا ليس واضحًا
I'd like to put this in your safe.	*c*a-wiz [*c*aw-za] a-**HuTT** dee fil-**khaz**-na.	أريد أن أضع هذا في الخزنة
I'd like my things from your safe.	*c*a-wiz [*c*aw-za] 'eh-khud il-ha-**geht** bit-*tu*c-tee min il-**khaz**-na.	أريد أشيائي من الخزنة من فضلك

CHECKING OUT

I'm leaving <u>today</u>.	*a*-na mi-**seh**-fir [mi-**saf**-ra] <u>in-na-**haar**-da/il-**yohm**</u>.	سأرحل اليوم
▪ tomorrow (morning)	▪ **buk**-ra (iS-**SubH**)	غداً (صباحاً)

I'd like the bill, please	*id-**dee**-nee il-Hi-**sehb** min **faD**-lak.*	أريد الحساب. من فضلك.
My room number is —.	*il-'**oh**-Da nim-ra —.*	رقم غرفتي —
There seems to be a mistake.	*fee gha-laT*	يبدو هناك خطأ
What is this amount for?	*il-**mab**-lagh da ᶜa-shehn 'eyh?*	لماذا هذا المبلغ؟
Please check it again.	*law sa-**maHt** reh-giᶜ ᶜa-leyh teh-nee.*	أرجوك راجعها ثانية
Can I leave my luggage here till <u>noon</u>?	***mum**-kin a-**seeb** ish-shu-naT hi-na li Hadd <u>iD-**Duhr**</u>?*	هل أستطيع ترك أمتعتي هنا حتى الظهر؟
▨ evening	▨ *il-mi-seh'*	المساء
Please have my luggage brought down.	*min **faD**-lak **naz**-zil ish-**shu**-nat*	أرجوك أنزل أمتعتي
I'm in a hurry.	*a-na mis-**taᶜ**-gil [mis-**taᶜ**-gi-la]*	أنا مستعجل [مستعجلة]
Please call a cab.	*min **faD**-lak uT-**lub**-lee tak-**see**.*	أرجوك أطلب تاكسي
I'm going to the airport.	*a-na reh-yiH [ray-Ha] il-ma-**Taar**.*	أنا ذاهب إلى المطار

OTHER ACCOMMODATIONS

I want to rent <u>a house</u>.	*^ca wiz [^caw-za] a-'ag-gar beyt.*	أريد استئجار بيت
■ an apartment	■ *sha"-"a*	شقة
■ an (un)furnished apartment	■ *sha"-"a (mish) maf-roo-sha*	شقة (غير) مفروشة
■ a furnished room	■ *'oh-Da/ghur-fa maf-roo-sha*	غرفة مفروشة
■ a houseboat	■ *^caw-weh-ma*	عوامة
Do you know a good boarding house?	*ti^c-raf pin-si-yohn kway-yis?*	هل تعرف بنسيون جيداً؟
Do you know know a good real estate agent?	*ti^c-raf sim-saar kway-yis?*	هل تعرف سمساراً جيداً؟
I need <u>one (two) bedroom(s)</u>.	*^cu-wiz [^caw-za] 'oh-Dit- ('ohT-teyn) nohm.*	أريد غرفة (غرفتين نوم)
■ a living room	■ *'oh-Dit gu-loos*	غرفة جلوس
■ a good bathroom	■ *Ham-mehm-kway-yis*	حمام جيد
How much is it <u>per week</u>?	*kam fil-'is-boo^c?*	كم إيجارها في الأسبوع؟
■ per month	■ *fish-shahr*	في الشهر
■ per year	■ *fis-sa-na*	في السنة

I'll be staying <u>two weeks</u>.	ha"-^cud '<u>is-boo-^ceyn</u>	سأبقى أسبوعين
■ one month	■ shahr	شهر
■ two months	■ shah-reyn	شهرين
■ (about) three months	■ (Ha-weh-lee) ta-lat-tush-hur	(حوالي) ثلاثة أشهر
Do you need a deposit?	^ca-wiz ^car-boon?	هل تحتاج لمقدم؟
Shall I pay in dollars?	ad-fa^c bid--do-laar?	هل أدفع بالدولار؟
Do you take key money?	bi-teh-khud khu-luww?	هل تريد وديعة/ خلو؟
Can I use the kitchen?	mum-kin as-ta^c-mil il-maT-bakh?	هل أستطيع استعمال المطبخ؟
Is there hot water?	fee may-ya sukh-na?	هل هناك ماء ساخن؟
Is there a <u>refrigerator</u>?	fee tal-leh-ga?	هل هناك ثلاجة؟
■ a freezer	■ free-zar	فريزر
Is there a youth hostel in town?	fee beyt sha-behb fil-ba-lad?	هل هناك بيت شباب في المدينة؟
Can I park the car here?	mum-kin ar-kin il-ca-ra-bee-ya hi-na?	هل أستطيع ترك السيارة هنا؟
Can I leave it here overnight?	mum-kin a-bay-yit-ha hi-na?	هل أستطيع ترك السيارة هنا ليلاً

Do you have a meter?	*ᶜan-dak ᶜad-dehd?*	هل عندك عداد؟
How much do you charge per day?	*bi-teh-khud **kam** fil-yohm?*	كم الأجرة اليومية؟
I want to go and come back.	*ᶜa-wiz [ᶜaw-za] a-rooH war-gaᶜ.*	أريد الذهاب والعودة
Will you wait for me here?	*mum-kin tis-tan-neh-nee hi-nehk?*	هل ستنتظرني هناك؟
Slow down!	*ᶜa-la **mah**-lak!*	قلل السرعة!
Please wait here a moment.	*is-**tan**-na **hi**-na shway-ya*	من فضلك انتظر هنا لحظة
I will be right back.	*har-gaᶜ **Heh**-lan.*	سأعود حالاً
Turn <u>left</u> here.	*Haw-wid shi-mehl hi-na*	إلى اليسار هنا
▪ right	▪ *yi-meen*	إلى اليمين
Straight on.	*dugh-ree.*	إلى الأمام
Stop here.	*'u-"af hi-na.*	قف هنا
I'll get out here.	*han-zil hi-na.*	سأنزل
How much do I owe you?	*ᶜa-wiz kam?*	كم تريد؟
Thanks. That's for you.	*shuk-ran. da ᶜa-la-sheh-nak.*	شكراً. هذا لك
Please tell me where to get off.	*min faD-lak "ul-lee an-zil feyn.*	أرجوك قل لي أين أنزل

SIGHTSEEING

Because the Arabic-speaking countries span such a vast area, each offers different attractions to the traveler. In North Africa, Morocco and Tunisia have the most developed tourist industries. A holiday there can combine relaxing on superb beaches with visits to medieval walled cities and to ancient Greek and Roman sites, or trips into the dramatic Atlas Mountains. Recently, Libya has been opening up to tourism: its Roman sites are the best preserved — but still the least visited — in the world.

At the eastern end of the Mediterranean, in Syria, Jordan, and Lebanon, you will find some of the most spectacular monuments of the ancient world and of Islamic civilization, as well as marvelous swimming off the Mediterranean and Red Sea coasts. Though political turmoil in the area has discouraged foreign visitors, the intrepid traveler will be well rewarded. Not only will people be delighted to see you and want to show you the best of their country, you will be blissfully free of the hype and hassle that popular tourist centers tend to attract.

Egypt is understandably the Arab country best known to the foreign tourist. It has literally hundreds of miles of unspoiled beaches on its Mediterranean and Red Sea coasts; the coral reefs of the Red Sea and Sinai Peninsula offer some of the best snorkeling and scuba diving in the world.

Most visitors with limited time to spend will want to concentrate on the great temples, pyramids, and tombs of the Nile Valley. The daily flights from Cairo to Luxor and Aswan, as well as comfortable trains, make it easy to stop off at lesser-known sites en route. Or you can travel one way by Nile steamer, the best of which retain an old-world elegance and charm.

Travel facilities in Egypt are being improved all the time, so that it is now possible to combine visits to the major Pharaonic monuments with trips to the chain of oases in the Western Desert and to Sinai in the east, where the famous Greek

Orthodox monastery of St. Catherine stands at the foot of Mount Sinai. This *can* all be done in a couple of weeks, but it is much more rewarding to take a little longer, to rest up in a quiet corner, absorb your impressions of the country, and get to know the people.

The main tourist centers offer accommodations ranging from the absolutely basic to international five-star standard. In the oases and smaller coastal resorts accommodations will be inexpensive and simple, if not Spartan.

In the Gulf, Dubai has been marketing itself very successfully as a winter destination for luxurious beach holidays, which also include golf — and unlimited shopping opportunities.

Where is the Tourist Office?	*mak-tab is-si-yeh-Ha feyn?*	أين مكتب السياحة؟
Do you have tourist information?	ᶜ*an-du-kum is-ti*ᶜ*-la-meht si-yeh-Hee-ya?*	هل عندكم معلومات سياحية؟
Do you have a guidebook?	ᶜ*an-du-kum da-leel si-yeh-Hee?*	هل عندكم دليل سياحي؟
Are there tours of the city?	*fee riH-leht si-ya-Hee-ya fil-ba-lad?*	هل هناك جولات في المدينة؟
When does the bus leave?	*bi-yiT-la*ᶜ *'im-ta il-'u-tu-bees?*	متى سيرحل الأوتوبيس؟
Where does it leave from?	*il-ma-HaT-Ta feyn?*	من أين سيرحل الأوتوبيس؟
How much does it cost?	*bee-kal-lif kam?*	كم تكلف؟
How long does it take?	*ha-yeh-khud kam seh-*ᶜ*a?*	ما مدة الجولة؟

What are the main attractions?	'eyh 'a-hamm il-'a-meh-kin is-si-yeh-Hee-ya?	ما هي أهم الأماكن السياحية؟
I have only <u>one day</u>.	^can-dee <u>yohm</u> bass.	لم يبق لي إلا يوم واحد
■ two days	■ yoh-meyn	يومين
■ three days	■ ta-lat tee-yehm	ثلاثة أيام
■ one week	■ 'is-boo^c	أسبوع
I need a guide with good English.	^ca-wiz [^caw-za] da-leel bi-yit-kal-im in-gi-lee-zee kway-yis.	أحتاج لمرشد يتكلم الانجليزية بطلاقة
How much does he charge <u>per hour</u>?	bi-yeh-khud kam <u>fis-seh-^ca</u>?	كم يطلب في الساعة؟
■ per day	■ fil-yohm	في اليوم
I want to go to <u>the Islamic Museum</u>.	^ca-wiz [^caw-za] a-rooH <u>il-mat-Haf il-is-leh-mee</u>.	أريد أن أذهب إلى المتحف الاسلامي
■ the Egyptian Museum	■ il-mat-Haf il-maS-ree	المتحف المصري
■ Khan ElKhalili bazaar	■ khan il-kha-lee-lee	خان الخليلي
■ the Azhar mosque	■ geh-mi^c il-'az-har	جامع الأزهر
■ the Sultan Hasan mosque	■ geh-mi^c is-sul-Taan Ha-san	جامع السلطان حسن
■ the Citadel	■ il-"al-^ca	القلعة

■ the pyramids	■ *il-ha-ram*	الهرم
■ the zoo	■ *gi-ney-nit il-Ha-ya-wa-neht*	حديقة الحيوانات
■ the market, bazaar	■ *is-soo"*	السوق
■ the old city	■ *il-ma-dee-na*	المدينة القديمة
■ Sakkara	■ *saq-qaa-ra*	سقارة
■ Fayyoum	■ *il-fay-yoom*	الفيوم
■ the Valley of the Kings	■ *weh-di l-mu-look*	وادي الملوك
■ the Temple of Luxor	■ *ma^c-bad lu"-Sur*	معبد الأقصر
■ the Temple of Hatshepsut	■ *ma^c-bad Hat-ship-soot*	معبد الملكة حتشبسوت
■ Abu Simbel	■ *'a-boo sim-bil*	أبو سمبل
mosque	*geh-mi^c*	جامع
monuments, antiquities	*il-'a-saar*	الآثار
temple	*ma^c-bad*	معبد
tomb	*maq-ba-ra*	مقبرة
Can I enter?	*mum-kin ad-khul?*	هل يمكن أن أدخل؟
At what time does it open?	*bi-yif-taH is-seh-^ca kam?*	متى يفتح؟
When does it close?	*bi-yi"-fil is-seh-^ca kam?*	متى يغلق؟

Is it open every day?	*bi-**yif**-taH **kul**-li yohm?*	هل يفتح كل يوم؟
What is the admission price?	*'eyh si^cr id-du-khool?*	كم رسم الدخول؟
How much for children?	*bi kam lil-'aT-**faal**?*	كم رسم دخول الأطفال؟
Do you know a good restaurant near here?	*ti^c-raf **maT**-^cam **kway**-yis "u-**ray**-yib min **hi**-na?*	هل تعرف مطعماً جيداً قريباً من هنا؟
Is photography allowed?	*it-taS-**weer** mas-**mooH**?*	هل التصوير مسموح؟
Do I need a permit?	***leh**-zim taS-**reeH**?*	هل أحتاج لتصريح؟
I have a permit from the Ministry.	*ma-^ceh-ya taS-**reeH** min il-wi-**zaa**-ra.*	معي تصريح من الوزارة
Let's rest and have a drink.	*nis-ta-**ray**-yaH wi **nish**-rab Ha-ga.*	فلنستريح ونشرب شيئاً
Can you pick us up in one hour exactly?	***mum**-kin tir-ga^c-**li**-na ba^cd <u>**seh**-^ca</u> biZ-ZabT?*	هل تستطيع أن ترجع لنا هنا بعد ساعة بالضبط؟
▦ two hours	▦ *sa^c-**teyn***	بعد ساعتين

MOSQUES

Some of the most beautiful and historic buildings to be found in the Middle East are mosques; you will certainly want to visit a number on your trip.

Attitudes toward non-Muslim visitors vary a good deal. Many famous mosques, such as Ibn Tulun and AlAzhar in Cairo, are recognized as national monuments as well as places of worship, and it is easy to visit them as long as you are suitably dressed. Often, however, visitors are not admitted to some parts of the mosque while prayers are in progress. Check whether photography is permitted (you may have to leave your camera at the door).

The mosque is the social as well as the religious center of the community; in the early days of Islam especially all important public announcements were made from the pulpit (***min**-bar*) Schools (*mad-**ra**-sa*) have always been associated with mosques, primarily to teach the Koran but also reading, writing, and arithmetic. A feature of the **geh** *mi*^{c}, or congregational mosque, is the large inner courtyard, where prayer or teaching may take place; this is usually absent from the smaller ***mas**-gids*, less monumental but often gems of Islamic architecture.

At the entrance to most mosques is a place to leave your shoes. Ask there whether it is all right to go in. Apart from removing your shoes, be sure you are properly dressed: shorts and halter tops are not acceptable. A skirt should cover the knee, and arms should be covered to the elbow. It is appreciated if women wear a headscarf.

Don't disturb anyone who is praying, and avoid walking between them and the ***mih**-rab* (niche) indicating the direction of Mecca. On leaving, you may want to put a contribution in the offerings box, which will go toward the upkeep of the mosque.

PLANNING A TRIP

TRAVEL BY AIR

When is there a flight to Aswan?	*Tay-yaa-rit <u>'aS-waan</u> 'im-ta?*	متى تكون الرحلة إلى أسوان؟
■ to Luxor	■ *lu"-Sur*	إلى الأقصر
■ to Sinai	■ *see-na*	إلى سيناء
I'd like a single (one-way) ticket.	*^ca-wiz [^caw-za] taz-ka-ra reh-yiH bass*	أريد تذكرة ذهاب
■ a return ticket	■ *taz-ka-ra reh-yiH gayy*	تذكرة ذهاب وعودة
I want to <u>cancel</u> my reservation.	*^ca-wiz [^caw-za] <u>al-ghee</u> il-Hagz*	أريد إلغاء الحجز
■ confirm	■ *a-'ak-kid*	تأكيد الحجز
When should I be at the airport?	*leh-zim a-koon fil-ma-Taar 'im-ta?*	متى يجب أن أكون بالمطار؟
I'd like a seat —.	*^ca-wiz [^caw-za] kur-see —.*	أريد مقعداً —
■ by the window	■ *gamb ish-shib-behk*	بجانب الشباك
■ on the aisle	■ *^cal-ma-marr*	على الممر
Tourist class	*da-ra-ga si-yeh-Hee-ya*	درجة سياحية
First class	*da-ra-ga 'oo-la*	درجة أولى

Business class	*da-ra-git il-'a^c-mehl*	درجة الأعمال

Business class | *da-ra-git il-'a^c-mehl* | درجة الأعمال

Business class	*da-ra-git il-'a^c-mehl*	درجة الأعمال
What is the fare?	*bi kam it-taz-ka-ra?*	بكم التذكرة؟
Can I pay by credit card?	*mum-kin ad-fa^c bi kri-dit kard?*	هل أستطيع الدفع ببطاقة اعتماد؟
Is there an <u>earlier</u> flight?	*fee ma-^cehd <u>bad-ree</u> shway-ya?*	هل هناك رحلة قبل هذا الموعد
■ later	■ *mit-'akh-khar*	بعد هذا الموعد
Is there a daily flight?	*fee Tay-yaa-ra kul lı yohm?*	هل هناك رحلة يومية؟
When does it arrive?	*bi-tiw-Sal 'im-ta?*	متى تصل؟
Where do I check my bags?	*a-sag-gil ish-shu-naT feyn?*	أين أسجل حقائبي؟
I have only hand luggage.	*ma-^ceh-ya shu-naT yad bass.*	ليس معي حقائب يد
What gate do we leave from?	*bi-nu-khrug min 'an-hee behb?*	من أي بوابة سنرحل؟

TRAVEL BY TRAIN AND BUS

Where is the ticket office?	*shib-bekh- it-ta-zeh-kir feyn?*	أين مكتب بيع التذاكر؟
May I see a schedule?	*mum-kin a-shoof gad-wal il-ma-wa-^ceed?*	هل أستطيع أن أرى جدول المواعيد؟

When does <u>the bus</u> to Alexandria leave?	_il-'-tu-bees_ lis-kin-di-ree-ya bi-yiT-la^c 'im-ta?	متى يرحل الأوتوبيس إلى الاسكندرية؟
■ the train	■ il-"aTr	القطار
Is there a student rate?	fee takh-feeD liT-Ta-la-ba?	هل يوجد تخفيض للطلبة؟
I have a student card.	ma-^ceh-ya kar-ney Taa-lib.	معي بطاقة طالب
Does it take the desert road?	bi-yeh-khud iT-Ta-ree" iS-SaH-reh-wee?	هل يأخذ الطريق الصحراوي؟
Does it stop en route?	bi-yu-"af fis-sik-ka?	هل يقف على الطريق؟
I'd like a seat at the front.	^cas-wiz [^caw-za] kur-see "ud-dehm.	أريد مقعداً في المقدمة
Are the seats numbered?	ik-ka-reh-see ^ca-ley-ha ni-mar?	هل المقاعد مرقمة؟
<u>A first class</u> ticket, please.	taz-ka-ra da-ra-ga-'oo-la, min faD-lak.	أريد تذكرة درجة أولى من فضلك
■ second class	■ da-ra-ga tan-ya	درجة ثانية
Two tickets, please.	taz-kar-teyn, min faD-lak.	تذكرتين من فضلك
Which platform?	ra-Seef nim-ra kam?	ما هو رقم الرصيف؟
I'd like <u>a berth (couchette)</u> to Luxor.	^ca-wiz [^caw-za] ma-kehn fi ^ca-ra-bee-yit in-nohm li lu"-Sur.	أريد مكاناً بعربة النوم إلى الأقصر

■ two berths (couchettes)	■ ma-ka-**neyn**	مكانين
Is it air-conditioned?	fee tak-**yeef**?	هل هو مكيف الهواء؟
Where is the checked luggage office?	feyn **mak**-tab il-'a-ma-**neht**?	أين مكتب الامانات؟
Is this <u>the train</u> for Asyut?	da "**aTr** 'as-**yooT**?	هل هذا قطار أسيوط؟
■ the bus	■ 'u tu **bees**	أوتوبيس
Is there a <u>dining car</u> on the train?	fee ^ca-ra-**bee**-yit 'akl fil-"**aTr**?	هلَ هناك عربة طعام في القطار؟
■ a buffet car	■ bu-**feyh**	بوفيه
What do you have <u>to eat</u>?	^can dak '**ak** li 'eyh?	ما هي أنواع الأكل عندكم؟
■ to drink	■ mash-roo-**beht**	المشروبات
Is this seat taken?	fee Hadd **hi**-na?	هل هذا المقعد محجوز؟
Can I change to first class?	**mum**-kin a-ghay-**yar**-ha li **da** ra ga '**oo** la?	هل أستطيع أن أغير للدرجة الأولى؟
Where are we now?	**iH**-na **feyn** dil-wa"-tee?	أين نحن الآن؟
What's the next stop?	'eyh il-ma-**HaT**-Ta g-**gay**-ya?	ما هي المحطة القادمة؟

TRAVEL BY BOAT

I'd like to take a boat —.	*ᶜa-wiz [ᶜaw-za]* **'eh**-khud **mar**-kib —.	أريد أن آخذ سفينة
■ from Cairo to Luxor.	■ *min maSr li lu"-Sur*	من القاهرة للأقصر
■ from Luxor to Aswan	■ *min lu"-Sur li-'aS-waan*	من الأقصر لأسوان
I want to return by air.	*ᶜa-wiz [ᶜaw-za]* ar-gaᶜ biT-Tay-**yaa**-ra.	أريد العودة بالطائرة
How long does the cruise take?	*ir-**riH**-la bi-teh-khud kam yohm?*	ما مدة الرحلة؟
I would like a cabin <u>for one</u>.	*ᶜa-wiz [ᶜaw-za]* ka-**bee**-na <u>li waH-dee</u>.	أريد حجرة/ كابينة لشخص واحد
■ for two people	■ *lit-**neyn***	لشخصين

Does it have a private bathroom?	*fee-ha Ham-mehm khaSS?*	هل لها حمام خاص؟
Where does it stop?	*bi-tu-"af feyn?*	أين تتوقف؟
Is there a <u>ferry</u>?	*fee mi-^cad-dee-ya?*	هل هناك عبارة/ معدية؟
■ hydrofoil	■ *hay-dro-feel*	هيدروفيل
What time do we have to be back on board?	*leh-zim nir-ga^c lil-mar-kib is-seh-^ca kam?*	متى يجب أن نعود إلى السفينة؟
I'd like to take a sailboat ride —.	*ca-wiz [^caw-za] 'eh-khud fa-loo-ka —.*	أريد أن أذهب في نزهة على مركب شراعي
■ around the island	■ *Hu-wu-leyn ig-gi-zee-ra*	حول الجزيرة
■ across the river	■ *lin-naH-ya t-tan-ya*	عبر النهر
■ for a couple of hours	■ *li mud-dit sa^c-teyn*	لمدة ساعتين
When will we get back?	*ha-nir-ga^c 'im-ta?*	متى سنعود؟
Is the wind right?	*ir-reeH mu-nas-ba?*	هل الرياح مناسبة؟

OTHER MODES OF TRANSPORT

Where does the river bus leave from?	*feyn ma-HaT-Tit il-'u-tu-bees in-nah-ree?*	أين محطة الأوتوبيس النهري؟

Can I take a streetcar/tram?	*mum*-kin '*eh*-khud tur-*maay*?	هل أستطيع أن آخذ الترام؟
Can I take a microbus?	*mum*-kin '*eh*-khud mee-kro-bus?	هل أستطيع أن آخذ ميكروبس؟
Can I hitchhike from here?	*mum*-kin *ar*-kab oh-toh-stop min *hin*-na?	هل أستطيع ركوب سيارة مارة من على الطريق؟
Could you give me a lift to —?	*mum*-kin ti waS-*Sal*-nee li —?	هل تستطيع توصيلي إلى —؟
Where can I get a shared taxi to —?	mi-*neyn* '*eh*-khud tak-see mush-*ta*-rak li —?	أين آخذ تاكسي مشترك (تاكسي بالنفر) إلى —؟
I'd like to hire —.	*ᶜa*-wiz [*ᶜaw*-za] a-'*ag*-gar —.	أريد استئجار —
■ a motorbike/ scooter	■ mo-to-*sikl*	دراجة بخارية
■ a bicycle	■ *ᶜa*-ga-la	دراجة
■ a horsedrawn carriage	■ Han-*Toor*	حنطور
■ a donkey	■ Hu-*maar*	حمار
■ a camel	■ ga-mal	جمل

ENTERTAINMENT AND DIVERSIONS

BEACH AND POOL

I love swimming.	ba-**Hibb** il-*c*ohm.	أحب السباحة
It's very hot.	id-**dun**-ya Harr **gid**-dan	الجو حار جداً
Is there a swimming pool?	fee Ham-**mehm** si-beh-Ha?	هل يوجد حمام سباحة؟
Is there a sandy beach?	fee plehj raml?	هل يوجد شاطئ رملي؟
The water's beautiful.	il-**may** ya Hil-wa **gid**-dan.	المياه جميلة
Is it safe to swim?	il-*c*ohm hi-na 'a-**mehn**?	هل السباحة مأمونة هنا؟
Is it deep?	il-**baHr** hi-na *c*a-**mee"**?	هل المياه عميقة هنا؟
Are there sharks?	fee "u-**roosh**?	هلو توجد أسماك القرش؟
I'd like to go scuba diving.	*c*a-wiz [*c*aw-za] agh-Tas.	أريد أن أغطس
Do they give diving lessons?	fee du-**roos** ghaTs?	هل هناك دروس غطس؟
I want to buy a mask.	*c*a-wiz [*c*aw-za] ash-ti-ree naD-**Daa**-rit baHr.	أريد شراء قناع

■ a snorkel	■ *payp*	أنبوبة للتنفس تحت الماء
■ flippers	■ *za-ᶜeh-nif*	زعانف
■ suntan lotion	■ *kreym li Hi-meh-yit il-bash-ra*	كريم لحماية البشرة
■ sunglasses	■ *naD-Daa-rit shams*	نظارات شمس
■ a sunhat	■ *bur-ney-Tit shams*	قبعة شمس
■ a swimsuit	■ *ma-yoh*	لباس بحر/مايوه
■ a beach towel	■ *foo-Tit baHr*	منشفة شاطئ
■ an inflatable mattress	■ *mar-ta-bit baHr*	مرتبة بحر
I want to go <u>waterskiing</u>.	*ᶜa-wiz [ᶜaw-za] <u>at-zaH-la" ᶜ al-may-ya</u>.*	أريد التزحلق على الماء
■ windsurfing	■ *ᵃc-mil wind-surf*	ركوب الأمواج
How much is it an hour?	*bi kam fis-seh-ᶜa?*	كم في الساعة؟
I'd like to rent an <u>umbrella</u>.	*ᶜa-wiz [ᶜaw-za] a-'ag-gar shams-see-ya*	أريد استئجار شمسية
■ a deck chair	■ *kur-see baHr*	كرسي شاطئ
■ a surfboard	■ *lohH ru-koob il-'am-wehg*	لوح ركوب الأمواج
■ skin diving equipment	■ *'a-da-weht ghaTs*	أدوات الغوص

Is there a diving club?	fee **neh**-dee ghTs?	هل يوجد نادي غوص؟
shells	**Sa**-daf	أصداف
coral	mur-**gehn**	مرجان
coral reefs	**shu**-ᶜab mur-ga-**nee**-ya	شعب مرجانية
crabs	a-boo ga-**lam**-boo, ka-**boor**-ya	أبو جلمبو، سرطان البحر
sponges	sa-**fing**	إسفنج
Is swimming forbidden?	is-si-**beh**-Ha mam-**noo**-ᶜa?	هل السباحة ممنوعة؟
Will you keep an eye on my things?	**mum** kin ti-**khal**-li **beh**-lak min il-Ha-**geht** dee?	هل ترعى أشيائي؟
Is there a lifeguard?	fee ghuT-**Tuus**?	هل هناك عامل إنقاذ/غطاس؟

SAILING AND FISHING

I'd like to hire a sailboat.	ᶜa-wiz [ᶜaw-za] a-'ag-gar **mar**-kib shi-raa-ᶜee.	أريد استئجار مركب شراعي
■ a motorboat	■ lansh	قارب بخاري
■ a yacht	■ yakht	يخت
I want to spend the whole day on the water.	ᶜa-wiz [ᶜaw-za] a-"aD-Dee yohm keh-mil fil-**baHr**.	أريد قضاء يوم كامل في البحر

Let's take a picnic.	**neh-khud il-'akl ma-^ceh-na.**	دعنا نقوم بنزهة
the Mediterranean	**il-baHr il-'ab-yaD**	البحر الأبيض المتوسط
the Red Sea	**il-baHr il-'aH-mar**	البحر الأحمر
the Atlantic	**il-'aT-lan-Tee**	المحيط الأطلنطي
The sea is very <u>rough</u>.	**il-baHr <u>heh-yig</u> gid-dan.**	البحر هائج جداً
■ calm	■ **heh-dee**	هادئ
I don't feel very well.	**a-na Heh-sis [Has-s] in-nee ta^c-behn [ta^c-beh-na]**	أنا متعب
Let's head back to shore.	**nir-ga^c lil-barr.**	فلنرجع إلى الشاطئ
Is there a boat race?	**fee si-beh" ma-reh-kib?**	هل هناك سباق مراكب؟
I'd like to go fishing —.	**^ca-wiz [^caw-za] aS-Taad —.**	أريد الذهاب لصيد الأسماك —
■ with rod and line	■ **biS-Sin-naa-ra**	بصنارة صيد
■ with nets	■ **bish-sha-ba-ka**	بالشباك
Can I come with you?	**mum-kin a-rooH ma-^ceh-kum?**	هل أستطيع الذهاب معكم؟
What bait should I use?	**as-ta^c-mil Ta^cm 'eyh?**	ما الطعم الذي سأستعمله؟

Did you have a good catch?	*iS-Tad-too kway-yis?*	هل وفقت في الصيد؟
What's the name of this fish?	*is sa mak d 'is-moo 'eyh?*	ما اسم هذه السمكة؟

HUNTING

What do you hunt in this area?	*bi-tiS-**Taa**-doo 'eyh fil-man-**Ti**-"a dee?*	ماذا تصطادون في هذه المنطقة؟
I would like to go hunting in the desert.	*ᶜa-wiz [ᶜaw-za] aS-**Taad** fiS-**SaH**-ra.*	أريد أن أصطاد في الصحراء
Can I rent a shotgun?	*mum kin a-'ag-gar bun-du-"ee-yit rashsh?*	هل أستطيع استئجار بندقية رش؟
■ a rifle	■ *bun-du-"ee-yit Seed*	بندقية صيد
Do I need a permit?	*leh-zim taS-reeH?*	هل أحتاج لتصريح؟
Are there rabbits?	*fee 'a reh-nib?*	هل هناك أرانب
■ partridges	■ *Ha-gal*	حجل
■ pigeons	■ *Ha-mehm*	حمام
■ deer	■ *gha-zehl*	غزال
■ foxes	■ *ta-ᶜeh-lib*	ثعالب
Do you go hunting with hawks?	*bi-tiS-**Taa**-doo biS-Su-"oor?*	هل تصطاد بالصقور؟

Can you give me some cartridges?	**mum**-kin tid-**dee**-nee kha-ra-**Teesh**?	هل يمكنك أن تعطيني بعض الخراطيش؟

RIDING AND RACING

I'd like to hire <u>a horse</u>.	^ca-wiz [^caw-za] a-'**ag**-gar Hus-**Saan**.	أريد استئجار حصاناً
■ a camel	■ **ga**-mal	جمل
Let's go riding in the desert.	**yal**-la **nir**-kab kheyl fiS-**SaH**-ra.	فلنركب الخيل في الصحراء
I need some riding lessons.	^ca-wiz [^caw-za] du-**roos** ru-**koob** il-**kheyl**.	أحتاج لبعض الدروس في الفروسية
How much is <u>a lesson</u>?	<u>id-**dars**</u> bi kam?	بكم الدرس؟
■ a series of lessons	■ mag-**moo**-^cit du-**roos**	مجموعة دروس
This horse is <u>lazy</u>.	il-Hu-**Saan** da <u>kas-**lehn**</u>.	هذا الحصان كسول
■ bad-tempered	■ **shi**-ris	شرس
I want a <u>quiet</u> horse.	^ca-wiz [^caw-za] Hu-**Saan** <u>heh-**dee**</u>	أريد حصاناً هادئاً
■ lively	■ na-**sheeT**	نشيط
Is there a racecourse near Cairo?	fee **mal**-^cab si-beh" gam il-qaa-**hi**-ra?	هل هناك ميدان سباق قريب من القاهرة؟

When are the races?	*fee si-beh" 'im-ta?*	متى تجري السباقات؟
Are there camel races?	*fee si-beh" lig-gi-mehl?*	هل هناك سباق للجمال؟
Is betting allowed?	*ir-ri-hehn mas-mooH?*	هل الرهان مسموح؟

TENNIS, SQUASH, AND GOLF

Is there a tennis court here?	*fee **mal-cab ti-nis** hi-na?*	هل يوجد ملعب تنس هنا؟
■ a squash court	■ *mal-cab skwash*	ملعب إسكواش
Is it a private club?	*da **neh-dee khaaS?***	هل هذا نادي خاص؟
Do I have to be a member?	*leh-zim a-koon cuDw?*	هل يجب أن أكون عضواً؟
Can I rent a racquet and balls?	*mum-kin a-'ag-gar maD-rab wi ko-war?*	هل يمكن أن أستأجر مضرباً وكوراً؟
Would you like a game?	*ca-wiz [caw-za] til-cab [til-cah-bee]?*	هل تريد أن تلعب معي؟
Is there a golf course nearby?	*fee **mal-cab golf** "u-ray-yib?*	هل يوجد ملعب جولف قريب؟
Can I become a temporary member?	*mum-kin ab-"a cuDw mu-wa"-"at?*	هل يمكن أن أصبح عضواً مؤقتاً؟
Can I rent golf clubs?	*mum-kin a-'ag-gar ma-Daa-rib golf?*	هل يمكن أن أستأجر مضارب جولف؟

CAMPING

Is there a camp site near here?	*fee* mu-**khay**-yam si-yeh-**Hee** "u-**ray**-yib?	هل يوجد مخيم سياحي قريب
Can we spend the night here?	**mum**-kin ni-beht **hi**-na?	هل يمكن أن نبيت هنا؟
Is there <u>drinking water</u>?	*fee* <u>**may**-yit shurb</u>?	هل توجد مياه للشـرب؟
■ a grocery store	■ *ba"-"ehl*	محل بقالة
Are there <u>showers</u>?	*fee* <u>du-**sheht**</u>?	هل توجد دشات؟
■ toilets	■ *twa-**litt***	تواليت
Can we do some washing here?	**mum**-kin **nigh**-sil **hin**-na?	هل يمكن أن نغسل هنا؟

SOCCER

I'd like to see a soccer match.	^c*a-wiz [^caw-za]* a-**shoof** matsh koh-ra.	أريد أن أرى مباراة كرة القدم
Where is the match?	il-**matsh** feyn?	أين ستجري المباراة؟
When does it begin?	bi-yib-**ti**-dee 'im-ta?	متى تبدأ؟
Can you get tickets?	**mum**-kin ti-**gib**-lee ta-**zeh**-kir?	هل تستطيع أن تشتري تذاكرلي؟
Is it an international match?	da matsh **daw**-lee?	هل هي مباراة دولية؟
Who is playing?	**meen** il-lee bi-yil-^cab?	من يلعب؟

When is the Cup Final?	*ni-**heh**-'ee il-**kehs** '**im**-ta?*	متى يكون نهائي الكأس؟
Who won (the Cup)?	***meen keh** sib (il kehs)?*	س كسب (الكأس)؟
Who do you support?	*bit-**shag**-ga^c [bit-shag-ga-^cee] meen?*	أي فريق تشجع؟
What is the score?	*in-na-**tee**-ga-kam?*	ما هي النتيجة؟
It was a draw.	*kehn ta-^ceh-dul.*	كانت تعادل
Foul!	*fawl!*	خطأ!
Goal!	*gohn!*	هدف!
Will it be shown on television?	*hay-**gee**-boo fit-til-li-vis-**yohn**?*	هل ستذاع في التليفيزيون؟
Are they a famous team?	*dee fir-"a mash-**hoo**-ra?*	هل هذا الفريق مشهور؟

INDOOR ENTERTAINMENT

Do you play <u>chess</u>?	*til-^cab [til-^ca-bee] sha-Ta-**rang**?*	هل تلعب الشطرنج؟
■ backgammon	■ *Taw-la*	الطاولة
■ roulette	■ *ru-litt*	الروليت
■ poker	■ *poh-kar*	البوكر

■ blackjack	■ **blak**-jak	البلاك جاك
■ pool	■ bil-**yar**-du	البلياردو
Is gambling allowed?	il-"u-**maar** mas-**mooH**?	هل القمار مسموح؟
Do you have <u>videos</u>?	^can-dak <u>vi-dyo-heht</u>?	هل عندك أفلام فيديو؟
■ video games	■ 'al-^cehb vid-yo	ألعاب فيديو
■ a home computer	■ kam-**byoo**-tar man-**zi**-lee	كمبيوتر منزلي
How many TV channels are there?	fee kam qa-**naat** ti-li-vis-**yohn**?	كم قناة تليفزيونية عندكم؟
Is this an <u>Egyptian</u> serial?	da mu-**sal**-sal **maS**-ree?	هل هذا مسلسل مصري؟
■ American/ English	■ am-ri-**keh**-nee/ in-gi-**lee**-zee	أمريكي/انجليزي
What's on at the movies?	fee 'af-**lehm** 'eyh fis-**si**-ni-ma?	ماذا يعرض في السينما؟
Is there an <u>open air</u> cinema?	fee si-ni-ma <u>**Sey**-fee</u>?	هل توجد دار عرض صيفية؟
■ air-conditioned	■ mu-**kay**-ya-fa	مكيفة
Is it an <u>Egyptian</u> film?	da film **maS**-ree?	هل هذا فلم مصري؟
■ American/ English	■ am-ri-**keh**-nee/ in-gi-**lee**-zee	أمريكي/انجليزي

Is it dubbed <u>in English?</u>	*da mu-da-blaj bi-lin-gi-lee-zee?*	هل هو مترجم إلى الانجليزية؟
■ in Arabic	■ *bil-^ca ra bee*	إلى العربية
Is it subtitled in English?	*da mu-tar-gam bi-lin-gi-lee-zee?*	هل عليه ترجمة انجليزية؟
What time does the show <u>begin</u>?	*il-^carD bi-yib-ti-dee 'im-ta?*	متى يبدأ العرض؟
■ end	■ *bi-yin-ti-hee*	ينتهي
Can I book seats (now)?	*mum-kin aH-giz ka-reh-see (dil-wa"-tee)?*	هل أستطيع حجز الأماكن (الآن)؟
We would like to go to <u>the theater</u>.	*^caw-zeen ni-rooH il-mas-raH.*	نريد الذهاب للمسرح
■ the opera	■ *il-'o-bi-ra*	للأوبرا
■ the ballet	■ *il-ba-ley*	للباليه
■ folk dancing	■ *ir-ra"S ish-sha^c-bee*	لرقص شعبي
■ a concert	■ *Haf-la mu-si-qee-ya*	لحفل موسيقي
Is it Western or Oriental music?	*il-mu-si-qee-ya ghar-bee ya wal-la shar-"ee ya?*	هل هي موسيقى غربية أم شرقية؟
That singer is very famous isn't he (she)?	*il-mu-ghan-nee da [il-mu-ghan-nee-ya dee] mash-hoor [mash-hoor-ra] gid-dan, mish ki-da?*	هذا المغني (المغنية) مشهور(ة) جداً، أليس كذلك؟

What's his (her) name?	*'is*-moo [*'is*-**ma**-ha] *'eyh*?	ما اسمه (اسمها)؟
I'd like to go to a nightclub.	^c*a*-wiz [^c*aw*-za] a-**rooH** mal-ha **lay**-lee	أريد الذهاب إلى ملهى ليلي
Which <u>club</u> has good belly dancing?	an-hee <u>mal-ha</u> fee ra"S **ba**-la-dee **kway**-yis?	في أي ملهى يوجد رقص شرقي جيد؟
■ restaurant	■ *maT-^cam*	مطعم

Is there an <u>Oriental</u> cabaret?	*fee ka-ba-rey shar-"ee?*	هل هناك كباريه شرقي؟
■ Western-style	■ *ghar-bee*	غربي
Can you get us a table near the dance floor?	*mum-kin ti-leh-"ee-lee Ta-ra-bey-za gamb il-beest?*	هل تستطيع أن تجد لنا طاولة قريبة من حلبة الرقص؟
When does the floor show start?	*il-ᶜarD bi-yib-ti-dee 'im-ta?*	متى يبدأ العرض؟
Is there a disco-theque in the hotel?	*fee dis-ko fil-'u-teel?*	هل يوجد ديسكو في الفندق؟
It's very crowded.	*da zaH-ma gid-dan.*	إنه مزدحم جداً
I'd like to go home.	*ᶜa-wiz [ᶜaw-za] a-raw-waH.*	أريد العودة إلى المنزل
I'd like to go back to the hotel.	*ᶜa-wiz [ᶜuw-za] a-raw-waH lil-'u-teel.*	أريد العوده إلى الفندق

EATING OUT

Part of the fun of your trip will be experimenting with Middle Eastern cuisine — one of the most subtle and varied in the world. The dishes mentioned here are to be found in most Arab countries, though each has its own regional specialties.

In North Africa, couscous *(kus-ku-see)*, fine grains of semolina, steamed, forms the basis for many dishes, whereas further east rice and beans are the staple food. Meat is served either charcoal-grilled or braised slowly in the oven. Because most Arab countries border an ocean, seafood is abundant.

Lunchtime is from about one o'clock till three, dinner from eight till eleven. This means you can — in theory! — sleep off your lunch in the hottest part of the day, and make the most of the cool of the evening.

lunch	*il-**gha**-da*
dinner	*il-ca-sha*

Big hotels serve Western as well as local dishes, and French and Italian restaurants are to be found in most major cities. Cairo offers an incredible range, from Hungarian to Japanese, whereas in the Gulf you will have the chance to try excellent Indian food. American-style chicken and hamburger restaurants and take-outs are becoming increasingly popular throughout the region.

Good guidebooks, a helpful receptionist, or a tourist information office will direct you to the restaurants where local people go for a really good meal. These will often specialize in grilled meat, fish, or chicken and pigeon. Lower-priced restaurants specialize in a range of meatless dishes, served at tiny tables on tin plates; they are inexpensive and friendly places where you are likely to be engaged in conversation by your neighbors.

Do you know a good restaurant?	*ti^c-raf maT-^cam kway-yis?*	هل تعرف مطعماً جيداً؟
I want to eat <u>local</u> food.	*^ca-wiz [^caw-za] 'eh-kul 'akl ma-**Hal**-lee.*	أريد أن آكل أكلاً محلياً
■ Oriental	■ *shar-"ee*	شرقي
■ Western-style	■ *ghar-bee*	غربي
I'm looking for a <u>French</u> restaurant.	*ba-**daw**-war ^ca-la maT-^cam fa-ran-**seh**-wee.*	أبحث عن مطعم فرنسي
■ Italian	■ *ee-Tal-**yeh**-nee*	إيطالي
■ Indian	■ *hin-dee*	هندي
I want to have lunch at —.	*^ca-wiz [^caw-za] at-**ghad**-da fi —.*	أريد العداء في —
I want to dine at —.	*^ca-wiz [^caw-za] at-^cash-sha fi —.*	أريد العشاء في —
Is it expensive?	*da **geh**-lee?*	هل هو غالٍ؟
How much (roughly) for two people?	*"ad-di '**eyh** (ta"-**ree**-ban) li shakh-**Seyn**?*	كم تقريباً لشخصين؟

AT THE RESTAURANT

My name is —.	*'is-mee —.*	اسمي —
I have (haven't) a reservation.	*^can-dee (ma-^can-**deesh**) hagz.*	(ليس) لي حجز

I'd like a table <u>for four</u> please.	^c**a**-wiz [^c**aw**-za] Ta-ra-**bey**-za <u>li 'ar-ba-^ca</u> min faD-lak.	أريد طاولة لأربعة من فضلك
■ for two	■ li-'it-**neyn**	لشخصين
Waiter!	mitr!	جرسون!
Could I have the menu, please?	id-**dee**-nee il-**min**-yu min faD-lak.	أعطني قائمة الطعام من فضلك
What do you recommend?	'eyh '**aH**-san 'aT-**baa''** ^can-du-kum?	ماذا تقترح؟
Is it fresh?	da **Taa**-za?	هل هو طازج؟
Is it spicy?	da **Heh**-mee?	هل هو متبل (حار)؟
I'm a <u>vegetarian</u>.	a-na na-**beh**-tee [na-ba-**tee**-ya]	أنا نباتي
vegan	ma-ba-**kulsh** 'ay-yi man-tu-**geht** Ha-ya-wa-**nee**-ya	لا آكل أية منتجات حيوانية

SOMETHING TO DRINK

In Saudi Arabia and some of the countries in the Gulf, alcohol is prohibited; in others the sale of alcohol is strictly limited during Ramadan. But in most countries in the Middle East, beer, wine, and spirits are available. In North Africa, Egypt, and Lebanon, wine is produced locally, the best-known labels being Gianaclis in Egypt and Ksara in Lebanon. Local beers tend to be light lagers.

International hotels will have a wide range of alcoholic drinks, and open-air *casinos* or cafés catering to a middle-class clientele will probably serve beer. Many neighborhood restaurants will, however, be "dry."

Do you have —?	^can-du-kum —?	هل عندكم — ؟
■ beer	■ bee-ra	بيرة
■ wine	■ ni-beet	نبيذ
■ whiskey	■ wis-kee	ويسكي
■ arak	■ ^ca-ra"	عرق
■ soft drinks	■ Ha-ga sa"-^ca	مشروبات غير روحية
■ fruit juice	■ ^ca-Seer	عصير
■ mineral water	■ may-ya ma^c-da-nee-ya	مياه معدنية
Do you have any (fresh) <u>fruit juice</u>?	^can-du-kum ^ca-seer (Taa-za)?	هل عندكم عصير طازج؟
■ orange juice	■ ^ca-Seer bur-tu-"aan	عصير برتقال
We'd like some red/white wine.	^caw-zeen ni-beet 'aH-mar/'ab-yaD.	نريد نبيذاً أحمر/ أبيض
What is the best local wine?	'eyh 'aH-san ni-beet ma-Hal-lee?	ما هو أفضل نبيذ محلي؟
a bottle (two bottles) <u>of wine</u>.	"i-zeh-zit ("iz-zehz-teyn) ni-beet.	زجاجة (زجاجتين) نبيذ
■ of beer	■ bee-ra	بيرة
cold beer	bee-ra sa"-^ca	بيرة مثلجة
a glass	kub-bay-ya	كأس
a glass of wine	kub-bay-yit ni-beet	كأس نبيذ
with ice	bi talg	بثلج
without ice	min gheyr talg	بدون ثلج

TRAVEL TIP

Mineral Water is inexpensive and easily obtainable throughout the Middle East. It is better not to risk the tap water, though tempting glasses of iced water will be served automatically with almost any order in a café or restaurant. Remember, the ice will be made from tap water, even in many international hotels.

Tea — especially mint tea — is both safe and more thirst-quenching than sweet carbonated drinks.

GENERAL REQUESTS

Please bring <u>some bread</u>.	min *faD*-lak *gib*-lee ^ceysh/khubz	أرجوك أحضر لي خبزاً
■ Oriental bread	■ khubz *ba*-la-dee	خبز عربي
■ a napkin	■ man-*deel*	منديل
■ a glass	■ kub-*bay*-ya	كأس
■ butter	■ *zib*-da	زبدة
■ a plate	■ *Ta*-ba"	طبق
■ a spoon	■ ma^c-*la*"a	ملعقة
■ a knife	■ sik-*kee*-na	سكينة
■ a fork	■ *shoh*-ka	شوكة
■ toothpicks	■ sal-la-*keht*	أعواد لتنظيف الأسنان
■ salt and pepper	■ malH wi *fil*-fil	ملح وفلفل
We'd like more —.	^caw-*zeen* — ka-*mehn*.	نريد — أكثر

What desserts do you have?	^c*an-**du**-kum* *Hal-la-wee-**yeht** 'eyh?*	ما هي أنواع الحلوى عندكم؟

If you're not satisfied try these phrases:

I didn't order this.	*ma Ta-lab-**toosh**.*	لم أطلب هذا
This isn't properly cooked.	*da **mish** mis-**ti**-wee.*	هذا ليس ناضجاً
This is overdone (dry).	*da **neh**-shif.*	هذا زائد النضج
This is cold.	*da **beh**-rld.*	هذا بارد
I want to speak to <u>the headwaiter</u>.	^c*a-wiz [^caw-za]* *a-kal-lim il-**mitr**.*	أريد أن أكلم مدير غرفة الطعام
◼ the manager	◼ *il-mu-**deer***	المدير
Do you have any appetizers?	^c*an-**du**-kum **maz**-za?*	هل عندكم مزة؟

UNDERSTANDING THE MENU

Appetizers

The Middle East is famous for the variety of its *mezza*, snacks such as dips, pickles, cheese, and olives served either as appetizers to the main course or with drinks.

The best-known creamy dips, a specialty of Middle East cuisine, are:

dips (in general)	*sa-la-**Taat***	سلطات
tahina (pureed chick-peas and sesame seed paste)	*Ta-**Hee**-na*	طحينة
hummus (pureed chick-peas)	***Hum**-muS*	حمص
baba ghanoush (roast eggplant [aubergine] with tahina)	***ba**-ba ghan-**noog***	بابا غنوج
foul (broad beans, pureed and seasoned)	*fool*	فول
yogurt and cucumber dip with garlic	***la**-ban za-**beh**-dee bil-khi-**yaar***	لبن زيادي بالخيار

The best way of eating these is with Oriental bread *(khubz **ba**-la-dee)*.

Other appetizers include:

stuffed vine leaves	***wa**-ra" ᶜi-nab*	ورق عنب
fish roe	*ba-**Taa**-rikh*	بطارخ
olives	*zey-**toon***	زيتون
herring	***rin**-ga*	رنجة

cracked wheat with parsley, onion, and tomato	*tab-**boo**-la*	تبولة
pickles	***Tur**-shee, ma-**kha**-lil*	طرشي/ مخلل

Soups

soup	***shur**-ba*	شربة
vegetable soup	***shur**-bit khu-**Daar***	شربة خضار
onion soup	***shur**-bit **ba**-Sal*	شربة بصل
lentil soup	***shur**-bit ^{c}ads*	شربة عدس
fish soup	***shur**-bit **sa**-mak*	شربة سمك
consommé with noodles	***shur**-bit shi^c-**ree**-ya*	شربة شعرية
mulukhiyya (spinach-like vegetable soup served with rice and meat)	*mu-lu-**khee**-ya*	ملوخية

Salads

salad	*sa-la-Ta*	سلطة
mixed salad	*sa-la-Ta **khaD**-ra*	سلطة خضراء
tomato salad	*sa-la-Tit Ta-**maa**-tim*	سلطة طماطم
potato salad	*sa-la-Tit ba-**Taa**-Tis*	سلطة بطاطس
beet salad	*sa-la-Tit **ban**-gar*	سلطة بنجر

Meat Dishes

meat	*laH-ma*	لحم
kebab (grilled marinated meat)	*ka-behb*	كباب
kibba (baked minced meat with cracked wheat and spices)	*kib-ba*	كبة
kufta (minced grilled meat)	*kuf-ta*	كفتة
meat and vegetable casserole	*Taa-gin*	طاجن
(roast) lamb	*Daa-nee (rus-too)*	ضاني (رستو)
veal	*bi-til-loo*	بتلو
veal cutlets	*is-ka-loop bi-ti-loo*	اسكالوب بتلو
lamb cutlets	*kus-ta-ley-ta*	شرائح ضاني/ كستلية
beefsteak	*fi-ley, steyk*	بفتيك
■ well done	■ *mis-ti-wee*	مستوي/تام النضج
■ medium	■ *nuS-Si si-wa*	نصف ناضج
■ rare (unusual in the Middle East)	■ *ya doh-bak maH-TooT can-naar*	قليل النضج
liver	*kib-da*	كبدة
kidneys	*ka-leh-wee*	كلاوي

brains	*mukh*	مخ
spiced grilled meat, served in fine slices	*sha-**wir**-ma*	شاورمة
fatta (mutton stewed in broth with bread and rice)	***fat**-ta*	فتة

Poultry and Game

(grilled) chicken	*fi-**rehkh**/da-**jehj** (**mash**-wee)*	دجاج (مشوي)
(stuffed) pigeon	*Ha-**mehm** (**maH**-shee)*	حمام (محشي)
duck	*baTT*	بط
rabbit	*'**ar**-nab*	أرنب
quail	*sim-**mehn***	سمان
turkey	*deek-**roo**-mee*	ديك رومي

Because pork is forbidden to Muslims it is found only (occasionally) in international hotels and tourist restaurants:

ham, pork	*khun-**zeer***	خنزير

You may want to know how the dish is prepared:

roast	***rus**-too*	رستو
fried	*ma"-lee*	مقلي
grilled	***mash**-wee*	مشوي
boiled	*mas-**loo"***	مسلوق
stuffed	***maH**-shee*	محشي
baked	*fil-**furn***	في الفرن
minced (ground)	*maf-**room***	مفروم

Fish Dishes

What kind of fish do you have?	^can-**du**-kum 'as-**mehk** 'eyh?	ما هـي أنواع السـمك عندكم؟
fish	**sa**-mak	سمك
prawns	gam-**ba**-ree	جمبري
squid	ka-la-**mar**-ya	أم الحبر، حبار
octopus	okh-Tu-**booT**	أخطبوط
swordfish	a-boo-**seyf**	أبو سيف
crab	**a**-boo ga-**lam**-boo, ka-**boor**-ya	كابوريا، أبو جلمبو
lobster	is-ta-**koh**-za	سرطان بحري، استاكوزا
tuna	**too**-na	تونة
sardines	sar-**deen**	سردين
sole	**sa**-mak **moo**-sa	سمك موسى

Vegetables

What vegetables do you have?	^can-**du**-kum khu-**Daar** 'eyh?	ما هـي أنواع الخضروات عندكم؟
artichokes	khar-**shoof**	خرشوف
beans	fa-**Sul**-ya	فاصوليا
carrots	**ga**-zar	جزر
cauliflower	"ar-na-**beeT**	قرنبيط
cucumber	khi-**yaar**	خيار

lettuce	*khass*	خس
mixed vegetables	*khu-**Daar** mi-**shak**-kil*	خضروات مشكلة
okra ("ladies' fingers")	***bam**-ya*	بامية
onions	***bu**-Sal*	بصل
(fried) potatoes	*ba-**Taa**-Tis (ma"-**lee**-ya)*	بطاطس (مقلية)
peas	*bi-**sil**-la*	بسلة
radishes	*figl*	فجل
rice	*nuzz*	أرز
spinach	*sa-**beh**-nigh*	سبانخ
sweet potatoes	*ba-**Taa**-Ta*	بطاطا
tomatoes	*Ta-**maa**-Tim*	طماطم

The following vegetables are often served stuffed (***maH-shee***) with rice and herbs and sometimes minced meat:

aubergines, eggplants	*bi-din-**gehn***	باذنجان
cabbage	*ku-**rumb***	كرنب
zucchini, squash	***koh**-sa*	كوسة
green peppers	***fil**-fil '**akh**-Dar*	فلفل أخضر

Dishes may be served or cooked with:

garlic	*bi-**toom***	بالثوم

mint	*bi n^c-**neh**^c*	بالنعناع
lemon	*bi la-**moon***	بالليمون
olive oil	*bi zeyt zey-**toon***	بزيت الزيتون

Side Dishes

macaroni (and pasta generally)	*ma-ka-**roh**-na*	مكرونة
(fried) eggs	*beyD (**ma"**-lee)*	بيض (مقلي)
lentils	*^cads*	عدس
(cheese) omelette	*om-**leet** (big-**gib**-na)*	أومليت(بالجبنة)
eggs baked with onions, tomatoes, and green peppers	*^c**ig**-ga*	عجة
spiced sausages	*su-**gu"''***	سجق
pastrami	*bs-**Tir**-ma*	بسطرمة
hard, mild cheese	***gib**-na **roo**-mee*	جبنة رومي
soft white salty cheese	***gib**-na **bey**-Da*	جبنة بيضاء
yogurt	***la**-ban za-**beh**-dee*	لبن زبادي

Some North African Dishes

couscous	***kus**-ku-see*	كسكسي
peppery fish soup	***mar**-qa*	مرقة

paper-thin pancakes filled with egg and deep fried	*breek*	بريك
spiced sausages	*mer-**gez***	مرجاز

Desserts

Though Western-style restaurants will offer a range of desserts, it is not customary to end a meal with an elaborate sweet course, and many local restaurants may list only ice cream, créme caramel, or fruit.

ice cream	*ays-**kreem***	أيس كريم
■ chocolate	■ *sho-ko-**laa-**Ta*	شوكلاتة
■ vanilla	■ *va-**nil**-ya*	فانيلا
mixed ice cream	*ays-**kreem** mi-**shak**-kil*	أيس كريم مشكل
créme caramel	*kreym ka-ra-**mel***	كريم كرامل
rice pudding	*ruzz bi **la**-ban*	أرز بلبن
vanilla blancmange	*ma-hal-la-**bee**-ya*	مهلبية
Umm Ali (pastry and milk pudding with raisins)	*'umm ᶜeh-lee*	أم علي
qamar eldin (apricot jelly, sometimes served as a drink)	*"a-mar id-**deen**, mish mi-**shee**-ya*	قمر الدين، مشمشية
fatir (large baked pancakes often served with jam or honey)	*tif-**Teer** Hilw*	فطير

Fruit

fruit	*fak-ha*	فاكهة
apples	*tuf-fehH*	تفاح
apricots	**mish**-*mish*	مشمش
bananas	*mohz*	موز
dates	**ba**-*laH*	بلح
figs	*teen*	تين
grapefruit	**greyp** *froot*	جريبفروت
grapes	^{c}**i**-*nab*	عنب
guava	*ga-***weh**-*fa*	جوافة
lemon	*la-***moon**	ليمون
mangoes	**man**-*ga*	مانجو
melon	*sh-***mehm**	شمام
oranges	*bur-tu-"***aan**	برتقال
peaches	*khohkh*	خوخ
pears	*kom-***mit**-*ra*	كمثرى
plums	*bar-"***oo**"	برقوق
pomegranates	*rom-***maan**	رومان
strawberries	*fa-***raw**-*la*	فراولة
tangerines	*yu-sa-***fan**-*dee*	يوسف افندي
watermelon	*baT-***Teekh**	بطيخ

Oriental Pastries

Every visitor must experience the delights of the Oriental pastry shop *(il-Ha-la-weh-nee)*. Pastries are rich and very sweet, made with clarified butter and steeped in syrup, often stuffed with different kinds of nuts. A dollop of chilled cream *("ish-ta)* is an optional extra. You can eat your pastry on the spot, usually at a marble-topped bar, or buy a selection to take with you (they are generally sold by weight). Give a small tip to the person who deftly ties up your package with ribbon tape.

basbousa (semolina backed in the oven, often with nuts, and steeped in syrup)	*bas-**boo**-sa*	بسبوسة
baclava (layers of paper-thin pastry and crushed nuts, with syrup)	*ba"-**leh**-wa*	بقلاوة
kunafa (fine-spun pastry stuffed with nuts)	*ku-**neh**-fa*	كنافة
qatayif (tiny pancakes, layered with nuts, syrup, and cream)	*"a-**Taa**-yif*	قطايف
with cream	*bil-"**ish**-Ta*	بالقشطة
Turkish delight	***mal**-ban/lu-**koom***	ملبن. حلقوم

AFTER THE MEAL

The bill (check), please.	*il-Hi-sehb, min faD-lak.*	الحساب. من فضلك
Can I pay by credit card?	***mum-kin ad-fa^c bi kri-dit kard?***	هل أستطيع أن أدفع ببطاقة اعتماد
Is service included?	*da bil-khid-ma?*	هل هذا يشمل الخدمة؟
That's for you.	*da ^ca-la-sheh-nak.*	تفضل. هذا لك
The food was excellent.	*il-'akl kehn mum-tehz.*	كان الأكل ممتازاً
We will come again.	*ha-nee-gee teh-nee.*	سنأتي مرة ثانية

AT THE CAFÉ

Street cafés usually serve only tea, Turkish coffee, and soft drinks. They are excellent places to sit and rest and watch the world go by. Traditionally, men go there to chat and smoke a water pipe (*shee-sha*) or play backgammon. Tourists are welcome, though a woman on her own might feel uncomfortable.

If you order a coffee you will automatically be given a small black Turkish coffee and a glass of water. Tea is usually served black, sometimes already sweetened.

In the big cities elegant tearooms or tea gardens, such as the famous Groppi's in Cairo, also serve light meals and pastries. Service may be leisurely, because most people go there to spend an hour or two.

coffee	*"ah*-wa	قهوة
tea	*shayy*	شاي
fruit juice	*^ca-Seer*	عصير
soda	*Soh*-da	صودا
soft drinks	*Ha-ga sa"-^ca*	مشروبات غير روحية
Do you have <u>French</u> (i.e., filter coffee?)	*^can-du-kum "ah*-wa *fa-ran-seh-wee?*	هل عندكم قهوة فرنسية؟
▪ instant coffee	▪ *nes-ka-fey*	نسكافيه
I'd like a Turkish coffee <u>without sugar</u>.	*^ca-wiz [^caw-za] "ah*-wa *seh*-da.	أريد قهوة سادة
▪ medium sweet	▪ *maZ-booT*	مضبوط
▪ very sweet	▪ *suk*-kar *zee-yeh-da*	سكر زيادة
Do you have mineral water?	*fee may*-ya *ma^c-da-nee ya?*	هل عندكم مياه معدنية؟
tea <u>with lemon</u>	*shayy bi la-moon.*	شاي بالليمون
▪ with milk	▪ *bi la*-ban	باللبن
▪ with mint	▪ *bi ni^o-nen^o*	بالنعناع
▪ without sugar	▪ *min ghey suk*-kar	بدون سكر
Some sugar, please.	*su*-kar, *min faD*-lak.	سكر، من فضلك

Sahlab (a hot milky drink topped with chopped nuts and shredded coconut)	*saH-lab*	سحلب
hot chocolate	*sho-ko-laa-Ta, ka-kaw*	شوكولاتة، كاكاو
Do you have anything to eat?	^c*an-du-kum 'akl?*	هل عندكم أكل؟
Do you have sandwiches?	^c*an-du-kum sand-wit-sheht?*	هل عندكم سندويتشات؟

Some cafés and fruit juice bars sell chilled Middle Eastern drinks:

tamarind juice	*ta-mar hin-dee*	تمر هندي
karkaday (hibiscus drink)	*kar-ka-dey*	كركديه

SNACKS IN THE STREET

The Middle East is famous for the variety of its "street food": fried and grilled snacks sold from tiny kiosks and brightly decorated mobile stalls to be found on every street corner in cities such as Cairo. The flat "Oriental" bread (*khubz ba-la-dee*) is stuffed with fried bean cakes, grilled meat, or cheese. Fruit juice bars will squeeze oranges or puree bananas while you wait.

bean purée	*fool*	فول
ta'miyya (fried balls of ground beans or chickpeas)	*Ta^c-mee-ya, fa-leh-fil*	طعمية، فلافل

kushary (macaroni or rice with noodles, lentils, fried onion, and a hot tomato sauce)	*ku-sha-ree*	كشري
shawirma, doner kebab (spiced lamb or veal grilled on a vertical spit)	*sha-wir-ma*	شاورمة
sandwiches	*sand-wit-sheht*	سندويتشات
a <u>cheese</u> sandwich	*sand-witsh <u>gib-na</u>*	سندويتش جبنة
■ liver	■ *kib-da*	كبدة
■ ta'miyya	■ *Ta^c-mee-ya*	طعمية
peanuts	*fool su-deh-nee*	فول سوداني
popcorn	*fi shaar*	فشار

TRAVEL TIP

The visitor should naturally be cautious of what and when he or she eats; anything freshly fried or grilled is likely to be safe, whereas the usual rules about avoiding salads – even garnishes on sandwiches — and fruit that cannot be peeled, should be strictly observed.

GETTING TO KNOW PEOPLE

GREETINGS

It is customary to shake hands when you are formally introduced to someone. When close friends or relations — men or women — haven't met for some time, they usually exchange kisses on both cheeks.

At Any Time of Day

Hello!	*is-sa-**leh**-mu* *^ca-**ley**-kum!*	السلام عليكم!
(reply)	*^ca-**ley**-kum is-sa-**lehm***	عليكم السلام
Hi/Welcome!	*ah-lan wa sah-lan!* *ah-lan!*	أهلا وسهلا أهلا
(reply)	*ah-lan **beek** [**bee**-kee]*	أهلا بك
... to two or more	*ah-lan **bee**-kum*	أهلا بكم
Welcome!	*mar-**Ha**-ba!*	مرحباً
(reply)	*mar-Hab **beek** [**bee**-kee]*	مرحباً بك
... to two or more	*mar-Hab **bee**-kum*	مرحباً بكم
Good-bye!	*ma-^ca s-sa-**leh**-ma!*	مع السلامة
Remember me to —.	*sal-**lim**-lee ^cal-la —.*	سلم لي على —
Nice to have met you.	*fur-Sa sa-^cee-da gid-dan.*	فرصة سعيدة جداً
(reply) I'm (even) happier.	*a-na 'as-^cad*	أنا أسعد

In the Morning

| Good morning. | Sa-baH il-kheyr. | صباح الخير |
| (reply) | Sa-baH in-noor | صباح النور |

In the Afternoon/Evening

| Good evening. | mi-seh' il-kheyr. | مساء الخير |
| (reply) | mi-seh' in-noor | مساء النور |

At Night

Good night.	tiS-baH [tiS-ba-Hee] ^ca-la-kheyr.	تصبح [تصبحي] على خير
...to two or more	tiS-ba-Hoo ^ca-la kheyr.	تصبحون على خير
How are you? or	iz-zay-yak? [iz-zay-yik]? keyf Heh-lak? [keyf Heh-lik]?	ازيك؟ كيف حالك؟
...to two or more	iz-zay-yu-kum?	ازيكم؟
I'm fine, thanks.	bi kheyr, il-Ham-du lil-leh.	بخير. الحمد لله
or	kway-is [kway-yi-sa], il-Ham-du lil-leh.	كويس [كويسة] الحمد لله
or	il-Ham-du lil-leh ("praise be to God") may be used by itself	الحمد لله
Have a good trip!	riH-la kway-yi-sa!	أتمنالك رحلة بهيجة
Welcome back!	Ham-dil-la ^cas-sa-leh-ma!	حمد الله على سلامتك

CONSERVATIVE ETIQUETTE

In Saudi Arabia and some of the countries of the Gulf, very conservative traditions are maintained. Women are still secluded and rarely appear at social gatherings, though this is changing gradually. It is impolite to ask after someone's wife, although a general inquiry about the family is acceptable. In more orthodox circles it is not appropriate for a man and a woman who are not related to shake hands. Presenting the soles of one's feet to someone is considered ill-mannered. If you are being entertained in traditional style, seated on carpets and cushions, leave your shoes at the door and sit cross-legged or with your feet tucked under you. Showing a lot of arm or leg, whether you are a man or a woman, is to be avoided. During a meal, interest is focused on the food, and conversation drops to a minimum level.

Show deference to someone by insisting that they pass through a door in front of you. Always offer a drink or a snack to a visitor, however casual the visit. In other countries there are fewer social constraints, but when in doubt it is always safest to err on the side of conservatism.

NAMES AND POLITE FORMS OF ADDRESS

When talking to someone directly, the word *ya* is usually put in front of the name or title.

How are you, Ahmad?	*is-zay-yak, ya 'aH-mad?*	ازيك، يا أحمد؟
Good morning, madam.	*Sa-baH il-kheyr, ya ma-dehm.*	صباح الخير، يا مدام

When talking to an elderly person whose name you don't know, it's polite to address them as

ya Hagg   يا حاج [يا حاجة]

or (to a woman) ya **Hag**-*ga*

which is the title given to anyone who has been on the pilgrimage to Mecca.

In Egypt especially, you will find yourself being addressed as

ya beyh   يا بيه

ya **fan**-*dim*   يا افندم

ya **beh**-*sha*   يا باشا

— all honorific titles of Turkish origin, used mostly to men.

INTRODUCTIONS

May I introduce to you —.	**mum**-*kin a-"ad-dim-lak [a-"ad-dim lik]*	هل يمكن أن أقدم لك —
■ Mr. —	■ *is-***say**-*yid* —	السيد —
■ Mrs. —	■ *ma-***dehm**/ *is-say-***yi**-*da* —	مدام، السيدة —
■ Miss —	■ *il-'eh-***ni**-*sa* —	الآنسة —
■ Dr. —	■ *id-duk-***toor** *[id-duk-***too**-*ra]* —	الدكتور [الدكتورة] —
■ Professor —	■ *il-'us-***tehz** *[il-'us-***teh**-*za]* —	الاستاذ [الاستاذة] —

My name is —.	*'is-mee* —.	اسمي —
This is <u>my husband</u>.	da **goh**-zee.	هذا زوجي

- my father
  - *'a-**boo**-ya*
  - أبي
- my brother
  - *'a-**khoo**-ya*
  - أخي
- my son
  - *'ib-nee*
  - ابني
- my fiancé
  - *kha-**Tee**-bee*
  - خطيبي
- my friend
  - *SaH-bee*
  - صديقي

This is <u>my wife</u>.	dee <u>mi-raa-tee</u>.	هذه زوجتي

- my mother
  - *'um-mee, wal-di-tee*
  - أمي
- my sister
  - *'ukh-tee*
  - أختي
- my daughter
  - *bin-tee*
  - بنتي
- my fiancée
  - *kha-**Tib**-tee*
  - خطيبتي
- my friend (fem)
  - *SaH-**bi**-tee*
  - صديقتي

These are my children.	dohl 'aw-**leh**-dee.	هؤلاء أولادي
This is my family.	dee ^ceyl-tee/'us-**ri**-tee	هذه أسرتي

MAKING FRIENDS

    People will want to know all about you — and it's quite polite to ask them questions about their family and their work in return. Family are very important, so why not take a couple of snapshots with you — of your family and home.

Where are you from?	*in-ta [in-tee] mi-neyn?*	من أين أنت؟
I'm from —.	*a-na min —.*	أنا من —
■ America	■ am-**ree**-ka	أمريكا
■ Britain	■ bri-**Taan**-ya	بريطانيا
■ Canada	■ **ka**-na-da	كندا
■ Australia	■ os-**tral**-ya	أستراليا
What is your name?	*'is-mak ['is-mik] 'eyh?*	ما اسمك؟
Pleased to meet you (lit., "a happy occasion")	*fur-Sa sa-ᶜee-da.*	فرصة سعيدة
The pleasure's mine.	*a-na 'as-ᶜad*	أنا أسعد
What's your job?	*bi-tish-**ta**-ghal [bi-tish-**ta**-gha-lee] 'eyh?*	ماذا تعمل؟
Are you married?	*in-ta mit-**gaw**-wiz? [in-tee mit-gaw-**wi**-za?]*	هل أنت متزوج [متزوجة]؟
Do you have any children?	*ᶜan-dak [ᶜan-dik] 'aw-lehd?*	هل عندك أطفال؟
Are you here on holiday?	*in-ta [in-tee] fee 'a-**geh**-za?*	هل أنت في عطلة؟
Where are you staying?	*in-ta **neh**-zil [in-tee **naz**-la] feyn?*	أين تقيم؟
I'm staying at —.	*a-na **neh**-zil [**naz**-la] fee —.*	أنا أقيم في —
Yes, I'm married.	*'ay-wa, a-na mit-**gaw**-wiz [mit-gaw-**wi**-za].*	نعم، أنا متزوج [متزوجة].

No, I'm not married.	*la'*, *a-na mish mit-gaw-wiz* [*mit-gaw-wi-za*]	لست متزوجاً [متزوجة]

OCCUPATIONS

I'm a <u>businessman</u>.	*a-na* **raa**-*gil* *'a^c*-**mehl**/*teh*-*gir*	أنا رجل أعمال. تاجر
■ a businesswoman	■ *say*-**yi**-*dit a^c*-**mehl**	سيدة أعمال
■ a student	■ **Taa**-*lib* [**Taa**-*li*-*ba*]	طالب [طالبة]
■ a teacher	■ *mu*-**dar**-*ris* [*mu*-*dar*-**ri**-*sa*]	مدرس [مدرسة]. معلم [معلمة]
■ a doctor	■ *duk*-**toor** [*duk*-**too**-*ra*]	دكتور [دكتورة]. طبيب [طبيبة]
■ a farmer	■ *mu*-**zeh**-*ri^c*	مزارع
■ an engineer	■ *mu*-**han**-*dis* [*mu*-*han*-**di**-*sa*]	مهندس [مهندسة]
■ a secretary	■ *si*-*kir*-**teer** [*si*-*kir*-**tee**-*ra*]	سكرتير [سكرتيرة]
■ a company director	■ *mu*-**deer** [*mu*-**dee**-*rit*] **shir**-*ka*	مدير [مديرة] شركة
■ a consultant	■ *mus*-*ta*-**shaar** [*mus*-*ta*-**shaa**-*ra*], *kha*-**beer** [*kha*-**bee**-*ra*]	مستشار [مستشارة]
■ a housewife	■ **sit**-*ti beyt*	ربة منزل
■ a nurse	■ *mu*-*mar*-**ri**-*Da*	ممرضة

■ a journalist	■ **Sa**-Ha-fee [Sa-Ha-**fee**-ya]	صحفي [صحافية]
■ a lawyer	■ mu-**Heh**-mee [mu-**Heh**-mee-ya]	محامي [محامية]
I'm in <u>import/export</u>.	a-na fil-'<u>is-ti-raad</u> wit-taS-**Deer**.	أعمل بالاستيراد والتصدير
■ manufacturing	■ fiS-Si-**naa**-^{c}a	في الصناعة
■ banking	■ fi bank	في بنك
■ computing	■ fis-ti^c-**mehl** il-kom-**byoo**-tar	في استعمال الكمبيوتر
■ publishing	■ fi daar nashr	بالنشر
He is (is he?) —.	**huw**-wa —(?)	(هل) هو —
She is (is she?) —.	**hee**-ya — (?)	(هل) هي —

GENERAL CONVERSATION

Whenever you meet and talk with people, for example, when discussing a purchase or making a routine business call, you are likely to be presented with coffee or tea or a soft drink.

I'm here for <u>a few days</u>.	ha"-^{c}ud **ka**-za yohm.	سأبقى هنا عدة أيام
■ a week	■ 'is-**boo**^{c}	أسبوع
■ (about) a month	■ (Ha-**weh**-lee) shahr	مدة شهر (تقريبا)

It's the first time I've been to Egypt.	dee **'aw**-wil **mar**-ra **'eh**-gee maSr.	إنها المرة الأولى لي في مصر
I hope to visit —.	^ca-wiz [^caw-za] a-**zoor** —.	أريد أن أزور —
I'm travelling by myself.	a-na mi-**seh**-fir [mi-**saf**-ra] li **waH**-dee.	أنا مسافر [مسافرة] وحدي
I am with friends.	a-na ma-^ca 'aS-**Haab**.	أنا مع أصدقاء
I'm waiting for someone.	a-na mis-**tan**-nee [mis-tan-**nee**-ya] Hadd.	أنا منتظر [منتظرة] واحداً
I love the country.	ba-**Hibb** il-**ba**-lad.	أحب البلد
I love the people here.	ba-**Hibb** in-**nehs** **hi**-na.	أحب الناس هنا
The people are very <u>kind</u>.	in-**nehs** <u>Tay-yi-**been**</u> **gid**-dan.	الناس طيبون جداً
■ generous	■ **ku**-ra-ma	كرماء
I've had no problems.	ma-^can-**deesh** ma-**sheh**-kil khaa-**liS**	ليس عندي مشاكل
It is rather hot.	ig-**gaww** Harr shway-ya.	الطقس حار إلى حد ما
It is very humid.	fee ru-**Too**-b ki-**teer**.	الطقس رطب جداً
Do you speak English?	bi-tit-**kal**-lim [bi-tit-kal-**li**-mee] in-gi-**lee**-zee?	هل تتكلم الانجليزية؟
You speak English very well!	bi-tit-**kal**-lim [bi-tit-kal-**li**-mee] in-gi-**lee**-zee kway-yis **gid**-an!	تتكلم الانجليزية بطلاقة!

I have learned a little <u>Arabic</u>.	da-**rast** ^c**a**-ra-bee **shway**-ya	أنا تعلمت قليلا من العربية
■ Egyptian Arabic	■ ^ca-ra-bee **maS**-ree	اللهجة المصرية
It's very difficult!	da Sa^cb **gid**-dan!	هذه اللغة صعبة جداً
Please join us.	it-**faD**-Dal [it-faD-**Da**-lee]	تفضل [تفضلي]
...to two or more	it faD **Da** loo	تفضلوا

(it-**faD**-Dal can also mean "please take this," "do come in," "have a seat," etc.)

What will you have to drink?	**tish**-rab [tish-**ra**-bee] 'eyh?	ما ذا تريد أن تشرب؟
...to two or more	tish-**ra**-boo 'eyh?	ماذا تشربون؟
May I take a picture of you?	**mum**-kin a-Saw-wa-rak? [a-Saw-wa-rik]?	هل يمكن أن أصورك؟
Would you take a picture of me (us)?	**mum**-kin ti-Saw-**war**-nee (ti-Saw-**war**-na)?	هل يمكن أن تصورني؟
Many thanks!	'al-fi **shukr**!	شكراً جزيلاً!
I will send you the photos.	hab-^cat-lak iS-**So**-war.	سأرسل لك الصور

ARRANGING TO SEE SOMEONE AGAIN

When will I see you?	a-**shoo**-fak [a-**shoo**-fik] '**im**-ta?	متى أراك ثانية؟
Can I see you tomorrow?	a-**shoo**-fak [a-**shoo**-fik] **buk**-ra?	هل سأراك غداً؟
I'll see you <u>here</u>.	a-**shoo**-fak [a-**shoo**-fik] **hi**-na.	سأراك هنا
■ at the hotel	■ fil-**fun**-du", fil-'u-**teel**	■ في الفندق
■ at the office	■ fil-**mak**-tab	■ في المكتب
At what time?	is-**seh**-^ca kam?	متى؟
Do join us for lunch.	it-**faD**-Dal [it-faD-**Da**-lee] tit-**ghad**-da [tit-**ghad**-dee] ma-^c**eh**-na.	تفضل للغداء معنا
Do join us for dinner.	it-**faD**-Dal [it-faD-**Da**-lee] tit-^c**ash**-sha [tit-^c**ash**-shee] ma-^c**eh**-na.	تفضل للعشاء معنا
May I call you?	**mum**-kin a-kal-**li**-mak [a-kal-**li**-mik] bit-ti-li-**fohn**?	هل أستطيع الاتصال بك؟
What is your telephone number?	**nim**-rit ti-li-**foh**-nak [ti-li-**foh**-nik] 'eyh?	ما هو رقم تليفونك؟
This is my telephone number.	dee-**nim**-rit ti-li-**foh**-nee.	هذا هو رقم تليفوني
This is my address (in Egypt).	da ^cin-**weh**-nee (fi maSr)	هذا عنواني (في مصر)

...i-qaa'!   إلى اللقاء!

...or the future it's usual to add:

...naa' al-laah   إن شاء الله

...oo-fak buk-ra, 'in   أراك غداً إن شاء
...' al-laah   الله

...OMEONE'S HOME

...oints of etiquette to remember. No
...box of candy for the children or a
...a thoughtful gesture. The host will
...t pieces of meat and add these to
...oks as though it needs replenishing.
...are full, because you will definitely

...s it is still customary to eat some
... In this case use the right hand

...finished, sit back with a satisfied
...ise be to God!").

...owl and jug of water will be brought
...can wash your hands and rinse your
...gne may be passed around, so that
...selves (cologne, scent, and after-
...e gifts).

...served, and, if it is lunchtime, you
...est. More usually, it is polite to leave
...ps have been removed.

...eople eating a meal, they will, out
...to join them; but if you were not
...use unless they absolutely insist.

It was a lovely party.	*keh*-nit Haf-la mum-*teh*-za	كان الحفل ممتازاً
The food was delicious.	il-'akl kehn la-zeez gid-dan.	كان الأكل لذيذاً جداً
(lit.) Blessings on your hands (to the hostess).	tis-lam 'ee-dey-kee.	تسلم يديك
Thank you so much.	'*al*-fi shukr, mu-ta-*shak*-kir gid-dan	متشكر جداً
It's been lovely meeting you.	it-shar-*raf*-na	تشرفت بلقائك
Can I give you a lift?	*mum*-kin a-waS-*Sa*-lak [a-waS-*Sa*-lik]?	هل أوصلك؟
...to two or more	*mum*-kin a-waS-*Sal*-kum?	هل أوصلكم؟

HOT TOPICS

You will find that people throughout the Middle East are generally well informed about the politics of the whole area, and that this is a major topic of conversation. They will expect you to know something of the recent history and current situation in their country and will be interested to know your views. So it is rewarding to do some reading before you go — even if it is just a chapter in a guide book. (Often, Googling a particular country will provide independent websites with refreshingly different perspectives from those found in the mainstream media.) Be ready to listen and learn!

SHOPPING

Opening times of shops, offices, and banks vary from country to country and season to season; in summer, business may start and end early to avoid the heat of the day. Many shops close in the middle of the day and reopen in the late afternoon. In Saudi Arabia and some Gulf countries business comes to a halt briefly with the call to prayer; shops are either closed or simply left unattended while the shopkeeper goes to the local mosque or prays in a quiet back room.

In some countries businesses and institutions tend to close on Fridays, whereas in others the Western custom of Sunday closing has been retained.

The traditional *souk* (market or bazaar) — a maze of streets and tiny alleyways where you can buy everything from a frying pan to a silk carpet — is a fascinating place to visit, even if you don't want to buy. Because goods of particular kind   jewelry, spices, hardware, clothing, and so on — are sold in one area of the souk, it's easy to compare prices when you are buying a major item. This incidentally is considered the sensible way to shop, so there will be no hard feelings if you decide to "come back later." The most famous souks are perhaps the Hamidiyya in Damascus and the Khan ElKhalili in Cairo. Because these are both at the heart of the old cities, you can explore some of the early mosques and palaces at the same time.

GENERAL EXPRESSIONS

I'd like to go shopping.	*ca-wiz [^caw-za]* *ash-ti-ree Ha-geht*.	أريد الذهاب للتسوق

Can I see that?	*mum-kin a-shoof da?*	هل يمكن أن أرى هذا؟
I prefer this one.	*ba-faD-Dal da.*	أفضل هذا
How much is it?	*bi kam?*	بكم؟
That's (a bit) expensive.	*da gheh-lee (shway-ya)*	هذا غال إلى حد ما
Do you have anything cheaper?	*^can-dak Ha-ga 'ar-khaS?*	هل عندك شيء أرخص؟
Do you have anything better?	*^can-dak Ha-ga 'aH-san?*	هل عندك شيء أفضل
I owe you —.	*^can-dee — lak [lik]*	لك علي —
You owe me —.	*^can-dak [^can-dik]*	لي عليك —
Where can I find a —?	*a-leh-"ee — feyn?*	أين أجد —؟
■ bakery	■ *furn, makh-baz*	مخبز
■ bank	■ *bank*	بنك
■ barber	■ *Hal-leh"*	حلاق
■ beauty parlor	■ *Sa-lohn tag-meel*	صالون تجميل
■ bookshop	■ *mak-ta-ba*	مكتبة
■ butcher	■ *gaz-zaar*	جزار
■ pharmacy (chemist)	■ *'ag-za-kheh-na, Say-Da-lee-ya*	أجزاخانة، صيدلية

■ clothing store —	■ *ma-Hall ma-leh-bis* —	محل ملابس —
for men's clothes	*lir-rig-**geh**-la*	للرجال
for women's clothes	*li s-sit-**teht***	للسيدات
for children's clothes	*li l-'aT-**faal***	للأطفال
■ confectioner	■ *Ha-la-**weh**-nee*	حلواني
■ department store	■ *ma-Hall ki-**beer***	محل كبير
■ dressmaker	■ *khay-**yaa**-Ta*	خياطة
■ drugstore	■ *'ag-za-**kheh**-na, Say-Da-**lee**-ya*	أجزخانة، صيدلية
■ dry cleaner	■ *ma-Hall tan-**Deef***	محل تنظيف جاف
■ flower shop	■ *ma-Hall zu-**hoor***	محل زهور
■ greengrocer	■ *khu-**Da**-ree*	محل خضروات
■ grocery store	■ *ba"-"ehl*	محل بقالة
■ hairdresser	■ *kwa-**feer***	كوافير، مصفف الشعر
■ hardware store	■ *ma-Hall 'a-da-**weht** man-zi-**lee**-ya*	محل أدوات منزلية
■ jewelry store	■ *ga-wa-**hir**-gee*	جواهرجي
■ laundry	■ *magh-**sa**-la*	مغسلة
■ newsstand	■ *kushk ga-**reh**-yid*	كشك جرائد
■ optician	■ *naD-Da-**raa**-tee*	محل نظارات
■ pastry shop	■ *Ha-la-**weh**-nee*	حلواني

shoemaker	gaz-**ma**-gee	محل تصليح أحذية
shoe store	ma-**Hall gi**-zam	محل أحذية
shops	da-ka-**keen**, ma-Hal-**leht**	محلات
stationer	mak-**ta**-ba	مكتبة
tailor	**tar**-zee, khay-**yaaT**	خياط

BOOKS

Where can I buy English-language books?	ash-**ti**-ree **ku**-tub in-gi-**lee**-zee feyn?	أين أستطيع شراء كتب بالانجليزية؟
I would like —.	ᶜ**a**-wiz [ᶜ**aw**-za] —.	أريد —
a guidebook	da-**leel** si-yeh-**Hee**	دليل سياحي
a map	kha-**ree**-Ta	خريطة
a map of the city	kha-**ree**-Ta lil-**ba**-lad	خريطة للمدينة
Do you have any books in English?	ᶜan-**du**-kum ku-tub bi-lin-gi-**lee**-zee?	هل عندكم كتب بالانجليزية؟
Do you have books <u>about Egypt</u>?	ᶜan-**du**-kum **ku**-tub <u>ᶜan maSr</u>?	هل عندكم كتب عن مصر؟
about the Middle East	can ish-**sharq** il-**'aw**-SaT?	عن الشرق الأوسط
Do you have any <u>novels</u>?	ᶜan-**du**-kum <u>ri-wa-**yeht**</u>?	هل عندكم روايات؟

■ detective stories	■ *qi-SaS boo-li-See-ya*	قصص بوليسية
■ short stories	■ *qi-SaS qa-See-ra*	قصص قصيرة
■ dictionary	■ *qa-moos*	قاموس
■ English-Arabic dictionary	■ *qa-moos in-gi-lee-zee- ^ca-ra-bee*	قاموس إنجليزي-عربي
■ a pocket dictionary	■ *qa-moos geyb*	قاموس جيب
I'll take these books.	*heh-khud ik-ku-tub dee.*	سآخذ هذه الكتب

CLOTHING

I'm looking for —.	*ba-daw-war ^ca-la —.*	أريد —
■ a belt	■ *Hi-zehm*	حزام
■ a blouse	■ *bloo-za*	بلوزة
■ a bra	■ *soot-yehn*	حمالة صدر
■ briefs (men)	■ *kee-lott*	سروال داخلي
■ a cardigan	■ *ja-kitt tree-koh*	جاكيت (تريكو)
■ a coat	■ *bal-Too*	معطف
■ a dress	■ *fus-tehn*	فستان
■ handkerchiefs	■ *ma-na-deel*	مناديل
■ a hat	■ *bur-ney-Ta*	قبعة
■ a jacket	■ *ja-kit-ta*	جاكيت، سترة

■ jeans	■ *jeenz*	بنطلون جينز
■ a necktie	■ *ka-ra-vat-ta*	ربطة عنق
■ a nightgown	■ *"a-meeS nohm*	قميص نوم
■ panties	■ *kee-lott*	سروال داخلي نسائي
■ pantyhose, tights	■ *koo-lohn*	جوارب طويلة
■ a robe, dressing gown	■ *rohb*	ثوب، روب
■ sandals	■ *san-dal*	صندل
■ a scarf	■ *'i-sharb, ku-fee-ya*	كوفية
■ a shawl	■ *shehl*	شال
■ a shirt	■ *"a-meeS*	قميص
■ shoes	■ *gaz-ma*	حذاء
■ a skirt	■ *gu-nil-la*	جيبة، جونلة
■ a slip	■ *kom-bi-ney-zohn*	قميص داخلي
■ slippers	■ *shib-shib*	شبشب
■ socks, stockings	■ *sha-raab*	جوارب
■ a suit (man's)	■ *bad-la*	بدلة
■ a suit (woman's)	■ *tay-yeer*	طاقم حريمي
■ a sweater	■ *bu-loh-var*	بلوفر، كنزة صوفية
■ a swimsuit	■ *ma-yoh*	مايو، لباس بحري
■ a T-shirt	■ *fa-nil-la*	فانلة، قميص نصف كم
■ a tracksuit	■ *libs tad-reeb*	بدلة تدريب
■ trousers, pants	■ *ban-Ta-lohn*	بنطلون، سروال
■ an undershirt, vest	■ *fa-nil-la*	فانلة، قميص

■ underwear	■ *ma-leh-bis*	ملابس داخلية
	dakh-lee-ya	

You may find it comfortable to wear the long loose robe (usually made of cotton) that is still traditional dress in many parts of the Middle East — the *galabiyya* (*gal-la-bee-ya*) (known in the Arab countries further east as the *thawb* or the *dish-da-sha*) — or the more widely cut version, with broad sleeves — the *kaftan* (*"uf-Taan*). A long cloak, the *abaya* (*ᶜa-beh-ya*) — may be worn over these; or, in North Africa especially, the woolen *burnous* (*bur-noos*).

Colors, Styles, Fabrics

I want something in —.	*ᶜa-wiz [ᶜaw za]* *lohn* —.	أريد لون —
■ black	■ *'is-wid*	أسود
■ blue	■ *'az-ra"*	أزرق
■ red	■ *'aH-mar*	أحمر
■ green	■ *'akh-Dar*	أخضر
■ yellow	■ *'aS-far*	أصفر
■ white	■ *'ab-yaD*	أبيض
■ brown	■ *bun-nee*	بني
■ gray	■ *ra-maa-dee*	رمادي
■ beige	■ *beyj*	بني فاتح

■ loose	■ *weh-si^c*	واسع
■ tight	■ *day-ya"*	ضيق
Can you alter this for me?	*mum-kin tuZ-buT-heh-lee?*	هل يمكنك تغيير هذا لي؟
When will it be ready?	*hat-koon gah-za 'im-ta?*	متى ستكون جاهزة؟
The zipper doesn't work.	*is-sus-ta mak-soo-ra.*	السوستة مكسورة

ELECTRICAL APPLIANCES

Most countries in the Middle East use 220 volts, but there are exceptions; so check before you go, or take an adapter with you.

I want to buy —.	*^ac-wiz [^caw-za] ash-ti-ree —.*	أريد شراء —
■ an adapter	■ *mu-Haw-wil*	محول
■ an alarm clock	■ *mi-nab-bih*	منبه
■ a battery	■ *baT-Ta-ree-ya*	بطارية
■ a blender	■ *khal-laaT*	خلاط
■ a CD player	■ *gi-hehz li 'is-Ti-wa-naat ley-zar*	جهاز لاسطوانات ليزر
■ a calculator	■ *'eh-la Has-ba*	آلة حاسبة
■ a cassette player	■ *gi-hehz ka-sitt*	جهاز كاسيت
■ a curling iron	■ *gi-hehz li tag-^ceed ish-sha^cr*	جهاز لتجعيد الشعر
■ a shaver	■ *ma-ka-nit Hi-leh-"a*	آلة حلاقة

■ a hair dryer	■ sish-**waar**, mu-**gaf**-fif li sh-**sha**^cr	مجفف للشعر
■ a microcassette player	■ **wok**-man, gi-**hehz** ka-**sitt** Su-**ghay**-yar	ووكمان، جهاز كاسيت صغير
■ a plug	■ **fee**-sha	فيشة
■ a (portable) radio	■ **rad** yo (Su-**ghay**-yar)	راديو (صغير)
■ a television	■ ti-li-viz-**yohn**	تليفزيون
■ a videorecorder	■ gi-**hehz** vid-yo	جهاز فيديو
What voltage does this take?	kam il-**volt**?	ما هو الفولت الذي تستخدمه؟
Could you demonstrate it for me?	**mum**-kin ti-**shagh**-ghal-**hoo**-lee?	هل يمكن أن تشغله لي؟
It doesn't work.	mab-yish-ta-**ghalsh**.	لا يعمل

FOOD AND HOUSEHOLD ITEMS

(See p. 79–89 for food words)

I'd like —.	^c**a**-wiz [^c**aw**-za] —.	أريد —
■ a bar of soap	■ Sa-**boo**-na	صابونة
■ breakfast cereal	■ korn fleyks	كورن فلاكس
■ a can of sardines	■ ^cil-bit sar-**deen**	علبة سردين
■ chocolate (candy)	■ sho-ko-**laa**-ta	شكولاتة

■ cocoa (hot chocolate)	■ *ka-kaw*	كاكاو
■ (ground) coffee	■ *bunn*	بن
■ cookies (biscuits)	■ *bas-ka-weet*	بسكويت
■ candy	■ *bon-bo-**neht***	مسكّرات
■ cooking oil	■ *zeyt Ta-beekh*	زيت للطهي
■ a loaf	■ *ri-gheef*	رغيف خبز
■ matches	■ *ka-breet*	كبريت
■ milk	■ *la-ban, Ha-leeb*	حليب
■ paper tissues	■ *ma-na-deel wa-ra"*	مناديل ورق
■ paper towels	■ ***fu**-waT **wa**-ra"*	فوط ورق
■ salt	■ *malH*	ملح
■ soap powder	■ *Sa-boon bud-ra*	صابون بودرة
■ sugar	■ *suk-kar*	سكر
■ tea	■ *shayy*	شاي
■ toilet paper	■ *wa-ra" twa-litt*	ورق تواليت
■ shoe polish	■ *war-**neesh gaz**-ma*	طلاء لتلميع الحذاء
■ vinegar	■ *khall*	خل
■ liquid detergent	■ *Sa-boon seh-yil*	صابون سائل
■ yogurt	■ *la-ban za-beh-dee*	لبن زيادي

Containers

a bottle	*"i-**zeh**-za*	زجاجة
a bottle of —	*"i-**zeh**-zit —*	زجاجة —
a packet	***beh**-koo*	كيس
a tin, a can, a carton	*cil-ba*	علبة

| a can of — | *ᶜil-bit* — | علبة — |
| a jar | *bar-Ta-maan* | برطمان |

THE SPICE MARKET

Oriental spices are increasingly popular in the West. A selection bought from the great sacksful on display in the spice section of the bazaar makes an unusual gift for adventurous cooks back home. (Label them at once so that you know which is which!) The most common are:

- cardamon (*Hab-ba-hehn* حبهان) Small pods of highly aromatic seeds, used in both sweet and savory dishes and to flavor Turkish coffee.
- cumin (*kam-moon* كمّون) Sold as whole seeds or in powdered form, adds interest to simple foods like lentils and beans. It is often used in combination with coriander.
- coriander (*kuz-ba-ra* كسبيرة), either its ground seeds or leaves, which look like flat-leaved parsley and can also be used as a garnish.
- saffron (*zaᶜ-fruun* زعفران) Gives rice a subtle, slightly earthy flavor and delicate yellow color. (Turmeric is a cheaper substitute.)
- harissa (*ha-ree-sa* شطة), or ground red chilies, also sold as a paste, is an important ingredient in many North African dishes.

Nutmeg, cinnamon, and cloves — used for centuries in the West as ingredients in desserts, punches, and milk drinks— are also used in savory dishes in the Middle East, and can be bought there for a fraction of the price.

Every region has its own preferred mixture of ground spices. In North Africa the mixture known as *raas il-ha-noot* usually includes red pepper, coriander, and cumin.

Unless you are buying a ready-made mixture, buy the whole seeds, to be freshly ground when needed. In the spice bazaar you will also find dried fruit and nuts, again great bargains compared with the cost in Europe or the United States.

Quantities

The metric system is generally used, that is, kilos, grams, and liters. These words don't change in the plural in Arabic:

a kilo (X kilos of) —	(X) **kee**-loo —	كيلو —
a gram (X grams) of —	(X) grehm —	جرام —
a liter (X liters) of —	(X) litr —	لتر —
half a kilo	nuSS **kee**-loo	نصف كيلو
a quarter of a kilo	rub^c **kee**-loo	ربع كيلو

The traditional measure of one pound — about half a kilo — is still widely used:

a pound (of —)	raTl (—)	رطل
That's enough.	ki-**feh**-ya ki-da.	هذا يكفي
A little more.	ka-**mehn** shway-ya.	أكثر قليلاً
A little less.	'a-"all shaw-ya	أقل قليلاً
Can I see that, please?	**mum**-kin a-**shoof** da, min **faD**-lak?	هل يمكن أن أرى هذا من فضلك؟
Is it fresh?	da **Taa**-za?	هل هو طازج؟

AT THE JEWELER'S

I'd like to see —.	*ᶜa-wiz [ᶜaw-za] a-shoof* —.	أريد أن أرى —.
■ a bracelet	■ *ghi-wey-sh*	سوار
■ a brooch	■ *brohsh*	دبوس
■ a chain	■ *sil-si-la*	سلسلة
■ a charm, medallion	■ *ᶜul-li-"a*	مدالية، تعليقة
■ some earrings	■ *Ha-la"*	حلق
■ a necklace	■ *ᶜu"d*	عقد
■ prayer beads	■ *sib-Ha*	سبحة
■ a ring	■ *kheh-tim*	خاتم
■ a wristwatch	■ *seh-ᶜit yadd*	ساعة يد
■ an alarm clock	■ *mi-nab-bih*	منبه
■ a watch with an alarm	■ *seh-ᶜit yadd bi mi-nab-bih*	ساعة يد بها منبه
Is this —?	*da* —?	هل هذ —؟
■ gold	■ *da hab*	ذهب
■ platinum	■ *bleh-teen*	بلاتين
■ silver	■ *faD-Da*	فضة
■ stainless steel	■ *steyn-lis steel*	صلب لا يصدأ
■ solid gold	■ *da-hab Saa-fee*	ذهب صافي
■ gold plated	■ *maT-lee da-hab*	مطلي ذهب

■ MP3 player	*gi-hehz em-bee-sree*	جهاز صغير يخزن معلومات صوتية
Can I download this?	*mum-kin a-Ham-mil da?*	هل أستطيع تنزيل هذا؟
■ speakers	■ *sam-ma-^ceht*	سماعات
■ headphones	■ *sam-ma-^ceht ir-ra's*	سماعات رأس
■ recordable CDs	■ *is-Ti-wa-naht ley-zar far-gha, lit-tas-geel*	اسطوانات ليزر فارغة، للتسجيل
Will the warranty be honored in the US?	*yiS-laH iD-Da-mahn fi 'am-ree-ka?*	هل يصلح الضمان في أمريكا؟
Can I listen to this?	*mum-kin as-ma^c da?*	هلي يمكن أن أسمع هذا؟

NEWSPAPERS AND MAGAZINES

Do you have an English-language <u>newspaper</u>?	*^can-dak ga-ree-da in-gi-lee-zee?*	هل عندكم جريدة بالإنجليزية؟
■ magazine	■ *ma-gal-la*	مجلة
Do you have stamps?	*^can-dak Ta-waa-bi^c?*	هل عندك طوابع؟
■ postcards	■ *ku-root bus-teht*	بطاقات بريدية؟
■ a map of the town	■ *kha-ree-Ta lil-ba-lad*	خريطة للمدينة
■ a guidebook	■ *da-leel si-yeh-Hee*	دليل سياحي

PHOTOGRAPHIC SUPPLIES

Is there a camera shop near here?	*fee ma-**Hall** ka-me--**reht** "u-ray-ib?*	هل يوجد محل آلات تصوير قريب؟
I'd like a <u>good</u> camera.	*^ca-wiz [^caw-za] ka-me-ra <u>kwa-yi-sa</u>.*	أريد آلة تصوير جيدة
■ inexpensive	■ *ri-**khee**-Sa*	رخيصة
■ video	■ ***vid**-yo*	فيديو
■ digital camera	■ ***ka**-me-ra ra-qa-**mee**-ya*	كاميرا رقمية
■ SLR digital camera	■ ***ka**-me-ra ra-qa-**mee**-ya es-el-ar*	كاميرا رقمية إس إل آر
■ disposable camera	■ ***ka**-me-ra tir-**mee**-ha ba^cd il-is-ti^c-**mehl***	كاميرا معدة للطرح بعد الاستعمال
■ zoom lens	■ *^ca-da-sit zoom*	عدسة زوم
I want to charge the <u>battery</u>.	*a-na ^ca-wiz [^caw-za] ash-Han <u>il-baT-Ta-ree-ya</u>*	أريد أن أشحن البطارية
■ memory card	■ *bi-**Tah**-qit iz-**zeh**-ki-ra*	بطاقة الذاكرة
How many megabytes does it have?	*fee-ha kam me-ga-bayt?*	فيها كم ميغابايت؟
How many megapixels does it have?	*fee-ha kam me-ga-bik-sel?*	فيها كم ميغابيكسيل؟
Can I make prints from this card?	***mum** kin aT-ba^c **So**-war min il-bi-**Tah**-qa dee?*	هل أستطيع طبع صور من هذه البطاقة؟

Do you develop film?	*bit-Ham-ma-Doo 'af-lehm?*	هل تحمض الأفلام؟
A <u>print</u> with <u>glossy</u> finish.	*Soo-ra <u>lam-mee-^ca</u>.*	أريد طباعة لامعة
■ matte	■ *maT, maT-fee-ya*	مطفية
I want an <u>enlargement</u> of this one.	*^ca-wiz [^caw-za] <u>a-kab-bar</u> dee.*	أريد تكبير هذه
■ another print	■ *nus-kha tan-ya min dee*	نسخة أخرى من هذه
When will they be ready?	*hat-koon gah-za 'im-ta?*	متى ستكون جاهزة

SOUVENIRS

The Middle East is famous for ceramics, carpets, jewelry, copper and brassware, leather goods, and fine inlay work in metal and wood. There is no problem in having goods shipped or air-freighted home, though there are likely to be restrictions on the export of antiques. If you are considering buying an antique, make sure you get a government guarantee of authenticity.

Bargaining is normal practice in traditional markets and bazaars, though not in modern shops or supermarkets. The basic technique is to express mild shock and disbelief at the price suggested, propose a sum well below that, then gradually work up to a compromise between the two. Often the shopkeeper will make you a "final offer" as you are about to leave the shop. It is quite all right to shop around and compare prices, then return to a shop where you have already bargained strenuously. You will always be welcome!

Arabic has many elaborate phrases for use on such occasions. Some of the most useful are:

Be generous!	*khal-**leek** ka-**reem**!*	كن كريما!
You're putting me off (with the price)!	*khaD-**Deyt**-nee!*	أفزعتني!
Come down a bit.	***naz**-zil **shway**-ya.*	أخفض لي السعر
Let's split the difference.	*ni"-sim il-**ba**-lad nuS-**Seyn**.*	نقسم البلد نصفين
Here's the money.	*it-**faD**-Dal*	تفضل

When you do buy something, the shopkeeper — and friends, too — will congratulate you with:

Congratulations!	*mab-**rook**!*	مبروك!
To which the reply is:	*al-**laah** yi-beh-rik feek [**fee**-kee]*	الله يبارك فيك
Do you have <u>leather goods</u>?	^c*an-du-kum maS-nu-^c**aat** gil-dee-ya?*	هل عندكم مصنوعات جلدية؟
■ jewelry	■ *mu-gaw-ha-**raat***	مجوهرات
■ pottery, ceramics	■ *fukh-**khaar***	فخار، خزف
■ carpets	■ *sa-ga-**geed***	سجاجيد
■ (long narrow) rugs	■ *mash-sha-**yeht***	مشايات
■ woven rugs	■ *'**ak**-li-ma*	اكلمة
■ caftans	■ *"a-fa-**Teen***	قفاطين

■ galabiyyas (Arab robe)	■ *gal-la-bee-yeht*	جلاليب
■ brassware	■ *muS-nu-^caat ni-Hehs*	مصنوعات نحاس أصفر
■ copperware	■ *maS-nu-^caat ni-Hehs 'aH-mar*	مصنوعات نحاس أحمر
■ glassware	■ *maS-nu-^caat "i-zehz*	مصنوعات زجاجية
I'm looking for <u>a brass tray</u>.	*^ca-wiz [^caw-za] <u>Sa-nee-ya ni-Hehs</u>*	أريد صينية نحاس
■ a tray with inlay	■ *Sa-nee-ya mu-Ta^c-^ca-ma*	صينية مطعمة
■ a tray with a stand	■ *Sa-nee-ya bi kur-see*	صينية بكرسي
■ a box with inlay	■ *san-doo" mu-Ta^c-^cam*	صندوق مطعم
■ a coffee set	■ *Ta"m lil-"ah-wa*	طاقم للقهوة
■ a chess set	■ *sha-Ta-rang*	طاقم شطرنج
■ a coffeepot	■ *'ab-ree" "ah-wa*	إبريق قهوة
■ an ashtray	■ *Ta"-Too-"a*	طفاية
■ slippers	■ *shib-shib*	شبشب
■ sandals	■ *san-dal*	صندل
■ a leather bag	■ *shan-Ta gild*	حقيبة جلدية
■ a leather cushion (poufee)	■ *boof gild*	حشية جلدية

■ a water (hubble bubble) pipe	■ *shee-sha*	نارجيلة، شيشة
■ a vase	■ *zhu-ree-ya*	زهرية
■ prayer beads	■ *sib-Ha*	سبحة
Do you sell Oriental perfumes?	*^can-du-kum ^cu-Toor shar-"ee-ya?*	هل عندكم عطور شرقية؟
■ jasmine	■ *yas-meen*	ياسمين
■ rose	■	ورد
■ sandalwood	■	صندل
Is this handmade?	*da -shughl yadd?*	هل هذا شغل يد؟
Please wrap these for me.	*lif-fu-hum-lee, min faD-lak.*	أرجو أن تلف هذا لي
Will you airfreight this for me?	*mum-kin tib-^cat-hoo-lee bil-ba-reed il-gaw-wee?*	هل ترسل لي هذا بالبريد الجوي؟
Please send it by surface mail.	*ib-^cat-hoo-lee bil-ba-reed il-^ceh-dee*	أرجو أن ترسل لي هذا بالبريد العادي

STATIONERY ITEMS

I want —.	*^ca-wiz [^caw-za] —.*	أريد —.
■ a ballpoint pen	■ *"a-lam gaff*	قلم جاف
■ envelopes	■ *Zu-roof*	ظروف
■ an eraser	■ *as-tee-ka*	ممسحة
■ glue	■ *Samgh*	صمغ

■ emery boards	■ **mab**-rad **wa**-ra" liD-Da-**waa**-fir	مبرد ورق للأظافر
■ eyebrow pencil	■ "**a**-lam Ha-**weh**-gib	قلم حواجب
■ eyeliner	■ ay-lay-nar, kuHl	قلم كحل
■ eye shadow	■ Dill lil-^cu-**yoon**	ظل جفون
■ washcloth	■ foo-Ta lil-**wishsh**	فوطة/منشفة وجه
■ gargle	■ ghar-**gha**-ra	غرغرة
■ hairspray	■ is-**brey** lish-**sha**^cr	مثبت للشعر
■ lipstick	■ rooj	أحمر الشفاه
■ makeup	■ mak-**yaj**	مكياج
■ mascara	■ mas-**ka**-ra	ماسكره
■ mirror	■ mi-**reh**-ya	مرآة
■ mouthwash	■ gha-seel lil-**famm**	غسيل للفم
■ nail clippers	■ "aS-**Saa**-fa liD-Da-**waa**-fir	قصافة للأظافر
■ a nail file	■ **mab**-rad Da-waa-fir	مبرد للأظافر
■ nail polish	■ ma-nee-**keer**	طلاء أظافر
■ nail polish remover	■ a-see-**tohn**	مزيل طلاء الأظافر
■ nail scissors	■ ma-"aSS liD-Da-**waa**-fir	مقص أظافر
■ night cream	■ kreym lil-**leyl**	كريم لليل

■ razor blades	■ *'am-wehs Hi-leh-"a*	أمواس حلاقة
■ sanitary napkins	■ *fo waT SiH-Hee-ya*	فوط صحية
■ shampoo	■ *sham-poo*	شامبو
■ shaving soap	■ *Sa-boon Hi-leh-"a*	صابون حلاقة
■ soap	■ *Sa-boon*	صابون
■ a sponge	■ *sa-fin-ga*	إسفنجة
■ suntan lotion	■ *los-yohn li Hi-meh-yit il-bash-ra*	سائل حماية البشرة
■ suntan oil	■ *zeyt li Hı-meh-yit il-bash-ra*	زيت حماية البشرة
■ talcum powder	■ *bud-rit talk*	بودرة تلك
■ tampons	■ *tam-paks*	صمامات قطنية
■ tissues	■ *ma-na-deel wa-ra"*	مناديل ورق
■ toilet paper	■ *wa-ra" twa-litt*	ورق تواليت
■ a toothbrush	■ *fur-shit 'as-nehn*	فرشاة للأسنان
■ toothpaste	■ *mac-goon lil-'as-nehn*	معجون أسنان
■ tweezers	■ *mul-"aaT*	ملقاط

PERSONAL CARE AND SERVICES

AT THE BARBER

Does the hotel have a barber shop?	*fee Hal-**leh"** fil-**fun**-du"?*	هل يوجد حلاق بالفندق؟
Where is there a good barber shop?	*feyn a-**leh**-"ee Hal-**leh"** kway-yis?*	أين أجد حلاقاً جيداً؟
Do I have to wait long?	***leh**-zim as-**tan**-na ki-**teer**?*	هل يجب أن أنتظر فترة طويلة؟
I want <u>a shave</u>.	*^c**aw**-zak <u>tiH-**la**"-lee id-da"n</u>.*	أريد أن أحلق ذقني
■ a haircut	■ *ti-"**uS**-**Si**-lee sha^c-ree*	أقص شعري
■ just a trim	■ *ti-"**aS**-Sar-**hoo**-lee shway-ya*	مجرد تهذيب
Trim it <u>at the front</u>.	*khif-fu-**hoo**-lee <u>min "ud-**dehm**</u>.*	قصه قليلاً من الأمام
■ at the back	■ *min **wa**-ra*	من الخلف
■ at the sides	■ *min ig-gi-**nehb***	على الجوانب
Leave it long.	*khal-**lee** Ta-weel shway-ya.*	اتركه طويل
I'd like it very short.	*"aS-Sar-**hoo**-lee khaa-liS.*	أريده قصيراً جداً

I'd like a razor cut.	**"uS-Soo bil-moos.**	قصه بالموسى
Please trim my —.	*min faD-lak uz-buT-lee —.*	من فضلك قص قليلاً—.
■ beard	■ *id-da''n*	ذقني
■ mustache	■ *ish-sha-nab*	شاربي، شنبي
■ sideburns	■ *is-sa-weh-lif*	سوالفي
I want to have <u>my beard</u> shaved off.	^c*a-wiz aH-la'' da''-nee.*	أريد أن أحلق ذقني
■ my mustache	■ *sha-na-bee*	شاربي، شنبي
I part my hair <u>on the left</u>.	*af-ri'' sha^c-ree ^cash-shi-mehl.*	أفرق شعري من اليسار
■ on the right	■ ^c*al-yi-meen*	من اليمين
■ in the middle	■ *fil-wuST*	من الوسط
A little more here.	*'ak-tar shway-ya hi-na.*	أكثر قليلاً من هنا
That's enough.	*ki-feh-ya ki-da.*	هذا يكفي
That's fine.	*kway-yis ki-da*	هذا حسن
I (don't) want —.	*(mish)* ^c*a-wiz —.*	(لا) أريد —
■ shampoo	■ *sham-poo*	شامبو
■ tonic	■ *ko-lon-ya*	كولونيا
■ hair oil	■ *zeyt sha^cr*	زيت شعر
■ hairspray	■ *is-brey*	مثبت الشعر

| Can I see it in the mirror? | ***mum*-kin a-*shoo*-foo fil-mi-*reh*-ya?** | أريد أن أنظر في المرآة |
| How much do I owe you? | ^c***a*-wiz kam?** | كم الحساب؟ |

AT THE BEAUTY PARLOR

[For cutting and trimming terms, see "At the Barber"]

Is there a <u>beauty parlor</u> near here?	fee Sa-***lohn*** tag-meel "u-***ray*-yib?**	هل يوجد صالون تجميل قريب؟
■ hairdresser	■ kwa-***feer***	مصفف شعر. كوافير
Can I make an appointment —?	***mum*-kin aH-giz ma-^c*ehd* —?**	أريد حجز موعد
■ this afternoon	■ ba^cd iD-***Duhr***	بعد الظهر
■ tomorrow	■ ***buk*-ra**	غداً
Can you give me —?	***mum*-kin ti^c-*mil*-lee —?**	أريد —؟
■ a color rinse	■ sham-***poo*** bil-***lohn***	شامبو تلوين
■ a facial massage	■ tad-***leek***	تدليك وجه
■ a steam massage	■ tad-***leek*** bil-bu-***khaar***	تدليك بالبخار
■ a manicure	■ ma-nee-***keer***	مانيكير
■ a pedicure	■ pi-di-***keer***	باديكير
■ a permanent	■ ber-ma-***nant***	برماننت

■ a shampoo	■ *sham-***poo**	شامبو
■ a tint	■ ***Sab***-gha	صبغة
■ a touch up	■ ***Sab***-gha *lig-gu-***zoor**	صبغة الجذور
■ a wash and set	■ ***mee***-zam plee	غسيل وتصفيف
■ a wash and blow dry	■ *gha-***seel** *wi sish-***war** *bass*	غسيل وتجفيف
I (don't) want hairspray.	(*mish*) ^c*aw-za is-***brey**.	(لا) أريد مثبت للشعر
Just a little.	*shway*-ya *bass*.	قليل فقط
I'd like to see a color chart.	^c*aw-za a-***shoof** *da-leel 'al-***when**.	أريد أن أرى دليل الألوان
I want this color.	^c*aw-za il-***lohn** *da*.	أريد هذا اللون
■ the same color	■ *nafs il-***lohn**	نفس اللون
■ a darker color	■ *lohn '***agh**-ma"	لون أعمق
■ a lighter color	■ *lohn '***af**-taH	لون أفتح

THE HAMMAM

Known in the West as the "Turkish bath," the *Hammehm* is in fact a general Middle East development of the Roman communal bath house — a social as well as a hygienic institution. Gossip, intrigue, and sometimes serious debate were as important to the clientele as the steaming, bathing, and massage that took place.

Many hammams still function; if you decide to use their services establish first what you want and how much it will cost. The price quoted may well not include tips to whoever hands out the towels, minds the clothes, and so on.

LAUNDRY AND DRY CLEANING

You may see the *mak-wa-gee* working in a tiny shop open to the street. He will press clothing and bed linens and have them delivered to your door within 24 hours if you are staying in the neighborhood. Note that the quality of dry cleaning services is highly variable. It is safest to take clothes with you that can be washed.

Is there a <u>laundry service</u> in the hotel?	*fee gha-**seel** wi **mak**-wa fil-**fun**-du"?*	هل يوجد غسيل ومكواة في الفندق؟
■ a dry cleaning service	■ *tan-**Deef** neh-shif*	تنظيف جاف
Is there a <u>laundry</u> near here?	*fee **magh**-sa-la "u-ray-**yi**-ba?*	هل توجد مغسلة قريبة؟
■ an ironer	■ *mak-**wa**-gee*	مكوجي. محل للكي
I want to have these —.	*dee —.*	هذه — .
■ washed	■ *lil-gha-**seel***	للغسيل
■ dry cleaned	■ *lit-tan-**Deef** in-**neh**-shif*	للتنظيف الجاف
■ mended	■ *lit-taS-**leeH***	للتصليح
■ ironed	■ *lil-**mak**-wa*	للكي
Here's the list.	*it-**faD**-Dal il-"**ay**-ma.*	هذه هي القائمة

[See Shopping section for clothes words.]

When will it/they be ready?	Hat-**koon** gah-za 'im-ta?	متى ستكون جاهزة؟
I need them <u>for tonight</u>.	a-na miH-**tehg**-ha [miH-ta-**geh**-ha] bil-**leyl**.	أريدهم الليلة
■ tomorrow	■ buk-ra	غداً
■ the day after tomorrow	■ ba^c-di buk-ra	بعد غد
I am leaving <u>soon</u>.	a-na mi-seh-fir [mis-**saf**-ra] "u-**ray**-yib.	سأسافر قريبا
■ tomorrow	■ buk-ra	غداً
Is my laundry ready?	il-gha-**seel** bi-**teh**-^cee geh-hiz?	هل غسيلي جاهز؟
This isn't my laundry.	dee mish bi-ta^c-tee.	هذه ليست لي
There's something missing.	fee **Ha**-ga na"-Sa.	ينقص شيء ما
There is a button missing.	fee zu-**raar** naa-"iS.	ينقص زر
This is silk.	da Ha-reer.	هذا حرير

SHOE REPAIRS

| Can you repair these shoes for me? | **mum**-kin ti-Sal-**laH**-lee ig-**gaz**-ma dee? | هل يمكن أن تصلح لي هذه الأحذية؟ |

They need new <u>heels</u>.	*leh-zim <u>ka^cb</u> gi-deed*	تحتاج لكعب جديد
■ soles	■ *na^cl*	لنعل
Can you fix it while I wait?	*mum-kin ti-Sal-laH-ha Heh-lan?*	هل يمكن تصليحها حالاً؟
Would you polish them too?	*mum-kin ti-lam-ma^c-heh-lee ka-mehn?*	هل يمكن أن تلمعها أيضاً؟
I need them tomorrow.	*a-na miH-tehg-ha [miH-ta-geh-ha] buk-ra.*	أحتاجها غداً

WATCH REPAIRS

Can you fix this <u>watch</u> for me?	*mum-kin ti-Sal-laH-lee <u>is-seh-^ca</u> dee?*	هل تستطيع إصلاح هذه الساعة لي؟
■ alarm clock	■ *il-mi-nab-bih da?*	هذا المنبه
I need a new <u>strap</u>.	*^caw-za 'us-teek gi-deed*	تحتاج لأوستيك جديد
■ crystal (glass)	■ *"i-zehz*	لزجاج
■ hour hand	■ *^ca"-rab sa-^ceht*	لعقرب ساعات
■ minute hand	■ *^ca"-rab da-"eh-yi"*	لعقرب دقائق
■ second hand	■ *ca"- rab sa-weh-nee*	لعقرب ثواني
■ battery	■ *baT-Ta-ree-ya*	لبطارية
It's stopped.	*wi"-fit*	توقفت

It's fast.	*bit-"ad-dim.*	تقدم
It's slow.	*bit-'akh-khar.*	تؤخر
It needs cleaning.	*ᶜaw-za tan-Deef.*	تحتاج لتنظيف
When will it be ready?	*hat-koon gah-za 'im-ta?*	متى ستكون جاهزة؟
May I have a receipt?	*mum-kin tid-dee-nee waSl?*	أرجوك أعطني إيصالاً

CAMERA REPAIRS

Can you fix this camera?	*mum-kin ti-Sal-laH-lee ik-ka-me-ra dee?*	هل يمكن تصليح آلة التصوير هذه؟
There's a problem with —.	*fee mush-ki-la ma-ᶜa —.*	هناك مشكلة في —
■ the exposure counter	■ *ᶜad-dehd iS-So-war*	عداد الصور
■ the film winder	■ *di-rehᶜ it-tagh-yeer*	ذراع التغيير
■ the light meter	■ *gi-hehz it-taᶜ-reeD/ miq-yehs iD-Doh'*	مقياس الضوء
■ the rangefinder	■ *Daa-bit il-ma-seh-fa*	ضابط المسافة
■ the shutter	■ *il-gheh-li", ish-sha-tar*	الغالق

How much will it cost to fix it?	*it-taS-**leeH** hay-**kal**-lif kam?*	كم يكلف تصليحها؟
When can I come and get it?	*as-ti-**lim**-ha '**im**-ta?*	متى أحضر لاستلامها؟
I need it as soon as possible.	^c*a-**wiz**-ha [^caw-**zeh**-ha] fi '**a**"-rab wa"t **mum**-kin.*	أحتاجها في أقرب وقت ممكن

MEDICAL CARE

AT THE PHARMACY

Where is the nearest <u>pharmacy</u>?	*feyn 'a"-rab 'ag-za-kheh-na/ Say-Da-lee-ya?*	أين أقرب أجزخانة/ صيدلية؟
■ all-night pharmacy	■ *'ag-za-kheh-na ley-lee-ya*	أجزخانة ليلية
At what times does it open (close)?	*bi-yif-taH (bi-yi"-fil) is-seh-^ca kam?*	متى تفتح (تغلق)؟
I need something for —.	*^ca-wiz [^caw-za] Ha-ga li —.*	أريد دواء —
■ asthma	■ *ir-rabw*	للربو
■ a cold	■ *zu-kehm, il-bard*	للبرد
■ constipation	■ *il-'im-sehk*	للامساك
■ a cough	■ *kuH-Ha*	للسعال
■ diarrhea	■ *il-'is-hehl*	للاسهال
■ a fever	■ *su-khu-nee-ya*	للحمى
■ hay fever	■ *Ha-seh-see-ya ra-bee-^cee-ya*	للحساسية الربيعية
■ headache	■ *Su-daa^c*	للصداع
■ indigestion	■ *soo'il-haDm*	لسوء الهضم
■ insomnia	■ *^ca-dam in-nohm*	للأرق

■ nausea	■ *gham-ma-mehn*	لغثيان النفس
■ sunburn	■ *Hu-roo" ish-shams*	حروق الشمس
■ toothache	■ *wa-ga^c fiD-Dirs*	لألم الأسنان
■ an upset stomach	■ *ta-^{c}ab fil-mi^c-da*	لاضطراب المعدة

Do I need a prescription for this medicine?	*leh-zim ru-shit-ta lid-da-wa da?*	هل أحتاج لروشتة لهذا الدواء؟
Can you fill this prescription for me now?	*mum-kin tiS-rif-lee ir-ru-shit-ta dee dil-wa'"-tee?*	هل يمكنك أن تصرف الروشتة لي الآن؟
Do you stock this medicine?	*^{c}an-du-kum id-da-wa da?*	هل عندكم هذا الدواء؟
It's an emergency.	*da Ta-waa-ri'.*	هذه طوارئ
Can I wait for it?	*as-tan-neh-ha?*	هل أنتظره؟
How long will it take?	*ha-yeh-khud "ad-di 'eyh?*	كم من الوقت يحتاج؟
I would like —.	*^{c}a-wiz [^{c}aw-za] —.*	أريد —.

■ adhesive tape	■ *mu-sham-ma^c laa-Siq*	شريط لاصق
■ antacid	■ *da-wa Didd il-Hu-moo-Da*	دواء ضد الحموضة
■ an antiseptic	■ *mu-Tah-hir*	مطهر
■ aspirins	■ *as-bi-reen*	أسبرين

■ bandages	■ *ru-baaT*	رباط
■ Band-Aids	■ *blaas-tir*	ضمادات لاصقة
■ corn plasters	■ *blaas-tir ^ca-shehn i-kal-loo*	ضمادات لاصقة للمسامير
■ (absorbent) cotton	■ *"uTn Tib-bee*	قطن طبي
■ cough drops	■ *bas-til-ya liz-zohr*	باستيليا طبية
■ cough syrup	■ *da-wa kuH-Ha*	دواء للسعال
■ ear (nose) drops	■ *nu-"aT lil-widn (lil-ma-na-kheer)*	نقط للأذن (للأنف)
■ eye drops	■ *"aT-ra lil-^ceyn*	نقط للعين
■ an inhaler	■ *bakh-kheh-kha*	جهاز للاستنشاق
■ insect repellent	■ *kreym Taa-rid lil-Ha-sha-raat*	كريم طارد للحشرات
■ iodine	■ *Sab-ghit yood*	يود
■ a (mild) laxative	■ *mu-lay-yin*	مسهل
■ milk of magnesia	■ *maH-lool il-magh-nee-sya*	محلول المغنيزيا
■ painkillers	■ *mu-sak-ki-neht*	مسكنات
■ potassium permanganate	■ *ber-min-ga-neht il-bu-tas-yoom*	برمنجنات البوتاسيوم
■ sanitary napkins	■ *fo-waT SiH-Hee-ya*	فوط صحية

■ sleeping pills	■ *Hu-boob mu-naw-wi-ma*	حبوب منومة
■ suppositories	■ *lu-boos, mu-sah-hil*	لبوس
■ tampons	■ *tam-paks*	تامبونات طبية
■ a thermometer	■ *tir-mo-mitr, mi-zehn Ha-raa-ra*	ثرمومتر
■ tranquilizers	■ *mu-had-di-'eht*	مهدئات
■ vitamins	■ *vi-ta-mi-neht*	فيتامينات
Do you have care products for <u>contact lenses</u>?	^c*an-du-kum maH-lool lil-*^c*a-da-seht il-laS-qa?*	هل عندكم محلول عدسات لاصقة؟
■ hard lenses	■ *li l-*^c*a-da-seht in-nash-fa*	عدسات صلبة
■ soft lenses	■ *li l-*^c*a-da-seht iT-Ta-ree-ya*	عدسات لينة

FINDING A DOCTOR

Most doctors you will come across in the Middle East are likely to have a good working knowledge of English, because English is used in the teaching of medicine in many Arab countries.

I need a doctor.	*a-na miH-tehg [miH-teh-ga] Ta-beeb.*	أنا محتاج لطبيب

Do you know a doctor who speaks English?	*ti^c-raf* Ta-**beeb** *bi-yit-**kal**-lim in-gi-**lee**-zee **kway**-yis?*	هل تعرف طبيبا يتكلم الانجليزية بطلاقة؟
Where is his office (his clinic)?	*mak-ta-**boo** (^cee-**yat**-too) feyn?*	أين مكتبه (عيادته) ؟
Where is the hospital?	*il-mus-**tash**-fa feyn?*	أين المستشفى؟

TALKING TO A DOCTOR

I don't feel well.	*a-na-ta^c-**behn** [ta^c-**beh**-na].*	أشعر بتعب
I feel sick.	*nif-see **gham**-ma ^ca-**leh**-ya.*	أشعر بغثيان النفس
I feel dizzy.	*a-na **deh**-yikh [**day**-kha].*	أشعر بدوخة
It hurts me here.	*bi-yiw-**ga**^c-nee **hi**-na.*	الألم هنا
My <u>ear</u> hurts.	<u>wid</u>-nee bi-tiw-**ga**^c-nee	اذني تؤلمني
■ eye	■ ^c**ey**-nee	عيني
■ foot	■ **rig**-lee	قدمي
■ fand	■ '**ee**-dee	يدي
■ head	■ **raa**-see	رأسي
■ neck	■ ra-"**ab**-tee	عنقي
■ knee	■ ruk-**bi**-tee	ركبتي
■ leg	■ **rig**-lee	رجلي

■ wrist	■ *khun-"it 'ee-dee*	رسغي
My <u>arm</u> hurts.	<u>*di-reh*</u>-^c*ee*	ذارعي يؤلمني
■ ankle	■ *ka*^c-*bee*	كعب القدم
■ back	■ *Dah-ree*	ظهري
■ chest	■ *Sid-ree*	صدري
■ elbow	■ *koo-*^c*ee*	كوعي
■ finger	■ *Su-baa-*^c*ee*	اصبعي
■ heart	■ *"al-bee*	قلبي
■ hip	■ *ra-da-fee*	ردفي
■ mouth	■ *bu"-"ee*	فمي
■ shoulder	■ *kit-fee*	كتفي
■ tooth	■ *Dir-see*	ضرسي
■ throat	■ *zoh-ree*	حنجرتي
I've broken my —.	*ka-sart —.*	— مكسور
My whole body aches.	*kul-li gis-mee bi-yiw-ga*^c*-nee.*	كل جسمي يؤلمني
I feel feverish.	^c*an-dee su-khu-nee-ya.*	أشعر بحمى
I'm constipated.	^c*an-dee 'im-<u>sehk</u>*	عندي إمساك
I have a <u>cold</u>.	^c*an-dee zu-kehm.*	عندي برد
■ an abscess	■ *khar-raag*	خراج

■ something in my eye	■ *Ha*-ga fi ^c*ey-nee*	شيء في عيني
■ an infection	■ *'il-ti-***hehb**	التهاب
■ diabetes	■ *ma-raD is-***suk**-*kar*	مرض السكر
■ diarrhea	■ *'is-***hehl**	إسهال
■ dysentery	■ *du-sin-***tar**-*ya*	دوسنتاريا
■ hepatitis	■ *'il-ti-***hehb** *ka-bi-dee*	التهاب كبدي
■ a stomachache	■ *ta*^c-*ab fil-***mi**^c-*da*	ألم في المعدة
I'm pregnant.	*a-na* **Heh**-*mil.*	أنا حامل
I'm (not) allergic to —.	*can-dee (ma-*^c*an-***deesh***) Ha-sa-***see**-*ya min —.*	(ليس) عندي حساسية —
■ antibiotics	■ *mu-Da-***Daat** *ha-ya-***wee**-*ya*	للمضادات الحيوية
■ penicillin	■ *bi-ni-sil-***leen**	للبنسلين
I had a heart attack — years ago.	*gat-lee 'az-ma qal-***bee**-*ya min — sin-***neen**.	أصبت بأزمة قلبية من — سنة
I have high (low) blood pressure.	^c*an-dee Daght* ^c*eh lee (**waa**-Tee).*	عندي ضغط دم مرتفع (منخفض)
Do I have <u>appendicitis</u>?	^c*an-dee <u>'il-ti-***hehb** *iz-***zay**-*da</u>?*	هل عندي التهاب الزائدة؟
■ tonsillitis	■ *'il-ti-***hehb** *il-***li**-*waz*	التهاب اللوز
■ flu	■ *in-floo-***in**-*za*	إنفلونزا
Do I have to go to hospital?	*leh-zim **ad**-khul il-mus-***tash**-fa?*	هل يجب أن أذهب للمستشفى؟

What can I eat and drink?	*mum-kin 'eh-kul wash-rab 'eyh?*	ماذا أستطيع أن آكل واشرب؟

Doctor's Instructions

Open your mouth.	*if-taH bu"-"ak/fum-mak.*	افتح فمك
Stick out your tongue.	*Tal-la^c li-seh-nak.*	اخرج لسانك
Cough.	*kuHH.*	اسعل
Breathe deeply.	*khud na-fas Ta-weel.*	خذ نفساً طويلاً
Take off your clothes (to the waist).	*i"-la^c hu-doo-mak (il-lee foh")*	اخلع ملابسك (حتى الوسط)
Lie down on your back.	*nehm ^ca-la Dah-rak.*	ارقد على ظهرك
■ on your stomach	■ *^ca-la baT-nak*	على بطنك
Get dressed.	*il-bis [il-bi-see].*	البس

Patient

Are you going to give me a prescription?	*ha-tid-dee-nee ru-shit-ta?*	هل ستعطيني روشتة؟
How often should I take this?	*a-khud-ha kul-li "ad-di 'eyh?*	كم مرة في اليوم سآخذ من هذا؟
(How long) do I have to stay in bed?	*leh-zim a"-^cud fis-si-reer ("ad-di 'eyh)?*	(حتى متى)سأبقى في السرير؟
Do you need a blood sample?	*in-ta ^ca-wiz ^cay-yi-nit damm?*	هل تحتاج لعينة دم؟

■ a urine sample	■ *^cuy-yi-nit bool*	عينة بول

Will you test my blood pressure?	*hat-shoof DakhT id-damm?*	هل ستقيس ضغط الدم؟
Should I have X rays taken?	*ha-ti^c-mil-lee 'a-shi^c-^ca?*	هل أقوم بعمل أشعة؟
What is your fee?	*kam 'at-^ceh-bak?*	كم أتعابك؟
I have medical insurance.	*^can-dee ta'-meen SiH-Hee.*	عندي تأمين صحي
Thank you very much.	*'al-fe shukr.*	شكراً جزيلاً

ACCIDENTS AND EMERGENCIES

Help!	*il-Ha-"oo-nee!*	النجدة!
Quickly, get a doctor!	*uT-lub Ta-beeb Heh-lan!*	اطلب الطبيب بسرعة
Call an ambulance!	*heht il-'is-^cehf*	اطلب الاسعاف
We must go to the hospital.	*leh-zim ni-rooH il-mus-tash-fa.*	يجب أن نذهب للمستشفى
I've (he's) lost a lot of blood.	*na zaft (na-zaf) damm ki-teer.*	فقدت (فقد) دماً كثيراً
I've (he's) had a heart attack.	*gat-lee (gat-loo) 'az-ma qal-bee-ya.*	أصبت (أصيب) بأزمة قلبية
I think the bone is broken.	*a-Zunn inn il-^caDm in-ka-sar.*	أعتقد أن العظم مكسور

I cut myself.	*in-ga-raHt.*	جرحت نفسي
I burned myself.	*it-Ha-ra"t*	حرقت نفسي
I was (he was) knocked down.	*kha-ba-Tit-nee (kha-ba-Ti-too) ca-ra-bee-ya.*	صدمتني (صدمته) سيارة
I was (he was) bitten by a dog.	*kalb caD-Di-nee (caD-doo).*	عضني (عضه) كلب
rabies	*ma-raD il-kalb*	مرض الكلب

AT THE DENTIST

Can you recommend a dentist?	*mum-kin ti-"ul-lee ca-la Ta-beeb 'as-nehn kway-yis?*	هل تستطيع أن تقترح طبيب أسنان؟
I'd like to make an appointment.	*ca-wiz [caw-za] aH-giz ma-cehd.*	أريد أن أحجز موعداً
I must see him as soon as possible.	*leh-zim a-shoo-foo fi 'a"-rab wa"t mum-kin.*	يجب أن أراه في أقرب وقت ممكن
I have an awful toothache.	*'as-neh-nee bi-tiw-gac-nee gid-dan.*	عندي ألم أسنان رهيب
I've lost a filling.	*il-Hashw wi-"ic.*	وقع الحشو
I've lost a crown.	*iT-Tar-boosh wi-"ic.*	وقع الطربوش
I've broken a tooth.	*fee sin-na in-ka-sa-rit.*	عندي سن مكسور

My gums hurt me.	*Il-Il-su bi-tiw-ga^c noo.*	لثتي تؤلمني
Is there an infection?	*fee "il-ti-hehb?*	هل هناك التهاب؟
Will it have to be extracted?	*leh-zim tit-khi-li^c?*	هل يجب أن تخلع السن؟
Will you fill it —?	*ha-tiH-shee-ha —?*	هل ستحشوه —؟
■ temporarily	■ *mu-'aq-qa-tan*	مؤقتاً
■ with amalgam	■ *bi Hashw ^ceh-dee*	بحشو عادي
■ with gold	■ *bi Hashw da-hab*	بذهب
■ with silver	■ *bi Hashw faD-Da*	بفضة
■ with platinum	■ *bi Hashw bla-teen*	ببلاتين
I need a painkiller.	*^ca-wiz [^caw-za] mu-sak-kin*	أحتاج لمسكن
Can you fix —?	*mum-kin ti Sal-laH —?*	هل تستطيع إصلاح ؟
■ this bridge	■ *ik-kub-ree da*	هذا الكوبري
■ this crown	■ *iT-Tar-boosh da*	هذا الطربوش
■ this denture	■ *iT-Ta"-mi da*	هذا الطاقم
When should I come back?	*ar-ga^c 'im-ta?*	متى أعود؟
What is your fee?	*kam 'at-^ceh-bak?*	كم أتعابك؟

WITH THE OPTICIAN

Is there an optician near here?	*fee na-Da-Da-raa-tee "u-ray-yib min hi-na?*	هل يوجد محل للنظارات قريب؟
Can you repair these glasses for me?	*mum-kin ti-Sal-laH-lee in-naD-Daa-ra dee?*	هل يمكنك إصلاح هذه النظارة لي؟
Can you put in a new lens?	*mum-kin ti-rak-kib Ha-gar gi-deed?*	هل تستطيع تركيب عدسة جديدة؟
Can you repair the frame?	*mum-kin ti-Sal-laH-lee ish-sham-bar?*	هل يمكنك أن تصلح الإطار؟
I (don't) have the prescription.	*ᶜan-dee (ma-ᶜan-deesh) il ma-"ehs.*	(ليس) معي قياس نظر
Can you do an eye test now?	*mum-kin tiᶜ-mil-lee ma-"ehs na-Zar dil-wa"-tee?*	هل يمكن عمل قياس النظر الآن؟
Do you sell contact lenses?	*ᶜan-du-kum ᶜa-da-seht laS-qa?*	هل تبيع عدسات لاصقة؟
■ hard	■ *nash-fa*	صلبة
■ soft	■ *Ta-ree-ya*	لينة
I've lost a lens.	*Daa-ᶜit ᶜa-da-sa*	فقدت عدسة
Can you replace it right away?	*mum-kin tid-dee-nee waH-da dil-wa"-tee?*	هل تستطيع استبدالها حالاً؟

COMMUNICATIONS

POST OFFICE

Where's the nearest post office?	*feyn 'a"-rab mak-tab ba-reed?*	أين أقرب مكتب بريد؟
Where's a mailbox?	*feyn san-doo" il-bus-Ta?*	أين صندوق البريد؟
What's the postage on — to America?	*'eyh 'ug-rit il-ba-reed li 'am-ree-ka ^ca-shehn —?*	كم أجرة البريد لأمريكا —؟
■ this letter	■ *ig-ga-wehb-da*	لهذا الخطاب
■ an airmail letter	■ *ga-wehb bil-ba-reed ig-gaw-wee*	لخطاب بالبريد الجوي
■ a postcard	■ *kart bus-tehl*	لبطاقة بريدية
■ this package	■ *iT-Tar-di da*	لهذا الطرد
I'd like to send this —.	*^ca-wiz [^caw-za] ab-^cat da —.*	أريد إرسال هذا —
■ by surface mail	■ *bil-ba-reed il-^ceh-dee*	بالبريد العادي
■ by registered post	■ *bil-ba-reed il-mu-sag-gal*	بالبريد المسجل
■ by special delivery (express)	■ *bil-ba-reed il-mis-ta^c-gil*	بالبريد المستعجل
■ cash on delivery	■ *id-daf^c ^cand ititas-leem*	الدفع عند التسليم

May I use your phone?	**mum**-kin as-ta**ᶜ**-mil it-ti-li-**fohn**?	هل أستطيع استعمال هذا التلفون؟
country code	**nim**-rit il-**ba**-lad	رقم البلد
area code	in-**nim**-ra il-ma-Hal-**lee**-ya	الرقم المحلي
If we get cut off, call me back.	**i**-za il-**xaTT** in-qa-Taᶜ, kal-**lim**-nee **teh**-nee.	إذا قطع الخط اتصل بي مرة ثانية
I have a mobile phone.	**ᶜan**-dee mo-**bayl**	عندي تليفون قابل للحمل
I will send you a text message.	hab-**ᶜat**-lak tekst	سأرسل لك رسالة تليفونية مكتوبة
Is there network coverage here?	feeh tagh-Tee-ya **hi**-na?	هل توجد هنا تغطية تليفونية؟
Do you have an answerphone?	**ᶜan**-dak an-sir-**fohn**?	هل عندك آلة تسجيل للرسائل التليفونية؟
I will send you an e-mail.	hab-**ᶜat**-lak ee-meyl.	سوف أبعث لك رسالة إلكترونية
This is my e-mail address.	it-**faD**-Dal ᶜin-**wehn** il-ee-**meyl** bit-teh-**ᶜ**ee	هذا عنواني الإلكتروني
I want access to the internet.	**ᶜa**-wiz [**ᶜaw**-za] at-**far**-rag ᶜal-**in**-ter-net.	أريد قراءة الإنترنت
I want to make —.	**ᶜa**-wiz [**ᶜaw**-za] **a**ᶜ-mil mu-**kal**-ma —.	أريد عمل —
■ local call	■ ma-Hal-**lee**-ya	مكالمة محلية
■ person-to-person call	■ shakh-**See**-ya	مكالمة شخصية

Can I call direct?	*fee khaTT mu-heh-shir?*	هل أستطيع الاتصال مباشرة؟
I'd like to reverse the charges	*^ca-wiz [^caw-za] inn ish-shakhS il-maT-loob yid-fa^c.*	أريد أن يدفع الشخص المطلوب
I'd like to book a call to —.	*^ca-wiz [^caw-za] aH-giz mu-kal-ma li —.*	أريد حجز مكالمة لـ —.
How long will it take?	*ha-yeh-khud kam wa"t?*	هل يجب أن أنتظر مدة طويلة؟
I'd like to cancel the call.	*^ca-wiz [^caw-za] al-ghee il-mu-kal-ma*	أريد إلغاء المكالمة
How much does it cost —?	*— bi kam?*	كم سعر—؟
■ per minute	■ *id-da-"ee-"a*	الدقيقة
■ for three minutes	■ *ta-lat da-"eh-yi"*	الثلاث دقائق
Please give me Cairo 4810572.	*min faD-lak id-dee-nee il qaa-hi-ra ar-ba-^ca tu-man-ya weh Hid Sifr kham-sa sab-^ca it-neyn* (see p. 17 for numbers)	من فضلك أعطني القاهرة ٤٨١٠٥٧٢
My number is —.	*nim-ri-tee —.*	رقمي—.
Is Mr. [Mrs.] — in?	*is-say-yid [ma-dehm/ is-say-yi-da]?*	هل السيد — موجود [السيدة — موجودة]؟

(see p. 17 for numbers)

— isn't in.	— *mish maw-good*.	— ليس موجود.
May I speak to —.	*mum*-kin a *kal*-lim —?	هل يمكن أن أتكلم مع —؟
Hello.	'*a-loh*.	آلو
This is —.	*a-na* —.	أنا —
Who is calling?	*meen bi-yit-kal-lim*?	من يتكلم؟
One moment.	*laH-Za*.	لحظة
I can't hear.	*mish seh-mi^c [sam-^c a]*.	لا أسمع
Speak louder.	*ir-fa^c Soh-tak [ir-fa-^c ee Soh-tik]*.	ارفع صوتك
Don't hang up.	*khal-leek [khal-lee-kee] ma-^c eh-ya*.	لا تغلق
It's a bad line.	*il-khaTT wi-Hish*.	الخط سيئ
I'll try again.	*ha-gar-rab khaT-Ti teh-nee*.	سأحاول مرة ثانية
There's no reply.	*ma-Had-dish bee-rudd*.	لا إجابة
The line is busy.	*il-khaTT mash-ghool*.	الخط مشغول
Wrong number.	*nim-ra gha-laT*.	الرقم خطأ
I was cut off.	*il-khaTT in-"a-Ta^c*.	قطع الخط
Please dial it again.	*uT-lub in-nim-ra teh-nee min-faD-lak*.	أرجوك حاول ثانية
I want to leave a message.	*^c a-wiz [^c aw-za] a-seeb ri-seh-la*.	أريد أن أترك رسالة
How much was the call?	*keh-nit bi kam il-mu-kal-ma?*	كما كان سعر المكالمة؟

AT THE CYBER-CAFÉ

Is there a cyber-café near here?	*feeh qah-wit in-ter-net "u-ray-yib?*	هل هناك مقهى الإنترنت قريب؟
How much is it an hour?	*is-seh-^ca bi kam?*	بكم الساعة؟
a laptop	*lab-tob*	كمبيوتر صغير نقال
keyboard	*loo-Hit il-ma-fa-teeH*	لوحة المفاتيح
mouse	*il-faar*	فأر الكمبيوتر
I need an adaptor for my computer.	*a-na miH-tehg [miH-teh-ga] mu-Haw-wil lil-kom-byoo-tar bi-teh-^cee.*	أريد محوّل للكمبيوتر
password	*kil-mit is-sirr*	كلمة السر
user name	*ism taw-qee^c*	اسم توقيع
memory stick	*sha-ree-Hit iz-zeh-ki-ra*	شريحة الذاكرة
I want to —	*a-na ^ca-wiz [^caw-za] —*	أريد —
■ download this file	■ *a-Ham-mil il-ma-laff da*	تنزيل هذا الملف
■ print out this document	■ *aT-ba^c il-wa-see-qa dee*	طبع هذه الوثيقة
Do you have an e-mail address?	*^can-dak ^cin-wehn ee-mayl?*	هل عندك عنوان إلكتروني؟

DRIVING A CAR

SIGNS

No parking	mam-**noo**[c] il-'in-ti-**Zaar**	ممنوع الانتظار
No stopping	mam-**noo**[c] il-wu-"**oof**	ممنوع الوقوف
Caution	**iH**-dar	احذر
Stop	qif	قف
Slow	hadd is-**sur**-[c]a	هدئ السرعة
Danger	**kha**-Tar	خطر
Work in progress	man-**Ti**-qit [c]a-mal	منطقة عمل
School	mad-**ra**-sa	مدرسة
Hospital	mus-**tash**-fa	مستشفى
Motorway	Ta-**ree**" sa-**ree**[c]	طريق سريع
One Way	it-ti-**geh** **weh**-Hid	اتجاه واحد
No Entry	mam-**noo**[c] id-du-**khool**	ممنوع الدخول
Detour	taH-**wee**-la	تحويلة
Dangerous bends	mun-**Ha**-na kha-Tar	منحنى خطر
Keep right (left)	**il**-zim il-yi-**meen** (**ish**-shi-mehl)	الزم اليمين (اليسار)

CAR RENTALS

Where can I rent <u>a car</u>?	*min feyn a-'ag-gar <u>^ca-ra-bee-ya/say-yaa-ra</u>?*	من أين أستأجر سيارة؟
■ a motorcycle	■ *mo-to-sikl*	دراجة بخارية
■ a bicycle	■ *^ca-ga-la*	دراجة
■ a scooter	■ *skoo-tar*	دراجة صغيرة
I want a — car.	*^ca-wiz [^caw-za] ^ca-ra-bee-ya/say-yaa-ra —.*	أريد سيارة —.
■ small	■ *Su-ghay-ya-ra*	صغيرة
■ large	■ *ki-bee-ra*	كبيرة
■ sports	■ *spoor*	سبور
■ automatic	■ *'u-tu-ma-teek*	أوتوماتيكي
How much does it cost —?	*bi kam —?*	بكم —؟
■ per day	■ *fil-yohm*	في اليوم
■ per week	■ *fil-'us-boo^o*	في الأسبوع
Does that include full insurance?	*da bit-ta'-meen ik-keh-mil?*	هل هذا يشمل التأمين الكامل؟
Is the gas included?	*da bil-ban-zeen?s*	هل هذا يشمل البنزين؟
Do you accept credit cards?	*bi-ti"-ba-loo kri-dit kard?*	هل تقبلوا بطاقات اعتماد؟

إحترس توجد حيوانات
Caution: Animal Crossing

طريق غير ممهد
Bumpy Road

كوبري متحرك
Draw Bridge

طريق ضيق
Narrow Road

منحنى مزدوج
الأول لليسار
Double curves (S-curve)
(First one to the left)

منحدر خطر
Dangerous Incli

إحترس
Caution

عبور المشاه
Pedestrian Crossing

مركز إسعاف
Ambulance Cen

لافتة تشير إلى الاتجاهات
Sign indicating directions

علامة نهاية المدينة
Sign indicating city limits

ممنوع الانتظار في الأيام الفردية
No standing on odd days

ممنوع الوقوف قطعا
Absolutely no parking

Low clearance
bridge

ممنوع الانتظار في الأيام الزوجية
No standing on even days

ممنوع الانتظار
No standing

Passage in
both directions

مزلقان مفتوح
Open crossing

طريق غير ممهد
Bumpy road (potholes)

ممنوع الدخول
No entry

أقصى عرض ٢ متر
Maximum Width 2 meters

إنتهاء نطاق تحديد الانتظار
End of no standing zone

Here is my driver's license.	*it-**faD**-Dal ir-**rukh**-Sa.*	تفضل ها هي الرخصة
Here's my passport.	*it-**faD**-Dal il-baS-**boor**/ ga-**wehz** is-sa-**far**.*	تفضل ها هو جواز السفر
Do I have to leave a deposit?	*leh-zim ad-fa^c ^car-**boon**?*	هل يجب أن أترك عربونا؟
I want to rent the car here and leave it in —.	*^ca-wiz [^caw-za] a-'ag-gar il-^ca-ra-bee-ya hi-na w a-seeb-ha fi —.*	أريد استئجار السيارة هنا وتسليمها في —.
What kind of gas does it take?	*a-Hut-**Til**-ha ban-**zeen** 'eyh?*	ما نوع البنزين الذي تستخدمه السيارة؟

Renting a car tends to be expensive, and facilities are usually rather limited; you may have little choice of drop-off points and if you break down it may take some time to repair or replace the car.

Driving techniques in the big cities can be hair-raising. You will encounter every kind of wheeled and four-legged transport, few of them respecting the highway code.

Bear in mind, too, that in the case of an accident, especially in Saudi Arabia and some of the Gulf countries, you could be involved in extremely lengthy legal proceedings, irrespective of who was at fault. You may well decide it is preferable to hire a driver for short periods of time or use public transportation, which is generally both cheap and efficient.

ON THE ROAD

[For more directions see Getting Around Town.]

Excuse me . . .	*law sa-**maHt** . . .*	. . . بعد إذنك

Can you tell me . . . ?	*tis-maH ti-"ul-lee* . . . ?	أرجوك أن تقول لي . . .
Which way is it to —?	*min feyn iT-Ta-ree" li —?*	ما هو الطريق إلى — ؟
We're lost.	*tuh-na.*	ضللنا الطريق. تهنا
Is this the road to —?	*da Ta-ree" —?*	هل هذا هو الطريق إلى — ؟
Where does this road go?	*iT-Ta-ree" da bee-wad-dee ^{c}a-la feyn?*	إلى أين يؤدي هذا الطريق؟
How far is it to the next town?	*'a"-rab ba-lad ^{c}a-la bu^{c}d 'ad-di 'eyh?*	كم نبعد عن البلدة القادمة؟
What's the next town called?	*'eyh 'ism il-ba-lad ig-gay-ya?*	ما هو اسم البلدة القادمة؟
Can you show me on the map?	*mum-kin ti-war-ri-heh-lee ^{c}al-kha-ree-Ta?*	هل ممكن أن توضح لي الطريق على الخريطة؟
Is the road in good condition?	*is sik-ka kway-yi-sa?*	هل حالة الطريق جيدة؟
Is the road to — open?	*iT-Ta-ree" li — maf-TooH?*	هل الطريق إلى — مفتوح؟
How far is the next filling station?	*feyn 'a"-rab ma-Hat-Tit ban-zeen?*	أين أقرب محطة بنزين؟

The keys are locked inside the car.	*"a-falt il-^ca-ra-bee-ya ^ca-la l-ma-fa-teeH.*	أنا قفلت السيارة على المفاتيح
Is there a garage near here?	*fee war-sha "u-ray-yib min hi-na?*	هل توجد ورشة قريبة؟
Do you know a good mechanic?	*ti^c-raf mi-ka-nee-kee kway-yis?*	هل تعرف ميكانيكياً جيداً؟
I need a mechanic (a tow truck).	*a-na miH-tehg [miH-teh-ga] mi-ka-nee-kee (wintsh yis-Hab-nee).*	أحتاج ميكانيكي (شاحنة لسحب السيارة)
Do you have the spare part?	*^can-dak qiT-^cit il-ghi-yaar?*	هل عندك قطعة الغيار؟
Do you have distilled water?	*^can-dak may-ya mi-"aT-Ta-ra?*	هل عندك ماء مقطر؟
I (don't) have a spare wheel.	*^can-dee (ma-^can-deesh) is-tab-na/ ^ca-ga-la stibn.*	(ليس) عندي إطار احتياطي؟
Can you —?	*mum-kin —?*	هل من الممكن أن — ؟
■ help me	■ *ti-sa-^cid-nee*	تساعدني
■ push me	■ *ti-zu"-"i-nee*	تدفعني
■ tow me	■ *ti-gur-ri-nee*	تجرني
I don't have any tools.	*ma-^cand-deesh ^ci-dad.*	ليس معي أدوات
Can you lend me —?	*mum-kin ti-sal-lif-lee —?*	هل يمكن أن تسلفني —؟
■ a flashlight	■ *kash-shehf*	كشاف كهربائي

■ a hammer	■ *sha-koosh*	مطرقة، شاكوش
■ a jack	■ *ku-reek, jehk*	جك، مرفاع
■ a monkey wrench	■ *muf-tehH ki-beer/in-gi-lee-zee*	مفتاح ربط
■ a spanner	■ *muf-tehH Sa-moo-la*	مفتاح صواميل
■ pliers	■ *zar-ra-dee-ya*	زردية
■ a screwdriver	■ *mu-fakk ma-sa-meer*	مفك مسامير
There's something wrong with the —.	*fee Ha-ga bay-Za fi —.*	هناك مشكلة في —
■ directional signal	■ *if-fla-shar*	الاشارة
■ electrical system	■ *ni-Zaam ik-kah-ra-ba*	الكهرباء
■ exhaust	■ *ish-shak-mehn*	أنبوبة العادم
■ fan	■ *il-mar-wa-Ha*	المروحة
■ fan belt	■ *seer il-mar-wa-Ha*	سير المروحة
■ fuel pump	■ *tu-rum-bit il-ban-zeen*	طلمبة البنزين
■ gas tank	■ *khaz-zehn il-ban-zeen*	خزان البنزين
■ gears	■ *in-na"-leht, it-tu-roos*	التروس
■ gearshift	■ ^{c}*a-Sa il-fee-tehs*	ناقل السرعة
■ horn	■ *ik-ka-laks, in-ne-feer*	البوق، الكلاكسون

■ ignition	■ *il-'ish-^cehl*	الإشعـال
■ radiator	■ *ir-rad-ya-teer*	الرادياتير
■ starter	■ *il-kon-takt*	مبدئ الحركة
■ steering wheel	■ *id-di-rik-syohn/ ^ca-ga-lit is-si-weh-"a*	عجلة القيادة
■ transmission	■ *na"l il-Ha-ra-ka*	نقل الحركة
■ water pump	■ *tu-rum-bit il-may-ya*	طلمية

EXTERNAL PARTS

bumper	*il-'ak-Si-daam*	الاكصدام
door	*il-behb*	الباب
door handle	*il-'uk-ra*	ممسكة الباب
fender, wing	*ir-raf-raf*	الرفرف
headlights	*ik-kash-sha-feht*	النور الأمامي
hood, bonnet	*ik-kab-boot*	الكبوت
taillight	*il-fa-noos*	النور الخلفي
trunk, boot	*ish shan-Ta*	صندوق
wheel	*il-^ca-ga-la*	عجلة
windshield	*"iz-zehz ish-shib-behk*	الحاجب الزجاجي

windshield wipers	*il-mas-sa-**Heht***	المساحات
What's the matter?	*'eyh il-mush-**ki**-la?*	ما هي المشكلة؟
Can you fix it today?	***mum**-kin ti-Sal-laH-**heh**-lee in-na-**har**-da/il-**yohm**?*	هل يمكن أن تصلحها لي اليوم؟
How long will it take?	*ha-**yeh**-khud "ad-di 'eyh?*	متى ستكون جاهزة؟
Can you give me a lift to —?	***mum**-kin ti-waS-**Sal**-nee li —?*	هل يمكن أن توصلني إلى —؟
How much do I owe you?	*kam il-Hi-**sehb**?*	كم الحساب؟

GENERAL INFORMATION

TELLING THE TIME

hour	**seh**-^{c}a	ساعة
half an hour	**muS**-Si **seh**-^{c}a	نصف ساعة
a quarter of an hour	**rub**-^{c}i **seh**-^{c}a	ربع ساعة
twenty minutes	**til**-ti **seh**-^{c}a	ثلث ساعة
What time is it?	is-**seh**-^{c}a **kam**?	كم الساعة؟
It is —.	is-**seh**-^{c}a —.	الساعة —
12:00	it-**naa**-shar	١٢
1:05	**waH**-da wi **kham**-sa	١،٠٥
2:10	it-**neyn** wi ^{c}**a**-sha-ra	٢،١٠
3:15	ta-**leh**-ta wi **rub**^{c}	٣،١٥
4:20	ar-**ba**-^{c}a wi **tilt**	٤،٢٠
5:25	**kham**-sa wi **kham**-sa wi ^{c}ish-**reen**	٥،٢٥
6:30	**sit**-ta wi **nuSS**	٦،٣٠
7:35	**sab**-^{c}a wi **kham**-sa wi ta-la-**teen**	٧،٣٥
7:40	ta-**man**-ya il-la **tilt**	٤،٤٠
8:45	**tis**-^{c}a il-la **rub**^{c}	٨،٤٥

9:50	^{c}a-sha-ra **il**-la ^{c}a-sha-ra	٩،٥٠
10:55	Hi-**daa**-shar **il**-la **kham**-sa	١٠،٥٥
11:00	Hi-**daa**-shar	١١

EXPRESSIONS OF TIME

At what time (is) — ?	— is **seh**-^{c}a kam?	في أي وقت —؟
When?	'im-ta?	متى؟
at — o'clock	is-**seh**-^{c}a —	في الساعة —
at exactly five o'clock	is-**seh**-^{c}a **kham**-sa biZ-**ZabT**	في الساعة الخامسة بالضبط
in (i.e., after) 1 hour	**ba**^{c}-di seh-^{c}a	بعد ساعة
in (i.e., within) 1 hour	fi seh-^{c}a	في خلال ساعة
in 2 hours	ba^{c}d (or fi) sa^c-**teyn**	بعد (في خلال) ساعتين
(not) before 3 o'clock	(mish) "abl is-**seh**-^{c}a ta-**leh**-ta	(ليس) قبل الساعة الثالثة
(not) after 4:30	(mish) ba^{c}d is-**seh**-^{c}a ar-**ba**-^{c}a wi **nuSS**	(ليس) بعد الرابعة والنصف

at about 7 o'clock	*Ha-weh-lee is-seh-^{c}a sab-ca*	في حوالي الساعة السابعة
between 8 and 9 o'clock	*beyn is-seh-ca ta-man-ya wi tis-^{c}a*	بين الساعة الثامنة والتاسعة
until 6:30	*li gheh-yit is-seh-^{c}a sit-ta wi nuSS*	حتى الساعة السادسة والنصف
I have been waiting —.	*a-na mis-tan-nee [mis-tan-nee-ya] —.*	انتظر — .
■ since 3 o'clock	■ *min is-seh-^{c}a ta-leh-ta*	من الساعة الثالثة
■ for half an hour	■ *ba-"eh-lee nuS-Si seh-^{c}a*	منذ نصف ساعة
■ for a quarter of an hour	■ *ba-"eh-lee <u>rub</u>-^{c}i seh-^{c}a*	منذ ربع ساعة
3 hours ago	*min ta-lat sa-^{c}eht*	منذ ثلاث ساعات
early	*bad-ree*	مبكر
late	*wakh-ree*	متأخر
late (in arriving)	*mut-'akh-khir*	متأخر
on time	*fil-ma-^{c}ehd*	في الموعد
noon	*iD-Duhr*	الظهر
midnight	*muSS il-leyl*	منتصف الليل
in the morning	*iS-SubH*	في الصباح
in the afternoon	*ba^{c}d iD-Duhr*	بعد الظهر
at night	*bel-leyl*	بالليل

DAYS OF THE WEEK

What day is today?	*in-na-har-da "eyh?*	أي يوم اليوم؟
Today is — .	*in-na-har-da/ il-yohm* — .	اليوم —
Monday	*(yohm) lit-neyn*	(يوم) الاثنين
Tuesday	*(yohm) it-ta-leht*	(يوم) الثلاثاء
Wednesday	*(yohm) lar-ba^c*	(يوم) الاربعاء
Thursday	*(yohm) il-kha-mees*	(يوم) الخميس
Friday	*(yohm) ig-gum-^{c}a*	(يوم) الجمعة
Saturday	*(yohm) is-sabt*	(يوم) السبت
Sunday	*(yohm) il-Hadd*	(يوم) الأحد
last Tuesday	*(yohm) it-ta-leht il-lee feht*	(يوم) الثلاثاء الماضي
yesterday	*im-beh-riH/'ams*	أمس
the day before yesterday	*'aw-wil im-beh-riH/ 'ams*	أول أمس
tomorrow	*buk-ra*	غداً
the day after tomorrow	*ba^c-di buk-ra*	بعد غد
next Monday	*(yohm) lit-neyn ig-gayy*	يوم الاثنين القادم
the same day	*nafs il-yohm*	نفس اليوم

two days	*yoh-**meyn***	يومان
three days	***ta**-lat ay-**yehn***	ثلاثة أيام
every day	***kul**-li yohm*	كل يوم
day off	*yohm 'a-**geh**-za*	يوم إجازة / عطلة
holiday	*'a-**geh**-za*	إجازة / عطلة
birthday	^c*eed mi-**lehd***	عيد ميلاد
from now on	*min **hi**-na wi **reh**-yiH*	في المستقبل
this week	*i-'is-**boo**^c da*	هذا الأسبوع
last week	*il-'is-**boo**^c il-lee **feht***	الأسبوع الماضي
next week	*il-'is-**boo**^c ig-**gayy***	الأسبوع القادم
month	*shahr*	شهر
two months	*sha-**reyn***	شهران
three months	***ta**-lat shu-**hoor***	ثلاثة أشهر
this month	*ish-**shah**-ri da*	هذا الشهر
next month	*ish-**shahr** ig-**gayy***	الشهر القادم
during the month of —	*fi shar* —	في خلال شهر —
■ Ramadan	■ *ra-ma-**Daan***	رمضان
since the month of —	*min shahr* —	منذ شهر —
every month	***kul**-li shahr*	كل شهر
per month	*fish-**shahr***	في الشهر

this year	is-sa-**neh** dee	هذه السنة
last year	is-**sa**-na il-lee **feh**-tit	السنة الماضية
next year	is-**sa**-na g-**gay**-ya	السنة القادمة
two years	sa-na-**teyn**	سنتان
three years	**ta**-lat si-**neen**	ثلاث سنوات
per year	fi-**sa**-na	في السنة
all year	**Tohl** is-**sa**-na	طوال السنة
every year	**kul**-li **sa**-na	كل سنة
during the year	ʃi khi-**lehl** is-**sa**-na	في خلال السنة

MONTHS OF THE YEAR

Western calendar

January	ya-**neh**-yir	يناير
February	fib-**reh**-yir	فبراير
March	**meh**-ris	مارس
April	ab-**reel**	أبريل
May	**may**-yoo	مايو
June	**yoon**-yoo	يونيو
July	**yool**-yoo	يوليو
August	a-**ghus**-Tus	أغسطس
September	sib-**tam**-bir	سبتمبر

COUNTRY		NATIONALITY
America	am-**ree**-ka	am-**ree**-kee [am-ree-**keh**-nee]
		[am-ree-**kee**-ya/am-ree-ka-**nee**-ya]
	أمريكا	أمريكي
Asia	**as**-ya	as-**ye**-wee [as-ya-**wee**-ya]
	آسيا	آسيوي
Australia	us-**tral**-ya	us-**traa**-lee [us-tra-**lee**-ya]
	استراليا	استرالي
Austria	in-**nim**-sa	nim-**seh**-wee [nim-sa-**wee**-ya]
	النمسا	نمساوي
Belgium	bal-**jee**-ka	bal-**jee**-kee [bal-jee-**kee**-ya]
	بلجيكا	بلجيكي
Brazil	ba-ra-**zeel**	ba-ra-**zee**-lee [ba-ra-zee-**lee**-ya]
	برازيل	برازيلي
Britain	bri-**Tan**-ya	bri-**Taa**-nee [bri-Ta-**nee**-ya]
	بريطانيا	بريطاني
Canada	**ka**-na-da	**ka**-na-dee [ka-na-**dee**-ya]
	كندا	كندي
China	iS-**Seen**	**See**-nee [See-**nee**-ya]
	الصين	صيني
Denmark	id-**di**-ni-mark	di-ni-**mar**-kee [di-ni-mar-**kee**-ya]
	الدنمرك	دنمركي
England	in-gil-**ti**-ra	in-gi-**lee**-zee [in-gi-lee-**zee**-ya]
	انجلترا	انجليزي
Europe	u-**rub**-ba	u-**rub**-bee [u-ru-**bee**-ya]
	أوروبا	أوروبي
Finland	fin-**lan**-da	fin-**lan**-dee [fin-lan-**dee**-ya]
	فنلندا	فنلندي

COUNTRY		NATIONALITY
France	*fa-**ran**-sa* فرنسا	*fa-ran-**seh**-wee [fa-ran-sa-**wee**-ya]* فرنسي
Germany	*al-**man**-ya* المانيا	*al-**meh**-nee [al-ma-**nee**-ya]* الماني
Greece	*il-yu-**nehn*** اليونان	*yu-**neh**-nee [yu-na-**nee**-ya]* يوناني
Holland	*ho-**lan**-da* هولندا	*ho-**lan**-dee [ho-lan-**dee** ya]* هولندي
Hungary	*il-**ma**-gar* المجر	***ma**-ga-ree [mu-ga-**ree**-ya]* مجري
India	*il-**hind*** الهند	***hin**-dee [hin-**dee**-ya]* هندي
Iran	*i-**raan*** ايران	*i-**raa**-nee [i-raan-**nee**-ya]* ايراني
Ireland	*ayr-**lan**-da* ايرلندا	*uyr-**lun**-dee [ayr-lan-**dee**-ya]* ايرلندي
Israel	*is-ra-'**eel*** اسرائيل	*is-ra-'**ee**-lee [is-ra-'ee-**lee**-ya]* اسرائيلي
Italy	*i-**Taal**-ya* ايطاليا	*i-**Taa**-lee/i-Tal-**yeh**-nee [i-Taa-**lee**-ya/i-Tal·ya-**nee**-ya]* ايطالي
Japan	*il-ya-**behn*** اليابان	*ya-**beh**-nee [ya-ba-**nee**-ya]* ياباني
Luxembourg	***luk**-sum-burg* لوكسمبرج	*min ...* من ...
Malaysia	*ma-**leyz**-ya* ماليزيا	*ma-**ley**-zee [ma-ley-**zee**-ya]* ماليزي

COUNTRY		NATIONALITY
New Zealand	*nyoo zee-**lan**-da*	*nyoo zee-**lan**-dee [nyoo-zee-lan-**dee**-ya]*
	نيوزيلندا	نيوزيلندي
Norway	*in-nur-**weyg***	*nur-**wey**-gee [nur-wey-**gee**-ya]*
	النرويج	نرويجي
the Philippines	*il-fi-li-**been***	*fi-li-**bee**-nee [fi-li-bee-**nee**-ya]*
	الفيليبين	فيليبيني
Portugal	*il-bur-tu-ghehl*	*bur-tu-**gheh**-lee [bur-tu-gha-**lee**-ya]*
	البرتغال	برتغالي
Russia	***roos**-ya*	***roo**-see [roo-**see**-ya]*
	روسيا	روسي
Scotland	*is-kut-**lan**-da*	*is-kut-**lan**-dee [is-kut-lan-**dee**-ya]*
	اسكتلندا	اسكتلندي
South America	*am-**ree**-ka l-ga-noo-**bee**-ya*	*min ...*
	أمريكا الجنوبية	من ...
Spain	*as-**ban**-ya*	*as-**beh**-nee [as-ba-**nee**-ya]*
	اسبانيا	اسباني
Sweden	*is-su-**weyd***	*su-**wey**-dee [su-wey-**dee**-ya]*
	السويد	سويدي
Switzerland	*su-**wis**-ra*	*su-**wis**-ree [su-wis-**ree**-ya]*
	سويسرا	سويسري
Turkey	*tur-**kee**-ya*	***tur**-kee [kur-**kee**-ya]*
	تركيا	تركي

COUNTRY		NATIONALITY
United States	*i-wi-lay-**yeht** il-mut-**ta**-Hi-da* الولايات المتحدة	*min ...* من ...
Wales	*weylz* ويلز	**weyl**-zee [weyl-**zee**-ya] ويلزي
Yugoslavia	*yu-ghus-**laf**-ya* يوغسلافيا	*yu-ghus-**leh**-fee [yu-ghus-la-**fee**-ya]* يوغسلافي

The Arab World

COUNTRY		NATIONALITY
Algeria	*al-ga-**zeh**-'ir* الجزائر	*ga-**zeh**-'i-ree [ga-zeh-'i-**ree**-ya]* جزائري
Bahrain	*baH-**reyn*** البحرين	*baH-**rey**-nee [baH-rey-**nee**-ya]* بحريني
Djibouti	*ji-**boo**-tee* جيبوتي	*min* من ...
Egypt	*maSr* مصر	**maS**-ree [maS-**ree**-ya] مصري
Iraq	*il-^{c}i-**reh"*** العراق	*^{c}i-**reh**-"ee [^{c}i-ra-"**ee**-ya]* عراقي
Jordan	*il-'**ur**-dun* الأردن	*'ur-**du**-nee ['ur-du-**nee**-ya]* أردني
Kuwait	*ik-ku-**weyt*** الكويت	*ku-**wey**-tee [ku-wey-**tee**-ya]* كويتي

COUNTRY		NATIONALITY
Lebanon	*lib-**nehn***	*lib-**neh**-nee [lib-na-**nee**-ya]*
	لبنان	لبناني
Libya	***lib**-ya*	***lee**-bee [lee-**bee**-ya]*
	ليبيا	ليبي
Mauritania	*mu-ri-**tan**-ya*	*mu-ri-**teh**-nee [mu-ri-teh-**nee**-ya]*
	موريتانيا	موريتاني
Morocco	*il-**magh**-rib*	*magh-**ri**-bee [magh-ri-**bee**-ya]*
	المغرب	مغربي
Oman	*^{c}u-**mehn***	*^{c}u-**meh**-nee [^{c}u-ma-**nee**-ya]*
	عمان	عماني
Palestine	*fa-laS-**Teen***	*fa-laS-**Tee**-nee [fa-laS-Tee-**nee**-ya]*
	فلسطين	فلسطيني
Qatar	***qa**-tar*	***qa**-Ta-ree [qa-Ta-**ree**-ya]*
	قطر	قطري
Saudi Arabia	*il-^{c}a-ra-**bee**-ya* *is-su-^{c}u-**dee**-ya*	*su-^{c}**oo**-dee [su-^{c}oo-**dee**-ya]* سعودي
	السعودية	
Somalia	*iS-Su-**maal***	*Su-**maa**-lee [Su-maa-**lee**-ya]*
	الصومال	صومالي
Sudan	*is-su-**dehn***	*su-**deh**-nee [su-da-**nee**-ya]*
	السودان	سوداني
Syria	***soor**-ya*	***soo**-ree [soo-**ree**-ya]*
	سوريا	سوري
Tunisia	***too**-nis*	***too**-ni-see [too-ni-**see**-ya]*
	تونس	تونسي

COUNTRY		NATIONALITY
United Arab Emirates	*il-'i-maa-raat* الامارات	*min ...* من ...
Yemen	*il-ya-man* اليمن	*ya-man-nee [ya-ma-nee-ya]* يمني

DIRECTIONS

north	*ish-shu-mehl*	الشمال
south	*il-ga-noob*	الجنوب
east	*ish-shar"*	الشرق
west	*il-gharb*	الغرب

COUNTING TIMES

once	*mar-ra waH-da*	مرة واحدة
twice	*mar-ri-teyn*	مرتان
three times	*ta-lat mar-raat*	ثلاث مرات
four times	*ar-ba^c mar-raat*	أربع مرات

FOR THE BUSINESS TRAVELER

[See also the sections on Banking and Money Matters and Telecommunications.]

Personal contacts and personal relationships will be a crucial factor in the success or failure of any business venture in the Middle East. There, one rarely finds the strict division between work and leisure so common in the West. Thus patience is needed to nurture a social/business relationship. Avoid a high-pressure approach, which may be perceived as crude and undignified. For instance, you may arrive for a business appointment to find other people in the office — friends, relations, or business associates. Be prepared for the exchange of quite lengthy social preliminaries before you can broach the topic you want to discuss.

So many stereotypes and prejudices have become associated with the Middle East that people will find it refreshing to do business with a foreigner who has actually taken the trouble to learn about the area. Read as much as you can about the social and political system of the countries you are going to visit, talk with people who know them well, and be ready to learn while you are there.

You will certainly be offered hospitality by business colleagues and should be ready to reciprocate enthusiastically on your home ground.

How you dress is important. Err on the side of formality — that means a jacket and tie despite high temperatures and humidity (you will understand the purpose of the traditional loose cotton robes of Saudi Arabia and the Gulf states!). It is rather unusual for women to do business in Saudi Arabia and the Gulf, though they are employed in high positions in hospitals, schools, universities, and so on. Being respectably dressed for a foreign woman means sleeves to below the elbow, skirts to below the knee, and not too much décolleté.

In Saudi Arabia (except in Jedda) all women are expected to wear the voluminous *abaya* when they go out in the street.

It is best to try to schedule a business trip during the winter, spring, or autumn, because in the summer months there is a mass exodus from the big cities and the people you were hoping to contact may be at the seaside or vacationing in Europe.

Avoid traveling to the Middle East on business during the month of Ramadan (see p. 200), because the pace of life is so much slower. Don't expect to accomplish much during the two big religious festivals of the Muslim year (p. 201), which are national holidays and a time for family celebrations and reunions.

MINI-DICTIONARY FOR BUSINESS

account	*Hi-**sehb***	حساب
accounts, accounting	*Hi-seh-**beht***	حسابات
■ deposit account	■ *Hi-**sehb** 'i-deh*^c	حساب إيداع
■ current account	■ *Hi-**sehb** geh-ree*	حساب جاري
amount	***mab**-lagh*	مبلغ
bank notes	*'aw-**reh"** na"d*	أوراق نقد
bill (noun)	*fa-**too**-ra*	فاتورة
bill of exchange	*kam-bee-**yeh**-la*	كمبيالة
bill of lading	*bu-**lee**-Sit shaHn*	بوليصة شحن

free trade zone	*man-**Ti**-qit ti-**gaa**-raa **Hur**-ra*	منطقة تجارة حرة
goods	*il-ba-**Daa**-yiᶜ*	البضائع
head office	*il-**mak**-tab ir-ra-'**ee**-see*	المكتب الرئيسي
import	*il-'is-ti-**raad***	الاستيراد
infringement of patent rights	*'ikh-**lehl** bi Ha" "il-'ikh-ti-**reh**ᶜ*	إخلال بحق الاختراع
insurance	*ta'-**meen***	تأمين
insurance against all risks	*ta'-**meen** ᶜamm*	تأمين عام
international law	*il-qa-**noon** id-**daw**-lee*	القانون الدولي
lawful ownership	*mil-**kee**-ya qa-noo-**nee**-ya*	ملكية قانونية
lawsuit	*qa-**Dee**-ya*	قضية
lawyer	*mu-**Heh**-mee*	محامي
letter of credit	*ri-**seh**-lit iᶜ-ti-**mehd***	رسالة اعتماد
manager	*il-mu-**deer***	المدير
manufacturers	*iS-Si-**naa**-ᶜa*	الصناع
the Middle East market	*soo" ish-**sharq** il-'**aw**-Sat*	سوق الشرق الأوسط

market value	*il-**qee**-ma is-soo-**qee**-ya*	القيمة السوقية
owner of company	***Saa**-Hib ish-**shir**-ka*	مالك الشركة
partner	*sha-**reek***	شريك
past due	*mus-ta-**Hi"** "id-**daf**ᶜ*	مستحق الدفع
payment	*id-**daf**c*	الدفع
partial payment	***duf**-ca guz-'**ee**-ya*	دفعة جزئية
we pay (you pay) customs	***nid**-fa*ᶜ *(tid-**fa**-ᶜoo) igg-ga-**meh**-rik*	ندفع (تدفعوا) الجمارك
percentage	***nis**-ba mi-'a-**wee**-ya*	نسبة مئوية
post office box	*san-**doo"** ba-**reed***	صندوق بريد
profit	*ribH*	ربح
profitable	***mur**-biH*	مربح
property	*'am-**lehk***	أملاك
purchasing agent	*wa-**keel** mush-ta-ra-**yeht***	وكيل مشتريات
refund (noun)	*'i-ᶜ**eh**-dit il-**mehl***	إعادة المال
sale	*il-**bee**ᶜ*	البيع
we (you) sell	*ni-**bee**ᶜ (ti-**bee**-ᶜoo)*	نبيع (تبيعوا)

refined oil	*bit-**rohl** mu-**kar**-rir*	بترول مكرر
refinery	*ma^c-mal tak-**reer***	معمل تكرير

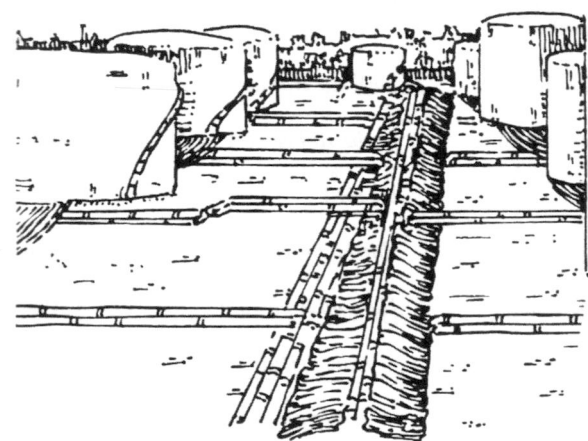

ISLAM

The Koran, the holy book of Islam, which contains the divine revelations received by the prophet Mohammed, is the cornerstone of the Muslim faith. The fundamental religious observances of Islam consist of the profession of faith, prayer, fasting, almsgiving, and the pilgrimage to Mecca in Saudi Arabia, birthplace of the prophet. Like Judaism and Christianity, Islam is monotheistic, believing in an omnipotent creator to whom all must answer.

A Muslim prays after ritual ablutions five times a day — at dawn, noon, in the afternoon, at sunset, and in the evening — facing the direction of Mecca. The call to prayer, or a-*thehn*, will become a familiar sound, as it is chanted or broadcast via loudspeakers from minarets all over town. A Muslim may pray in any quiet and secluded place, kneeling and prostrating himself on a small rug kept especially for that purpose. It is, however, considered important to attend midday prayers at the mosque on Fridays, when a sermon is preached. Sometimes the mosque is so full that the worshippers overflow onto the pavement outside.

There is no priesthood in Islam, no mediator between the worshipper and God. Prayers may be led by any Muslim well-versed in the ritual, though a sizeable community will appoint an Imam, or religious teacher, to officiate. Although there is no equivalent of an established church, schools of theologians and jurists (*cu-la-ma*) evolved, differing in their precise interpretations of Muslim doctrine.

Dissension within the Islamic state has focussed mostly on the rights and duties of the successive Caliphs. These elected successors to the Prophet played an essentially political and administrative rather than religious role. The

Caliphates were transformed into something more akin to traditional Middle Eastern dynasties, with the right to succession being violently disputed at many points in history. The last Caliphate of any real power was the Ottoman Empire based in Turkey, which finally collapsed in the early twentieth century, after a long period of decline.

The ancient Islamic state, stretching in medieval times from Spain to China, has long since fragmented into independent states. These have been secularized to varying degrees. Saudi Arabia, an absolute monarchy, retains the sharia (*sha-ree-^{c}a*), or Islamic legal system, while others are republics and have adopted and adapted Western legal systems. Sometimes the two operate in parallel, depending on the nature of the legal matter at issue.

The Prophet Mohammed

Mohammed was born in Mecca in West Arabia in about 571 A.D., into an essentially nomadic, tribal society in which a variety of local gods were worshipped. The Koran was revealed to him when he was about 40 years old, by the angel Gabriel. As more and more conversions took place, Mohammed was obliged to leave Mecca, and was welcomed with his followers in Medina, where he became a ruler and military leader as well as a religious teacher. His influence gradually spread throughout the peninsula, until at his death he left an organized and well-armed state unified in its adherence to the new faith.

According to Islam, Mohammed is the last and greatest of the line of prophets in the Judeo-Christian tradition. Abraham, Moses, and Jesus are all venerated as bearers of God's word, but the Koran is seen as the last in this series of divine revelations, completing and superseding all previous scriptures. Christians and Jews, as "people of the pact," traditionally enjoyed certain rights and privileges within the Islamic state, including freedom of worship.

Islamic Civilization

The Arabs founded, but were by no means the exclusive contributors to, a rich civilization that lasted for over a thousand years. There were two great waves of conquest, one immediately following the death of Mohammed, which took the Muslim armies north into Syria, west into Egypt, across North Africa, and into Persia in the east. Two centuries later, most of Spain came under Muslim rule, as did northern India and parts of China. The Arabs assimilated and built upon the scientific and technical knowledge of their subject nations, translating into Arabic works on mathematics, philosophy, astronomy, and medicine from the ancient Greek, Persian, and Indian civilizations. During what were the Dark Ages in Europe, great advances were also being made in the fields of chemistry, anatomy, geography, optics, and mechanical engineering. Universities, libraries, and hospitals flourished, often in close association with the great mosques of the period.

So in the Middle Ages it was to the East that Europe looked for scientific knowledge. (Our system of numerals, for example, was borrowed from the Arabs, who had themselves borrowed and adapted the system from an Indian source.)

In the arts, Islamic civilization can be seen at its most impressive in its great architectural creations, from the Taj Mahal in India to the Alhambra palace in Spain. In both, formal gardens, pools, and fountains perfectly complement the graceful architecture. (Garden motifs as well as complex geometric patterns often recur in textiles, ceramics, and carpet designs.) The bold and elegant shapes of dome, minaret, and monumental gateway are generally left unadorned; decoration is concentrated on interior surfaces, in the form of tiling, mosaic, and elaborate plasterwork.

In the museums of the Arab world you will see examples of other great artistic achievements of Islamic civilization, in the form of pottery, glassware, pierced and inlaid metalwork, carpets, and textiles — art forms that continue to flourish today.

Since pre-Islamic times poetry had been the favored literary genre, and the themes and forms of Arabic poetry are clearly reflected in the work of the medieval poets of southern Europe. Many believe that it was contact with this rich and varied culture that fostered new ideas in both the arts and sciences in Europe, culminating in the great flowering of the Renaissance.

The Muslim Calendar

The calendar is based on a key event in the history of the Islamic faith, the migration from Mecca to Medina by the Prophet and his followers in 622 A.D. This is therefore taken as the beginning of the Islamic era. In everyday conversation the years and months of the Western calendar are used, but for religious purposes and in published material of all kinds, Islamic dates are referred to. Both are used in newspapers.

The year is divided into 12 lunar months, each starting at the new moon, and consisting of about 29 days. This means that the Muslim year starts about 10 days earlier each year in relation to the Western calendar.

Here are the names of the months:

mu-**Har**-ram	محرّم
Sa-far	صفر
ra-**bee**^{c} il-'**aw**-wal	ربيع الأول
ra-**bee**^{c} it-**teh**-nee	ربيع الثاني
gu-**mehd** il-'**aw**-wal	جمادى الأولى
gu-**mehd** it-**teh**-nee	جمادى الآخرة
ra-gab	رجب
sha^c-**behn**	شعبان
ra-ma-**Daan**	رمضان
shaw-**wehl**	شوّال
zul-qa^c-da	ذو القعدة
zul-**Hig**-ga	ذو الحجة

Ramadan is the month of fasting, when Muslims neither eat, drink, nor smoke from dawn till sunset. Special dishes are eaten at the evening meal known as *il-fi-Taar*, which breaks the fast. In the early hours before dawn a second meal — *is-su-hoor* — is taken, to see people through the hours of fasting ahead.

Fasting is considered both a spiritual discipline and a reminder of those less fortunate than oneself who are hungry all year round. So it is a time to give generously to poor people in one's neighborhood. Devout Muslims gather to read aloud from the Koran, and go to the mosque more frequently during Ramadan.

The pace of life tends to slow down, with many people sleeping during the morning hours. In the evening, and often late into the night, there is a holiday atmosphere in the downtown areas of the cities, where shops and cafés stay open and the streets are thronged with people.

Hotels and all places catering to tourists function normally, but many neighborhood restaurants and cafés are closed during daylight hours. Non-Muslims are certainly not expected to fast, but it is polite not to eat, smoke, or drink in the street.

Muslim Festivals

Ramadan ends in the Feast of the Breaking of the Fast or the Small Feast — *ᶜeed il-fiTr* or *il-ᶜeed iS-Sugh-ghay-yar*, which is associated with all kinds of local customs, such as providing one's children with new clothes. The culminating day of the pilgrimage to Mecca is on the tenth of *zul Hig-ga*. This is known as the Great Feast, or Feast of Sacrifice — *il-ᶜeed il-ki-beer* or *ᶜeed il-'aD-Ha*, when every family that can afford it slaughters a sheep, in remembrance of the story of Abraham and Isaac, and meat is distributed to the poor.

The prophet's birthday — *moo-lid in-na-bee* — on the twelfth of *ra-bee^c il-'aw-wal* — is also celebrated; for days in advance mosques are illuminated and ceremonies and festivities abound.

During Ramadan, and on the occasion of any religious or secular festival — including birthdays — the equivalent to "Merry Christmas," "Happy Birthday," and so on is:

kul-li sa-na win-ta Tay-yib [win-tee Tay-yi-ba]

To which the reply is:

win-ta Tay-yib [win-tee Tay-yi-ba]

Or the more formal greeting is:

kul-li ^cehmm win-tum bi-kheyr

Saints' Days

In Egypt and North Africa especially there is a long tradition — probably dating back to pre-Islamic times —of venerating the memory of men and women of great piety and learning. Their tombs have become shrines, and even mosques have been founded to commemorate them, which may become places of pilgrimage. One of the liveliest public celebrations is a saint's day or *moo-lid*; miniature fairgrounds for children are set up, as well as street stalls selling food, toys, and souvenirs. Shops and cafés stay open till late at night, and bands of musicians and singers provide religious and secular music.

Secular Festivals

The Western New Year — *raas is-sa-na* — is celebrated wherever Western influence has made itself felt, but it is not generally an official holiday. May 1, Labor Day (May Day), is also accorded varying degrees of importance in different countries.

In Egypt an ancient spring festival, that of *shamm in-ni-seem*, is celebrated on Greek Orthodox Easter Monday throughout the country. Everyone flocks to the fields, parks, and gardens in their newest clothes, and huge amounts of spring onions and salted fish are consumed.

Christian Festivals

Large Christian communities are to be found throughout the Middle East; in Lebanon they constitute about half the population. Roughly 15 percent of Egyptians belong to the Greek Orthodox Church, one of the earliest established forms of Christianity, even today using the language of Ancient Egypt in its liturgy. The Greek Orthodox and Eastern Orthodox calendar does not coincide with the Western Christian calendar. The Eastern Christmas — ^{c}*eed il-mi-lehd* (literally, "Feast of the Birth") — and Easter — ^{c}*eed il-qi-yeh-ma* ("Feast of the Resurrection") — are celebrated about 12 days later than their Western equivalents.

THE ARAB WORLD
TODAY

The Arab world has a degree of cultural unity, based on shared religious beliefs, a common literary language of great prestige, and many shared social institutions such as the extended family, with its elaborate system of rights and obligations. But within this framework there is great diversity — of race, of wealth, of political systems, of attitudes to the West, and to modern technology.

In the West the stereotypical Arab as an oil-rich sheikh jet-setting around the capitals of Europe has tended to replace the more romantic image of the keen-eyed son of the desert, ascetic, proud, and bound by a strict code of honor. Both exist, but only as tiny pieces in a much larger mosaic. They are both vastly outnumbered by the hardworking fellaheen (*fel-la-Heen*), or peasant farmers, who still provide the economic base of the more populous Arab countries.

Urban centers increasingly attract workers to the factories from country towns and villages. Cairo, the town planner's nightmare — or ultimate challenge — has exploded from being a sizeable city of 3 million to a vast agglomeration of 16 million in the space of 30 years. Armies of government clerks (*mu-waZ-Za-feen*) — often university graduates — find it hard to make ends meet on their slender salary, and will often take a second job in the afternoon or evening.

There has been a massive emigration of the working population from the poorer to the richer countries within the Arab world and beyond, with all the social and economic turmoil that entails.

In this shifting scene two factors at least remain constant, which favor the foreign visitor: the innate sociability of the Arab people, and their abiding tradition of hospitality to strangers.

Women in Islam

Saudi Arabia, as the birthplace of the prophet Mohammed, sees itself as the guardian of traditional values, accepting changes to the established order with extreme caution. Attitudes that seem reactionary to Westerners, such as requiring women to go heavily veiled in public places and forbidding them to drive, should be viewed against some truly dramatic social reforms, like the provision of education for women at all levels, within the space of one generation.

Throughout the Middle East the trend has been toward greater emancipation for women and their increasing participation in every area of public life. In many ways they have enjoyed fuller legal rights than their Western sisters, from the early days of Islam, since they have always had individual property rights and legal protection against ill-treatment by their husbands.

Polygamy is still practiced in most Arab countries, although it is unusual among the mass of the population – since wives must be treated equally in every respect, few men can afford more than one! A woman must enter freely into the marriage contract, though frequently social and family pressures may mean that personal preference is not a major factor in the arrangement for either partner.

TRADITION AND CHANGE

In recent years, even in countries like Egypt, which have been open to Western influences for more than a century, a profound reevaluation of social and religious attitudes is taking place. The West is no longer synonymous with

k	q	f	gh	c	Z	T
ك	ق	ف	غ	ع	ظ	ط
y	w	h	n	m	l	
ي	و	ه	ن	م	ل	

ي (**y**) and و (**w**) can also be used to represent the long vowels **ee** and **oo** respectively.

Besides these 29 letters there are three additional "vowel marks," two written above, and one below the consonant they follow:

فَ = fa   فِ = fi   فُ = fu

بَ = ba   بِ = bi   بُ = bu

These short vowels are not generally written in, because Arabic speakers can recognize the word quite well without them (just as you don't usually need to put in the vowel marks in English shorthand).

Another "optional" symbol — ّ — is one used over a letter to indicate that letter is doubled, or long :

جزّار = *gaz-zaar*   شبّاك = *shib-behk*

The same glottal stop symbol ء (') rarely occurs by itself but is usually "carried" by ا , و , or ي : يء ؤ أ

In the "joining up" process letters tend to change their shape. Typically, letters coming at the end of the word (or occurring in isolation, as above) end in a flourish or "tail." They lose this tail if they occur at the beginning or in the middle of word.

First the letters that *don't* join up with the letters that follow them, and therefore do *not* change their shape:

ا   د   ذ   ر   ز   و

The following lose their tails:

ب   ت   ث   ج   ح   خ   ص   ض

ع   غ   ف   ق   ل   م   ن   ي

So if we were to join up ت + ح + ت (taHt — "under, below"), this would give تحت with only the final **t** ending in a flourish. Notice that dots are placed above or below the middle of the flourish if there is one. The same is true for the two forms of ب (**b**) and ث (**th**):

باب = *behb* ("door") and ثلث = *thilth* ("third")

Final ي sometimes loses its two dots: ى

Here are a few more examples of letters written first in their "full" form, and then as they would look joined up into words:

ب ح ر
بحر (*baHr*)

ج م ي ل
جميل (*ga-meel*)

ب ل د
بلد (*ba-lad*)

ش خ ص
شخص (*shakhS*)

ض ا ن ي
ضاني (*Daa-nee*)

ف و ل
فول (*fool*)

k has *three* variants forms, depending on whether they are intial, medial, or final in a word:

	FINAL	MEDIAL	INITIAL
k	ك	ـكـ	ك

Three other letters have initial, medial, and final shapes, the final one varying lightly if it is unjoined:

	FINAL Unjoined	Joined	MEDIAL	INITIAL
c	ع	ـع	ـعـ	عـ
gh	غ	ـغ	ـغـ	غـ
h	ه	ـه	ـهـ	هـ

This last letter may be written with two dots over it in final position: ة or ـة . Then it represents the feminine ending **-a**, as in طبيبة *Ta-**bee**-ba* — doctor (fem.) جميلة *ga-**mee**-la* — beautiful (fem.) Some examples of these last few letters in words:

*(^{c}**an**-dee)* عندي	*(**gum**-ruk)* جمرك	*(say-**yaa**-ra)* سيارة
*(**ma**-^{c}a)* مع	*(Say-da-**lee**-ya)* صيدلية	*(**maT**-cam)* مطعم
*(is-**seh**-^{c}a)* الساعة	*(ik-**kil**-ma)* الكلمة	*(il-^{c}in-**wehn**)* العنوان

The last three examples all begin with the definite article **il-** الـ (see Grammar Notes). Notice this is always written the same way, even if the **l** changes to match the following consonant in spoken Arabic.

You will occasionally come across three relatively new letters, which have been invented to cope with borrowed, foreign sounds. Arabic doesn't normally have a **v** sound, but this does occur in foreign borrowings such as "video." A variant of **f** with three dots is sometimes used: ڤ

vi-dyoo فيديو. Egyptian Arabic uses **g** rather than **j** in words like *ga-meel* جميل (beautiful) or *ga-mal* جمل (camel), but **j** may occur in foreign words such as "jeans." To make the difference clear, three dots can again be useds:

چينز jeenz مكياج mak-yaaj (makeup)

A **p** in foreign borrowings is usually Arabized to a **b**, as in *bu-loh-var* (pullover). But it can be represented by a modification of the **b** symbol ب again using three dots:

پ . For example:

سڤن اپ Seven Up

So you may find a word such as "jeep" being written جيب , or چيپ or جيپ !

DIALECTS OF THE ARAB WORLD

Considerable differences exist between the varieties of Arabic spoken throughout the Arab world; even within one country a good deal of local variation can be found. Although you will be able to make yourself understood very well with Egyptian Arabic, as the most widely known and prestigious form of the spoken language, if you are visiting other countries you may want to try to approximate the local dialect.

The differences lie in pronunciation and use of vocabulary rather than in grammatical structure. The following notes, indicating the most striking of these features, should help you "tune in" rapidly to another dialect. Dialects have been grouped together to simplify the picture, but it should be remembered that this simplification masks a lot of internal variation.

Egyptian Arabic

What identifies a speaker immediately as an Egyptian is his or her use of *g* as in *ga-**meel*** (beautiful), ***gid-dan*** (very), and so on; in virtually all other dialects (and in literary Arabic) this is a *j*, either as in "*jam*" or "*measure*": *ja-**meel***, ***jid-dan***, and so on.

The other feature (shared by some of the more Eastern dialects) is the use of the glottal stop " to replace what is elsewhere a *q*. The *q* has only survived in Egyptian in relatively few (usually rather learned) words. So other dialects will differentiate between ***qa-lam*** (pen) and ***'a-lam*** (pain), whereas in Egyptian they are pronounced the same, both with a glottal stop: ***"a-lam*** = ***'a-lam***. Two slightly different symbols have been used for the Egyptian glottal stop, so that you will know where you should switch to *q* in another part of the Arab world. So ***"ul-lee*** (tell me) will be pronounced ***qul-lee*** elsewhere, but *'is-**boo**[c]* (week) will stay the same.

South of Cairo a rather different dialect is spoken, in which *j* is used for *g* and *q* for ". This Upper Egyptian, or *'sa-[c]ee-dee'*, Arabic (sometimes made fun of by the educated city dweller) in fact has much in common with Sudanese.

Dialects of the Eastern Mediterranean
(*Lebanon, Jordan, Syria, Palestine*)

Egyptian *g* = *j* (as in mea<u>s</u>ure, rather than jam)

Some unstressed vowels are dropped. For example, Egyptian *ki-**teer*** = EM *kteer* (much, many).

As in Egyptian, *q* is usually replaced by ".

Here are some common expressions:

Not	*mish* or *ma*
Where?	*weyn?*
What?	*shoo?* or *'ehsh?*
Why?	*leysh?*
How much?	*"ad-**dehsh**?*
How?	*keyf?*

How are you?   **key**-fak [**key**-fik]?
Thing, something   shey'
Thus, so   heyk
Yes   'eyh
Nice, good   ma-**leeH**
I want   **bid**-dee or **bad**-dee
(You want . . . , etc.: the ending changes as after "ud-**dehm**-
(in front of); see p. 223: **bid**-dak, **bid**-dik, **bid**-doo, (etc.).

Sudanese

Very similar to Egyptian, except than j (as in "jam")
is used instead of g, so gi-**deed** = Sudanese ja-**deed**, and
Egyptian " is either q or g; for example, Egyptian "ah-wa
= Sudanese **gah**-wa (coffee), "i-**zeh**-za = gi-**zeh**-za.

Iraqi

Additional sounds: th as in "thing," corresponding to
Egyptian t (hence ka-**theer** = ki-**teer**) or s, and <u>th</u> as in
"this" corresponding to Egyptian d or z.
Egyptian g = Iraqi j (as in "jam").
Egyptian " = q or g: Ta-**ree**" = Iraqi Ta-**reeq**, "ah-wa =
Iraqi **gah**-wa.
k next to a or i often becomes tsh: Egyptian kam = Iraqi
tshehm.
Here are some common expressions:
What?   shi-**noo?**
Who?   min?
How?   keyf? shlohn?
How much?   kehm? tshehm?
Where?   weyn?
Why?   leysh?
When?   **mi**-ta?
Fine, good   zeyn
Bad   baT-**Taal**
Thus, so   **hee**-tshee
This, that   **heh**-<u>tha</u>
I want   a-**reed**
Not   moo, mush

Dialects of Saudi Arabia and the Gulf

th and *th* are used (as in "think" and "this"): *tha-leh-tha* (three), **heh**-*tha* (this, that).

k often becomes *tsh* next to *a, e, i*: *kam* = *tshehm*, *keyf* = *tsheyf*. Egyptian *"* is usually *g*, occasionally *q*: **gah**-*wa*, **fun**-*dug*, *ga-****leel****. Egyptian *g* = *j* (as in "jam").

Here are some common expressions:

What?	*shoo?*
Where?	*weyn?*
How?	*keyf?, tsheyf?, shlohn?*
How are you?	**shloh**-*nak [****shloh****-nik]?*
How much?	*kehm?, tshehm?*
Much, very	*ka-****theer***
I want	*a-****reed****, **a**-bee, **ab**-gha*
Good, fine	*zeyn*
Yesterday	*'ams*
This, that	**heh**-*tha [****heh****-thee]*
Thanks	*mash-****koor***

North African Dialects
(*Moroccan, Algerian, Tunisian, Libyan*)

These are possibly the furthest from Egyptian, particularly Moroccan, where there is a strong Berber influence.

Egyptian *g* = *j*

Egyptian *"* = *q* or *g*: *"alb* = *qalb*, *"****ah****-wa* = **gah**-*wa*.

Many unstressed vowels are lost: Egyptian *ta-leh-ta* = NA **tleh**-*ta*, *"a-****deem*** = *qdeem*.

Here are some common expressions:

Yes	*yeh*
Thank you	*ba-ra-kal-****laa****-hu **feek***
What?	*'ehsh? shnoo?*
Why?	*^{c}a-****lehsh****?*
When?	*waq-****tehsh****? foh-****gehsh****?*
How much/many?	*gad-****dehsh****? sh-****hehl****?*
How?	*keyf? key-****fehsh****?*

Who? *shkoon?*
Good, well *la-**behs**, **beh**-hee*
Nice, pleasant *mleeH, miz-**yehn***
Bad ***doo**-nee, **kheh**-yib*
Much, very ***yeh**-sir, biz-**zehf***
I want *ni-**Hibb**, **heb**-ghee [**bagh**-ya]*
Food ***mak**-la*
Tomorrow ***ghud** wa, **ghed**-da*

To form a "yes/no" question, add *-shee* to the verb or adjective: *beh-**hee**-shee?* — (Is it) O.K.?

GRAMMAR NOTES

The rules outlined here are those of spoken Egyptian Arabic, but most apply to other spoken forms of Arabic as well. The differences between the modern dialects are ones of pronunciation and vocabulary rather than of grammar.

Consonantal Roots and Word Patterns

The most striking feature of Arabic, like other Semitic languages, is the way a series of (usually three) consonants is used as the basis for forming many closely related words. Take the series *d-r-s*; from this are formed the words *dars* — "lesson," *da-ras* — "he studied," *dar-ras* — "he taught," *mad-**ra**-sa* — "school," *mu-**dar**-ris* — "teacher," and many others, all related to the concept of study. Once you know the meaning of a root you can often guess at the meaning of a word containing it, because the addition of particular patterns of vowels, plus prefixes or suffixes, modifies the meaning of the root in predictable ways.

"Place" nouns often follow the patterns of either ***mak**-tab* (office) or ***mak**-ta-ba* (library or bookstore), i.e., the

definite ("the . . .") the prefix *il-* is put at the beginning of the word:

*il-mu-**dar**-ris* the teacher   *il-**bee**-ra* the beer

The *l* of this prefix sometimes changes to match the first consonant of the noun:

*is-**suk**-kar* (the sugar)   — not *il-**suk**-kar*
*in-**nehs*** (the people)   — not *il-**nehs***

The consonants that trigger this change are:
  t d n s z sh r T D S Z

For *k*, *g*, and *j* the change is optional. So:

*il-**kart*** (the card)   or *ik-**kart***

Plurals

Sometimes an ending is added to make a noun plural (as in English):

*mu-dar-ri-**seen*** (teachers)   *do-la-**raat*** (dollars)

-een and *-aat* are among the most common plural endings. But even more frequently, the whole shape of the word changes, with only the consonantal root remaining intact. There are over a dozen different plural "patterns"; the most common are:

SINGULAR	PLURAL	SINGULAR	PLURAL
1 ***wa**-ra"* (paper)	*'aw-**reh**"*	***wa**-lad* (boy)	*'aw-**lehd***
2 *'is-**boo**^c* (week)	*'a-sa-**bee**^c*	*mif-**tehH*** (key)	*ma-fa-**teeH***
3 ***mak**-tab* (office)	*ma-keh-**tib***	*taz-**ka**-ra* (ticket)	*ta-**zeh**-kir*
4 *kart* (card)	*ku-**root***	*Deyf* (guest)	*Du-**yoof***
5 ***sik**-ka* (road)	*si-**kak***	***nim**-ra* (number)	*ni-**mar***

Unfortunately, most of the time you can't predict the plural from the singular; it just has to be learned. This is the hardest part of Arabic grammar, but if you use the wrong plural pattern or ending, people will probably still understand!

Duals

If two objects or people are being referred to, a special form of the noun is used. For masculine nouns the ending -*eyn* is added:

yohm	*yoh-**meyn***	*'alf*	*'al-**feyn***
(day)	(2 days)	(1000)	(2000)

For feminine nouns ending in -*a*, the *a* is removed and -*teyn* added:

seh-^ca	*sa^c-**teyn***	***Ha**-ga*	*Hag-**teyn***
(hour)	(2 hours)	(thing)	(2 things)

Noun ı Noun

When one noun immediately follows another, it usually indicates possession or the notion "of":

*beyt mu-**Ham**-mad*	Muhammed's house
***Saa**-Ḥiḥ ley-la*	Leila's friend

When the first noun is feminine, the -*a* ending changes to -*it*:

***shur**-ba* (soup)	but	***shur**-bit **ba**-Sal*
		(onion soup)
*"i-**zeh**-za* (bottle)	but	*"i-**zeh**-zit **bee**-ra*
		(a bottle of beer)

If you want to say "*the* bottle of beer" or "*the* teacher's daughter" only the second noun carries the definite *il-*:

*"i-**zeh**-zit il-**bee**-ra*	*bint il-mu-**dar**-ris*

Numbers

The numbers are given on page 17. 1 is the only number to have separate masculine and feminine forms:

***weh*-Hid** and ***waH*-da:** *yohm* ***weh*-Hid** one day, ***sa*-na *waH*-da** one year

Numbers 3 to 10 are followed by a plural noun:

ta*-lat 'a-sa-*bee*[c]** (3 weeks) **ar-*ba*[c] si-*neen (4 years)

Notice the final -*a* has been dropped before these plural nouns.

With all higher numbers, a *singular* noun is used:

ta-la-*teen* sa-na (30 years) **it-*naa*-shar shahr** (12 months)

When ordering in a restaurant, however, or when currency is being referred to, the singular is *always* used:

ta-*leh*-ta *bee*-ra (3 beers) **kham-sa do-*laar*** (5 dollars)

When the hundreds are followed by a noun, ***mee*-ya** becomes *meet*:

300 dollars	*tul-tu-meet do-laar*
500 pounds	*khum-su-meet gi-ney*

ADJECTIVES

Like nouns, adjectives have three different forms — masculine, feminine, and plural:

***kway*-yis** (good) masc.	*kway-yi-sa* fem.
	kway-yi-seen pl.
***Tay*-yib** (kind) masc.	*Tay-yi-ba* fem.
	Tay-yi-been pl.

The feminine ending is always *-a*, but as with nouns, the plural may take many forms:

*la-**Teef*** (pleasant) masc.   *la-**Tee**-fa* fem.   *lu-**Taaf*** pl.

*mag-**noon*** (crazy) masc.   *mag-**noo**-na* fem.
                                 *ma-ga-**neen*** pl.

Adjectives agree with the nouns they modify:

wa**-lad la-**Teef (a nice   *hint la-**Tee**-fa* (a nice girl)
boy)

Fortunately there is a strong tendency toward using the (regular!) feminine form with plural nouns as well. So you can say *either*

*nehs lu-**Taaf*** (nice people)   **or**   *nehs la-**Tee**-fa*

Adjectives also agree with the noun in being definite or indefinite, so the same definite prefix *il-* must be added to adjectives next to a definite noun.

wa**-lad la-**Teef   **but**   *il-**wa**-lad il-la-**Teef***
(a nice boy)   (the nice boy —
                                         lit., the boy the nice)

Comparatives and Superlatives

To say "bigger, biggest," "cheaper, cheapest," and so on, a special pattern is used:

*ki-**beer*** (big)   ***'ak**-bar* (bigger, biggest)
*ri-**kheeS*** (cheap)   ***'ar**-khaS* (cheaper, cheapest)
*ga-**meel*** (beautiful)   ***'ag**-mal* (more, most
                                beautiful)

When it means "the most . . ." it *precedes* the noun:

***'ar**-khaS si^{c}r*   *si^{c}r **'ar**-khaS*
(the cheapest price)   (a cheaper price)

Comparative/superlative adjectives are invariable:

'ak-bar **wa**-lad	(the biggest boy)
'ak-bar bint	(the biggest girl)
'ak-bar *'aw*-**lehd**	(the biggest boys)

NONVERBAL SENTENCES

There is no equivalent in Arabic to "am, is, are"; the subject is just followed directly by the rest of the sentence:

mu-**Ham**-mad **maS**-ree	Muhammed is Egyptian.
a-na min **lan**-dan	I'm from London.

To make these negative, *mish* is placed after the subject:

mu-**Ham**-mad mish **maS**-ree	Muhammed isn't Egyptian.
a-na mish min **lan**-dan	I'm not from London.

PRONOUNS

Personal Pronouns

These pronouns take the following form as subject of a sentence:

a-na	I	*iH*-na	we
in-ta	you (masc.)	*in*-**tum**-ma	you (pl.)
in-tee	you (fem.)		
huw-wa	he	**hum**-ma	they
hee-ya	she		

As in Spanish and Italian, these pronouns are used optionally with verbs — usually only when you want to emphasize the subject:

(a-na) ^c*a*-wiz *'eh*-kul	I want to eat.
(hee-ya) ^c*aw*-za *teh*-kul	She wants to eat.

Following a noun or preposition, they take the following forms:

-ee	"ud-**deh**-mee	in front of me
-ak	"ud-**deh**-mak	in front of you (masc.)
-ik	"ud-**deh**-mik	in front of you (fem.)
-oo	"ud-**deh**-moo	in front of him
-ha	"ud-**dehm**-ha	in front of her
-na	"ud-**dehm**-na	in front of us
-kum	"ud-**dehm**-kum	in front of you (pl.)
-hum	"ud-**dehm**-hum	in front of them

After a noun they have a possessive meaning:

bey-tee my house   *'ukh-tak* your sister
                                           (to a man)

After verbs, the same forms are used:

*yi-**shoof**-ha* he sees her   *ba **Hib**-boo* I like him.

The only exception is the "me" form, which is *-nee* after verbs:

*yi-**shoof**-nee* he sees me.

Demonstrative Pronouns

To say "this one" or "that one," *da* or *dee* is used (depending on whether the noun referred to is masculine or feminine):

*da **kway**-yis*   *dee kway-**yi**-sa*
that (masc.) one is good   that (fem.) one is good

Imperatives

Take the second person and omit the initial *t-*:

ish-rab!	drink! (masc.)
ish-ra-bee!	drink! (fem.)
ish-ra-boo!	drink! (pl.)

Future Tense

h(a)- is prefixed to the basic present:

*ha-**yish**-rab*	he will drink
*ha**sh**-rab*	I will drink

Negatives

In the present tense, *ma-* is added to the beginning, and *-sh* to the end of the verb:

*ma-bi-yish-**rabsh***	he doesn't drink/ isn't drinking

With the future, *mish* is placed before the verb:

*mish **hash**-rab*	I shall not drink

Past Tense

This will not be widely used in situations expressing immediate needs and feelings. The same consonantal root is combined with a set of suffixes:

*shi-**ribt*** I drank	*shi-**rib**-na* we drank
*shi-**ribt*** you (masc.) drank	*shi-**rib**-too* you (pl.) drank
*shi-**rib**-tee* you (fem.) drank	
*shi-**rib*** he drank	*shir-**boo*** they drank
*shir-**bit*** she drank	

The vowels separating the root consonants are either *i - i* (as in ***shi**-rib*) or *a - a* (as in *da-ras*: he studied).

As with the present tense, the negative is formed by placing *ma-* and *-sh* around the verb:

*ma-shi-**rib**-tish*	I did not drink, etc.

(See p. 7 for a note on the little "helping vowel" that avoids a heavy sequence of three consonants.)

"Want" and "Need"

"Verbs" such as *^Ca-wiz [^Caw-za]* (want) and *miH-tehg [miH-teh-ga]* (need) in fact behave more like adjectives, because they have only masculine, feminine, and plural forms. The plurals are *^Caw-zeen* and *miH-teh-geen*. They are negated by *mish* before the verb:

(a-na) mish ^Ca-wiz	I don't want

"Have"

There is no verb "to have" in Arabic; a preposition "with" (*^Cand* or *ma-^Ca*) is used with the object pronouns given above:

^Can-doo fi-loos	lit., with him money, that is, He has money
^Can-dee wa"t	lit., with me time, that is, I have time

These are negated like verbs, with *ma-* and *-sh* around the word:

ma-^Can-doosh fi loos	he has no money
ma-^Can-deesh wa"t	I have no time

QUESTIONS

Questions requiring "yes" or "no" as an answer have the same form as statements, but the voice rises at the end of the sentences.

mu-Ham-mad min maSr ↓	Muhammed is from Egypt (falling intonation)
mu-Ham-mad min maSr? ↑	Is Muhammed from Egypt? (rising intonation)

Questions beginning in English with "what," "where," "why," "how," and so on often have the question word at the beginning in Arabic too:

feyn il-'u-tu-**bees**?   Where is the bus?
iz-**zayy** il-'aw-**lehd**?   How are the children?

But many speakers put the question word at the end of the sentence:

il-'u-tu-**bees feyn**?   Where is the bus?
'**is**-mak '**eyh**?   What is your name?
in-ta za^c-**lehn leyh**?   Why are you angry?

COMPLEX SENTENCES

Once you are confident about using simple sentences that contain just one verb, you may want to create more elaborate structures.

Relative Clauses

Relative clauses are those following a noun and beginning with "who," "which," "that," "on which," "from whom," etc. in English.

In Arabic, if the noun is definite (begins with *il-*), the relative word is **il-lee**:

ish-rab il-**bee**-ra **il**-lee fit-tal-**leh**-ga.
Drink the beer that is in the refrigerator.

If the definite noun does not correspond to the subject of the relative clause, a matching pronoun has to be added to the second verb:

ish-rab il-**bee**-ra **il**-lee ish-ta-**reyt**-ha im-**heb**-riH.
Literally: Drink the beer that I bought *it* yesterday.

If the noun being modified by a relative clause is indefinite (no *il-*), no *il-lee* is used either:

***ti^c**-raf bint mish ^c**aw**-za tit-**gaw**-wiz?*
Do you know a girl (who) doesn't want to get married?

***hash**-rab **bee**-ra ish-ta-**reyt**-ha im-**beh**-riH.*
I will drink some beer that I bought yesterday.
(Literally: I will drink some beer I bought it yesterday.)

"That" Clauses

Clauses introduced by "that" usually begin with *inn* in Arabic:

*a-**Zunn** inn **seh**-mi fil-**beyt**.*
I think that Sami is at home.

*at-**man**-na inn **ley**-la ha-**tee**-gee **buk**-ra.*
I hope that Leila will come tomorrow.

Like verbs and prepositions (see above), *inn-* may carry a suffixed pronoun.

*a-**Zunn** in-noo fil-**beyt**.*
I think that he is at home.

*at-**man**-na in-**na**-ha ha-**tee**-gee **buk**-ra.*
I hope that she will come tomorrow.

While "that" can be dropped in English, *inn* should always be used in Arabic.

ENGLISH-ARABIC DICTIONARY

The feminine form is given in square brackets. When a plural is given, it is preceded by (pl.). Verbs are given in the third person singular present form ("he goes," etc.), beginning with *yi-*. For other forms of the verbs see Grammar Notes on page 215.

A

able *"eh-dir ["ad-ra]* قادر [قادرة]

about (approximately) *Ha-weh-lee* حوالي. تقربا

about (concerning) *^can* عن

above *foh"* فوق

absent *gheh-yib* غائب

accident *Hud-sa* حادثة

accidentally *Sud-fa* بالمصادفة

accompany *yi-waS-Sal* يرافق

account (financial) *Hi-sehb* حساب
(pl.) *Hi-seh-beht* حسابات

accountant *mu-Heh-sib* محاسب

ache (noun) *wa-ga^c/ 'a-lam* وجع/ ألم
(verb) *yiw-ga^c* يوجع
(head) — *Su-daa^c* صداع

actor *mu-mas-sil* ممثل

actress *mu-mas-si-la* ممثلة

adapter plug *mu-Haw-wil* محول

addicted (to) *mud-min (bi)* مدمن (على)

address *^cin-wehn* عنوان

administration *'i-daa-ra* إدارة

advertisement *'i^c-lehn* إعلان
(pl.) *'i^c-leh neht* إعلانات

advice *na-See Ha* نصيحة

advise *yin-SaH* ينصح

afraid *kheh-yif [khay-fa]* خائف

Africa *af-reeq-ya* إفريقيا

African *'af-ree-qee* إفريقي

after *ba^cd* بعد

afternoon *ba^cd iD-Duhr* بعد الظهر

afterwards *ba^c-deyn* بعد ذلك

again *teh-nee* مرة أخرى. ثانية

bag **shan**-Ta (pl.) **shu**-naT	حقيبة حقائب
baggage **shu**-naT/ ^cafsh	حقائب/ أمتعة
baked fil-**furn**	في الفرن
bakery furn/**makh**-baz	فرن. مخبز
ball **koh**-ra	كرة
ballpoint pen "al-lam gaff	قلم جاف
bananas mohz	موز
bandages ru-**baaT**	رباط
bank bank (pl.) bu-**nook**	بنك بنوك
bar baar	بار
barber Hal-**leh**"	حلاق
bargain (verb) yi-**faa**-Sil	يساوم
bargaining fi-**Saal**	مساومة
basket **sa**-bat	سلة
basketball **bas**-kit-bohl	كرة السلة
bath **ban**-yoo	بانيو
bathroom Ham-**mehm**, twa-**litt**	حمام. تواليت
bathe yis-ta-**Ham**-ma	يستحم
battery baT-Ta-**ree**-ya	بطارية
bazaar, market soo"	سوق
beach plehj/shaTT	شاطئ

beach umbrella sham-**see**-ya	شمسية
beans fa-**Sul**-ya, fool	فاصولية فول
beard da"n	لحية
beautiful Hilw/ga-**meel**	جميل
beauty parlor Sa-**lohn** tag-**meel**	صالون تجميل
because ^ca-**shehn**, li-'ann	لأن
become yib-"a	يصبح
bed si-**reer** (pl.) sa-**reh**-yir	سرير سراير
bedroom 'oh-Dit nohm	غرفة نوم
beef laH-ma ba-"a-ree	لحم بقر
beer **bee**-ra	بيرة
before (prep) "abl	قبل
beforehand "ab-li ki-da	من قبل
begin yib-**ti**-dee	يبدأ
behind wa-ra	خلف
believe yi-**sad**-da"	يصدق
bell ga-ras	جرس
belly dancing ra"S ba-la-dee	رقص شرقي
belt Hi-zehm	حزام
bet (verb) yi-**raa**-hin	يراهن
better, best 'aH-san/ kheyr	أحسن / أفضل
between beyn	بين

bicycle *c*a-ga-la   عجلة، دراجة

big ki-**beer**   كبير

bigger, biggest '**ak**-bar   أكبر

bill (check) Hi-**sehb**   حساب
  (pl.) Hi-seh-**beht**   حسابات

bills (currency)   أوراق نقدية
  'aw-reh" na"d

bird *c*aS-**foor**   طائر
  (pl.) *c*a-Sa-**feer**   طيور

birthday *c*eed mi-**lehd**   عيد ميلاد

biscuit bas-ka-**weet**   بسكويت

black '**is**-wid   أسود
  [**soh**-da]   [سوداء]

blanket baT-Ta-**nee**-ya   بطانية

blender khal-**laaT**   خلاط

blind '*a*c-ma   أعمى
  [*c*am-ya]   [عمياء]

blocked mas-**dood**   مسدود

blood pressure DakhT   ضغط الدم
  *i*d-**damm**

blouse **bloo**-za   بلوزة

blue '**az**-ra" [**zar**-"a]   أزرق، [زرقاء]

board looII   لوح

boat **mar**-kib   سفينة، سفن،
  (pl.) ma-**reh**-kib   مركب، مراكب

bobby pins **bi**-nas   دبابيس الشعر

body gism   جسد

boiled mas-**loo"**   مسلوق

bomb qum-**bi**-la   قنبلة
  (pl.) qa-**neh**-bil   قنابل

bone *c*aDm   عظم

book ki-**tehb**   كتاب
  (pl.) **ku**-tub   كتب

book (verb) yiH-**giz**   يحجز

booking Hagz   حجز

bookstore mak-**ta**-ba   مكتبة

boring mu-**mill**   مضجر

borrow yis-**ti**-lif   يسلف

boss **ray**-yis   رئيس

both lit-**neyn**   الاثنان

bottle "i-**zeh**-za   زجاجة
  (pl.) "a-**zeh**-yiz   زجاجات

box san-**doo"**   صندوق

boy **wa**-lad   ولد
  (pl.) 'aw-**lehd**   أولاد

bra soo-**tyehn**   حمالة
    الصدر

bracelet ghi-**wey** sha   سوار الصدر

brain mukhkh   مخ

brakes fa-**raa**-mil   فرامل

branch far*L*   فرع
  (pl.) fu-**roo**c   فروع

brand **mar**-ka   ماركة
  (pl.) mar-**keht**   ماركات

brass na-**Hehs** 'aS-far   نحاس أصفر

Brazil ba-ra-**zeel**   برازيل

Brazilian ba-ra-**zee**-lee   برازيلي
  [ba-ra-**zee**-lee-ya]

bread *c*eysh/khubz   خبز

break (verb) **yik**-sar — يكسر

    broken mak-**soor** — مكسور
[mak-**soo**-ra]

    broken (out of order) — معطل
^caT-**laan** [^caT-**laa**-na]

breakfast (noon) fi-**Taar** — إفطار

    (verb) **yif**-Tar — يفطر

breathe yit-**naf**-fis — يتنفس

bribe **rash**-wa — رشوة

bride ^ca-**roo**-sa — عروسة

bridegroom ^ca-**rees** — عريس

bridge **kub**-ree — كوبري
(pl.) ka-beh-**ree** — كباري

bring yi-**geeb** — يحضر

Britain bri-**Tan**-ya — بريطانيا

British bri-**Taa**-nee — بريطاني
[bri-Taa-**nee**-ya]

broke (bankrupt) — مفلس
mi-**fal**-lis

brother 'akhkh — أخ
(pl.) 'ikh-**weht** — أخوة

brown **bun**-nee — بني

brown-skinned 'as-mar — [أسمر]
[**sam**-ra]

brush **fur**-sha — فرشاة

buffet (dining) car — بوفيه.عربية
bu-**feyh** — الأطعمة

bug **Ha**-sha-ra — حشرة
(pl.) Ha-sha-**reht** — حشرات

building ^ci-**maa**-ra — عمارة
(pl.) ^ci-maa-**raat** — عمارات

burial dafn — دفن

burn yiH-**ra**" — يحرق

    burned maH-**roo**" — محروق

bus 'u-tu-**bees** — أوتوبيس
(pl.) 'u-tu-bee-**seht** — أوتوبيسات

bus stop ma-**HaT**-Tit — محطة
'u-tu-**bees** — أوتوبيس

business ti-**gaa**-ra, — تجارة
'a^c-**mehl** — أعمال

businessman **teh**-gir, — تاجر
raa-gil 'a^c-**mehl** — رجل أعمال

busy mash-**ghool** — مشغول

but bass, **leh**-kin — لكن

butcher gaz-**zaar** — جزار

butter **zib**-da — زبدة

button zu-**raar** — زر
(pl.) za-**raa**-yir — أزرار

buy (verb) yish-**ti**-ree — يشتري

by the hour fis-seh-^ca — في الساعة

by the way... — على فكرة
^ca-la **fik**-ra

C

cabaret ka-ba-**rey** — كلبلريه.عرض

cabbage ku-**rumb** — كرنب

café "**ah**-wa — مقهى

caftan "uf-**Taan** — قفطان
(pl.) "a-fa-**Teen** — قفاطين

cake *ga-toh*　كاتو
　(pl.) *ga-to-heht*

Cairo *il-qaa-hi-ra,*　القاهرة
　maSr

call (telephone)　مكالمة
　mu-kal-ma

call (verb) *yi-kal-lim*　يكلم

camel *ga-mal*　جمل

camera *ka-me-ra*　كاميرا، آلة تصوير

campsite *mu-khay-yam*　مخيم
　si-yeh-Hee　سياحي

can (noun) *ᶜil-ba*　علبة
　(pl.) *ᶜi-lab*　علب

Canada *ka-na-da*　كندا

Canadian *ka-na-dee*　كندي
　[*ka-na-dee-ya*]　[كندية]

cancel *yil-ghee*　يلغي

cancer *su-ra-Taan*　سرطان

candles *shamᶜ*　شمع

candy *bon-bo-neht*　مسكّرات

capital (finance)　رأس مال
　ra's mehl

capital (city) *ᶜaa-Si-ma*　عاصمة

car *ᶜa-ra-bee-ya/*　سيارة
　say-yaa-ra

carat *"i-raaT*　قيراط

card *kart* (pl.) *ku-root/*　كارت، كروت
　bi-Taa-qa　بطاقة،
　(pl.) *bi-Taa-qaat*　بطاقات

(be) careful! *Heh-sib!*　احذر
　[*Has-bee!*]

carpenter *nag-gaar*　نجار

carpet *sig-geh-da*　سجادة
　(pl.) *sa-ga-geed*　سجادات

carriage (horsedrawn)　حنطور
　Han-Toor

carry *yi-sheel, yiH-mil*　يحمل

cash (noun) *na"d*　نقد

cashier *Sar-raaf*　صراف

cassette *ka-sitt* (pl.)　كسيت
　kasit-teht　كسيتات

cassette player *gi-hehz*　جهاز
　ka-sitt　كسيت

cause (noun) *sa-bab*　سبب

ceiling *sa"f*　سقف

cemetery *mad-fan*　مدفن

center *wisT*　وسط

center (institution)　مركز
　mar-kaz

ceramics *fukh-khaar*　فخار

certain (sure) *mit'ak-kid*　متأكد
　[*mit-'ak-ki-da*]　[ةكأتم]

certainly *Haa-Dir*　حاضر، تحت أمرك

chain *sil-si-la*　سلسلة

chair *kur-see*　كرسي
　(pl.) *ka-reh-see*　كراسي

change (money)　يحوّل
　yi-Haw-wil

change (verb. intr.)　يتغير
　yit-ghay-yar

(verb. trans.)
*yi-**ghay**-yar* يغير

change (remainder)
beh-"ee باقي

small — **fak-ka** فكة

channel *qa-**naah*** قناة

chat (verb) *yi-**dar**-dish* يدردش

chauffeur *saw-**weh"*** سائق

cheap *ri-**kheeS***
[ri-**khee**-Sa] رخيص

cheaper, **'ar**-khaS رخيص
cheapest أرخص

cheat (verb) *yi-**ghishsh*** يغش

check, bill *Hi-**sehb*** حساب

check (personal) *sheek* شيك
(pl.) shee-**keht** شيكات

traveler's checks
shee-**keht** شيكات
si-ya-**Hee**-ya سياحية

check (examine) *yi-**shoof*** يفحص

check in (baggage)
*yi-**sag**-gil* يسجل

cheek *khadd* خد
(pl.) khu-**dood** خدود

cheese **gib**-na جبنة

chemist's (druggist's)
'ag-za-**kheh**-na, أجزخانة
Say-da-**lee**-ya صيدلية

chess *sha-**Ta**-rang* شطرنج

chest (box) *san-**doo"*** صندوق

chest (body) *Sidr* صدر

chick peas **Hum**-muS حمص

chicken *fi-**rehkh**/ فراخ/
da-**jehj*** دجاج

chicken soup **shur**-bit شربة
fi-**rehkh** فراخ
/ da-**jehj*** دجاج

child *Tifl* (pl.) *'aT-**faal**,* طفل أطفال،
wa-lad ولد
(pl.) 'aw-**lehd** أولاد

China *iS-**Seen*** الصين

Chinese **See**-nee صيني
[**See**-nee-ya] صيني

chocolate *sho-ko-**laa**-ta* شكولاتة

choose *yikh-**taar*** يختار

Christian *ma-**see**-Hee* مسيحي

Christmas
*ceed il-mi-**lehd*** عيد الميلاد

church *ki-**nee**-sa* كنيسة

cigarette *si-**gaa**-ra* سيجارة
(pl.) sa-**geh**-yir سجائر

cinema *si-ni-ma* سينما

city *ba-lad/ma-**dee**-na* مدينة

class, classroom *faSL* فصل

clean (adj.) *ni-**Deef*** نظيف
[ni-**Dee**-fa] نظيف

clean (verb)
*yi-**naD**-Daf* ينظف

cleansing cream *kreym li* كريم لإزالة
'i-**zeh**-lit il-mak-**yaj*** المكياج

clever **shaa**-Tir
[**shaT**-ra] شاطر

clock seh-^ca ساعة

alarm clock
mi-**nab**-bih منبه

close (verb) **yi"**-fil يغلق.يقفل

closed ma"-**fool** مغلق.مقفول

cloth "u-**mehsh** قماش

clothes hu-**doom** ملابس

club **neh**-dee نادي
(pl.) na-**weh**-dee نوادي

coast seh-Hil ساحل

coffee "**ah**-wa قهوة

ground – bunn بن

coffee shop "**ah**-wa مقهى

cold (things, weather)
beh-rid بارد

(people) bar-**dehn**
[bar-**deh**-na] بردان

(in the head)
zi-**kehm**/bard زكام

colleague zi-**meel** زميل
(pl.) zu-ma-la زملاء

college kul-**lee**-ya كلية

cologne ko-**lon**-ya كلونيا

color lohn (pl.) 'al-**wehn** لون.ألوان

color chart
da-**leel** 'al-**wehn** دليل ألوان

comb mishT مشط

come **yee**-gee يجيئ

come! (imp.) ta-^ceh-la!
[ta-^ceh-lee!] هيا بنا!

comfort (noun) **raa**-Ha راحة

coming gayy [**gay**-ya] قادم/جاي

commerce ti-**gaa**-ra تجارة

committee **lag**-na لجنة

communications
mu-waS-**laat** مواصلات

company **shir**-ka شركة
(pl.) sha-ri-**keht** شركات

complete (entire) **keh**-mil
[**kam**-la] كامل

computer kom-**byoo**-tar كمبيوتر

concert **Huf**-la حفلة
mu-si-**qee**-ya موسيقية

confectioner's
Ha-la-**weh**-nee حلواني

confectionery
Ha-la-wee-**yeht** حلويات

conference mu-**ta**-mar مؤتمر
(pl.) mu-ta-ma-**raat** مؤتمرات

confirm yi-'**ak**-kid يؤكد

congratulations!
mab-**rook**! مبروك!

constipation 'im-**sehk** إمساك

consulate qun-Su-**lee**-ya قنصلية

contact (verb)
yiT-**Ti**-Sil (bi—) يتصل (بـ)

contact lenses
^ca-da-**seht** عدسات لاصقة

soft — — Ta-**ree**-ya لينة -

hard — — **nash**-fa صلبة -

continue yi-**kam**-mil يستمر

contract ^ca"d عقد

cook (verb) yuT-bukh يطبخ

cook (noun) Tab-**baakh** طباخ

cookies bas-ka-**weet** بسكويت

Coptic "ib-Tee قبطي

copy (noun) **nus**-kha نسخة

coral mur-**gehn** مرجان

corn (maize) **du**-ra ذرة

corner (of street) naS-ya ناصية

correct maz-**booT** مضبوط

corruption fa-**sehd** فساد

cosmetics mak-**yaj** مكياج

cost (noun) ta-**man**/si^cr ثمن/سعر

cost (verb) yi-**kal**-lif يكلف

cotton "uTn قطن

cough (verb) yi-**kuHH** يسعل/يكح

(noun) **kuH**-Ha سعال/كحة

council **mag**-lis مجلس

country (nation) **ba**-lad بلد
(pl.) bi-**lehd** بلاد

country code
nim-rit il-**ba**-lad نمرة البلد

countryside reef ريف

(of course) Tab-^can طبعا

cows ba-"ar بقر

crab 'a-boo ga-**lam**-boo أبو جلمبو

crazy mag-**noon** مجنون
[mag-**noo**-na]

cream "ish-Ta قشطة

(cosmetic) cream kreym كريم

credit card **kri**-dit kard/ كريدت كارد/
bi-**Taa**-qit i^c-ti-**mehd** بطاقة اعتماد

crisis 'az-ma أزمة

crowded zaH-ma زحمة/مزدحم

crystal (watch) "i-**zehz** زجاج

cucumber khi-**yaar** قثاء، خيار

culture sa-**qaa**-fa ثقافة

cultured mu-saq-**qaf** مثقف

cup fin-**gehn** فنجان
(pl.) fa-na-**geen** فناجين

curling iron gi-**hehz** جهاز لتجعيد الشعر
li-tag-**ceed**
ish-sha^cr

currency ^cum-la عملة

hard — ^cum-la عملة
Sa^c-ba صعبة

customer zi-**boon** زبون
(pl.) za-beh-yin زبائن

customs ig-**gum**-ruk الجمرك

cut yi"-Ta^c يقطع

D

dam sadd سد

damage yi-**baw**-waZ يضر

dance (verb) **yur-"uS** يرقص

dancing **ra"S** رقص

danger **kha-Tar** خطر

dangerous **kha-Teer** خطير

date **ta-reekh** تاريخ

date (appointment)
ma-^cehd موعد،ميعاد

dates (fruit) **ba-laH** بلح

daughter **bint** بنت
(pl.) **ba-neht** بنات

dawn **fagr** فجر

day **yohm** (pl.) **'ay-yehm** يوم، أيام

two days **yoh-meyn** يومان

day after tomorrow
ba^c-di buk-ra بعد غد

dead **may-yit** ميت

deaf **'aT-rash [Tar-sha]** أطرش

death **moht** موت

December **di-sim-bir** ديسمبر

decide **yi-qar-rar** يقرر

delicious **la-zeez** لذيذ

deliver **yi-sal-lim** يسلم

demonstration
mu-Zah-ra مظاهرة

dentist **Ta-beeb
'as-nehn** طبيب أسنان

depart, leave **yim-shee/
yi-seh-fir** يمشي يسافر

department **qism** قسم
(pl.) **aq-sehm** أقسام

depend (on) **yi^c-ti-mid
(^ca-la)** يعتمد (على)

deposit (noun) **ta'meen,
^car-boon** تأمين، عربون

descend **yin-zil** ينزل

desert **SaH-ra** صحراء

desserts **Ha-la-wee-yeht** حلويات

destroy **yi-dam-mar** يدمر

detour **taH-wee-la** تحويلة

develop (film)
yl-Ham-maD يحمض

development
ta-Taw-wur تطور

dialect **lah-ga** لجهة
(pl.) **lah-geht** لهجات

diamond **'al-maaz** الماس

diarrhea **'is-hehl** إسهال

dictionary **qa-moos** قاموس

die **yi-moot** يموت

diesel (gas) **dee-zil** ديزل

diet **ri-jeem** نظام غذائي

different **mukh-ta-lif
[mukh-ta-li-fa]** مختلف

difficult **Sa^cb** صعب

difficulty **Su-^coo-ba** صعوبة

dig **yuH-fur** يحفر

digital camera **ka**-me-ra ra-qa-**mee**-ya   كاميرا رقمية

dine yit-**^cash**-sha   يتعشى

dining room (in hotel) **maT**-^cam   مطعم

dinner ^ca-**sha**   عشاء

direct (adj.) mu-**beh**-shir   مباشر

director mu-**deer**   مدير

directory da-**leel**   دليل

dirty **wi**-sikh [**wis**-kha]   قذر, وسخ

disaster mu-**See**-ba   مصيبة

disc disk   قرص
(pl.) dis-**keht**   أقراص

discount takh-**feeD**   تخفيض

disease (illness) ma-**raD**   مرض
(pl.) am-**raaD**   أمراض

dish **Ta**-ba"   طبق
(pl.) **aT-baa**"   أطباق

dishwasher ghas-**seh**-lit Su-**Hoon**   غسالة صحون

disposable camera **ka**-me-ra tir-**mee**-ha ba^cd il-is-ti^c-**mehl**   كاميرا ترميها بعد الاستعمال

distance ma-**seh**-fa   مسافة

distribution taw-**zee**^c   توزيع

district man-**Ti**-qa   منطقة

do yi^c-mil   يعمل

doctor Ta-**beeb**, duk-**toor**   طبيب, دكتور

documents 'aw-**reh**"   أوراق

dog kalb (pl.) ki-**lehb**   كلب, كلاب

dollar do-**laar**   دولار
(pl.) do-la-**raat**   دولارات

donkey Hu-**maar**   حمار

door behb   باب

doorman (doorkeeper) baw-**wehb** (pl.) baw-weh-**been**   بواب

down (stairs) taHt   تحت

downtown fi wiST il-**ba**-lad   في وسط البلد

dress (noun) fus-**tehn**   فستان

dressed **leh**-bis [**lab**-sa]   لابس

get dressed **yil**-bis   يلبس

drink (verb) **yish**-rab   يشرب

drinks mash-roo-**beht**   مشروبات

drive (verb) yi-**soo**"   يسوق

drugs mu-khad-da-**raat**   مخدرات

drugstore 'ag-za-**kheh**-na, Say-da-**lee**-ya   أجزخانة, صيدلية

drunk sak-**raan** [sak-**raa**-na]   سكران

dry **neh**-shif [**nash**-fa]   جاف, ناشف

dry cleaning it-tan-**Deef** in-**neh**-shif   التنظيف الجاف

Dutch ho-**lan**-dee [ho-lan-**dee**-ya]   هولندي

DVD af-**lehm** dee-vee-**dee**   أفلام دي في دي

DVD player gi-**hehz** dee-vee-dee   جهاز في دي دي

E

each kull   كل

ear widn   أذن

early **bad**-ree   مبكر باكر

earn yik-sab   يكسب

earrings Ha-la"   حلق

East (Orient) shar"   شرق

  Middle East ish-sharq il-'aw-Sat   الشرق الأوسط

Eastern shar-"ee [shar-"ee-ya]   شرقي

easy sahl   سهل

eat yeh-kul   يأكل

economics 'iq-ti-**Saad**   اقتصاد

education ta^c-leem   تعليم

eggs beyD   بيض

eggplant bi-din-**gehn**   باذنجان

Egypt maSr   مصر

Egyptian **maS**-ree [maS-**ree**-ya] (pl.) maS-ree-yeen   مصري

eight ta-**man**-ya   ثمانية

electricity kah-ra-ba   كهرباء

elevator 'a-san-Seer   مصعد

embarrassed mak-soof [mak-**soo**-fa]   مكسوف

embassy sa-**faa** ra   سفارة

emergency Ta-**waa**-ri'   طوارئ

employee mu-**waZ**-Zaf   موظف

empty **faa**-Dee, **feh**-righ   فارغ

energetic na-**shee**T'   نشيط

engine mo-**toor**, ^cid-da   موتور، محرك

engineer mu-**han**-dis   مهندس

engineering han-da-sa   هندسة

England in-gil-**ti**-ra   إنجلترا

English in gi-**lee**-zee [in-gi-lee-**zee**-ya]   إنجليزي

enjoy yit-**mat**-ta^c (bi—)   يتمتع (بـ)

enough ki-**feh**-ya   كفاية

enter **yud**-khul, yi-**khushsh**   يدخل

entertainment ma-**leh**-hee   ملاهي

entrance du-**khool**   دخول

  no entry mam-**noo**^c id du-khool   ممنوع الدخول

envelope Zarf (pl.) Zu-roof   ظرف ظروف

especially khu-**Soo**-San   خصيصا

Europe u-**rub**-ba   أوروبا

European u-**rub**-bee   أوروبي

even **Hat**-ta   حتى

evening mi-**seh**', **magh**-rib   مساء مغرب

every kull   كل

fresh **Taa**-za طازج

Friday (yohm) يوم
ig-**gum**-^ca الجمعة

fried **ma**"-lee مقلي

friend **Saa**-Hib صاحب. صديق
(pl.) 'aS-**Haab**

friendship Sa-**daa**-qa صداقة

frighten yi-**khaw**-wif يخوف

from min من

in front of "ud-**dehm** أمام. قدام

fruit **fak**-ha فاكهة

fry **yi**"-lee يقلي

full mal-**yehn** مليء
[mal-**yeh**-na]

fundamentalist
'u-**Soo**-lee أصولي
(pl.) 'u-**Soo**-lee-**yeen** أصوليون

furniture farsh فرش

G

galabiyya gal-la-**bee**-ya جلابية

garbage zi-**beh**-la زبالة

garbage collector
zab-**behl** زبال

garden gi-**ney**-na جنينة.
(pl.) ga-**neh**-yin حديقة

garlic tohm ثوم

gasoline ban-**zeen** بنزين

gas station ma-**HaT**-Tit محطة
ban-**zeen** بنزين

gate ba-**weh**-ba بوابة

gears na"-**leht**, tu-**roos** تروس

generous ka-**reem** كريم
[ka-**ree**-ma] (pl.)
ku-ra-ma كرماء

German al-**meh**-nee ألماني
[al-ma-**nee**-ya]

Germany al-**man**-ya ألمانيا

get yi-**geeb** يحضر

get in, on (vehicle) يركب
yir-kab

ghee **sam**-na سمن

gift ha-**dee**-ya هدية
(pl.) ha-**deh**-ya هدايا

girl bint (pl.) ba-**neht** بنت. بنات

glass "i-**zehr** زجاج

glass (drinking) kub- كأس
beh-ya

go yi-**rooH** يذهب

Let's go! **yal**-la! هيا بنا

go away **yim**-shee يرحل.يغادر

go home yi-**raw**-waH يرجع البيت

go in **yud**-khul يدخل

God 'al-**laah** الله

gold da-**hab** ذهب

golf golf جولف

good (things) **kway**-yis جيد. كويس
[kway-**yi**-sa]

good (people) **Tay**-yib
[*Tay-yi-ba*] طيب

Good afternoon. *mi-seh'*
il-kheyr مساء الخير

Good-bye. **ma-**^ca
s-sa-leh-ma مع السلامة

Good evening. *mi-seh'*
il-kheyr مساء الخير

Good morning. *Sa-baH*
il-kheyr صباح الخير

Good night. **tiS**-baH
^ca la **kheyr** تصبح على خير

government *Hu-koo-ma* حكومة

grandfather *gidd* جد

grandmother **gid**-da جدة

grapes ^ci-nab عنب

grateful *mam-noon* ممنون

grave *ma"-ha-ra* مقبرة
(pl.) ma-"eh-bir مقابر

gray *ra-maa-Dee* رمادي

great ^ca-**Zeem** عظيم

Greece *il-yu-nehn* اليونان

greedy *Tam-maac*
[*Tam-maa-^ca*] طماع

Greek *yu-neh-nee*
[*yu-neh-nee-ya*] يوناني

green **'akh**-Dar
[*khaD-ra*] أخضر

grilled **mash**-wee مشوي

grocery store
ba"-"ehl محل بقالة. بقال

ground *'arD* أرض

guard **Heh**-ris
(pl.) Hur-**raas** حارس
حراس

guest *Deyf* ضيف
(pl.) Du-**yoof** ضيوف

guide, guidebook *da-leel* دليل

guilty **muz**-nib مذنب

gulf *kha-leeg* خليج

H

hair *sha^cr* شعر

hairdresser *Hal-leh"*,
kwa-feer حلاق

hairdryer *sesh-waar* مجفف الشعر

half *nuSS* نصف

hand *'eed* (pl.) *'a-yeh-dee* يد. أيدي

hanger *sham-meh-^ca* شماعة

happen *yiH-Sal* يحصل

happy *mab-SooT*
[*mab-Soo-Ta*],
far-Haan [*far-Haa-na*] مبسوط
فرحان

harbor **mee**-na ميناء

hashish *Ha-sheesh* حشيش

hat *bur-ney-Ta* قبعة. برنيطة

have ^cand —
or ma-^ca — +
pronoun
I have ^can-dee,
ma-^ceh-ya عند - مع -
عندي. معي

hay fever *zu-kehm ra-bee-^cee*	زكام ربيعي
he *huw-wa*	هو
head *raas*	رأس
headache *Su-daa^c*	صداع
headlight *kash-shehf*	النورالأمامي
headphones *sam-ma-^ceht ir-ra's*	سماعات الرأس
health *SiH-Ha*	صحة
hear *yis-ma^c*	يسمع
heart *"alb*	قلب
heart attack *'az-ma qal-bee-ya*	أزمة قلبية
heat (verb) *yi-sakh-khan*	يسخن
heavy *ti-"eel*	ثقيل
heel *ka^cb*	كعب
Hello. (on the phone) *a-loh*	آلو
help (verb) *yi-seh-^cid*	يساعد
Help! *il-Ha-"oo-nee!*	النجدة!
here *hi-na*	هنا
hide (verb) *yi-khab-bee*	يخبئ
high *^ceh-lee*	عالي
highway *Ta-ree" ra-'ee-see*	طريق رئيسي
hire *yi-'ag-gar*	يؤجر يستأجر
historical *ta-ree-khee*	تاريخي
history *ta-reekh*	تاريخ

hit *yiD-rab*	يضرب
hobby *hi-weh-ya*	هواية
hold *yim-sik*	يمسك
holiday *'a-geh-za*	عطلة/إجازة
Holland *ho-lan-da*	هولندا
home *beyt*	بيت، منزل
at home *fil-beyt*	في البيت
honest *sha-reef, 'a-meen*	شريف، أمين
honey *^ca-sal*	عسل
(I/we) hope so *'in shaa' al-laah*	إن شاء الله
horse *Hu-Saan*	حصان
hospital *mus-tash-fa*	مستشفى
hostage *ra-hee-na* (pl.) *ra-haa-yin*	رهينة رهائن
hot (weather) *Harr*	حار
(people) *Har-raan*	حران
(food, etc.) *sukhn*	ساخن
hot (spicy) *Heh-mee*	متبل،حامي
hotel *'u-teel, fun-du"*	أوتيل، فندق
hour *seh-^ca* (pl.) *sa-^ceht*	ساعة ساعات
per hour *fis-seh-^ca*	في الساعة
house *beyt* (pl.) *bu-yoot*	بيت، منزل
housewife *sit-ti beyt*	ربة منزل

how? *iz-zayy/keyf?* ازي، كيف؟

How do you do?
iz-zay-yak?
[iz-zay-yik?] ازيك!

How are you?
keyf il-Hehl? كيف حالك؟

How much/many? *kam?* كم،
bi kam? بكم؟

hubble bubble *shee-sha* شيشة
(water) pipe

humidity *ru-Too-ba* رطوبة

hundred *mee-ya* مئة
(pl.) *mee yeht* مئات

hungry *ga-^cehn*
[ga-^ceh-na] جائع جوعان

(in a) hurry *mis-ta^c-gil* مستعجل
[mis-ta^c-gi-la]

hurt *yiw-ga^c* يؤلم، يوجع

husband *gooz/zohj* زوج

I

I *a-na* أنا

ice *talg* ثلج

ice cream *ays kreem* آيس كريم

idea *fik-ra* (pl.) *'af-kaar* فكرة، أفكار

if *law* لو

ill *^cay-yehn* [*^cay-yeh-na*], مريض
ma-reeD [*ma-ree-Da*]

immediately *Heh-lan* فورا

import *is-ti-raad* استيراد

important *mu-himm* مهم

impossible *mish mum-kin* غير ممكن

improve *yi Has-sin* يحسن

in *fi* في، بـ

incense *bu-khoor* بخور

indeed *fi^c-lan* حقا

independence *is-tiq-lehl* استقلال

India *il-hind* الهند

Indian *hin-dee* هندي
[hin-dee-ya]

indigestion
Hu-moo-Da حموضة سوء هضم

industry *Si-naa-^ca* صناعة

inexpensive *ri-kheeS* رخيص

infection *'il-ti-hehb* التهاب

influenza *il-floo-in-za* انفلونزا

information معلومات،
is-ti^c-lu-meht استعلامات

injection *Hu''-na* حقنة

insect *Ha-sha-ra* حشرة
(pl.) *Ha-sha-raat* حشرات

inside *gow-wa* في الداخل

insomnia
^ca-dam in-nohm أرق

instead of *ba-dal* بدلا من

insult (verb) *yish-tim* يشتم

insurance ta'-**meen**   تأمين

intelligent **za**-kee
    [za-**kee**-ya]   ذكي

interested (in —)
    muh-**tamm** (bi —)   مهتم (بـ)

interesting mu-**himm**   مهم

international **daw**-lee   دولي

interview, encounter
    (noun) mu-"**ab**-la   مقابلة

introduce X to Y
    yi-"**ad**-dim X li Y   يقدم X لـ Y

invitation ^cu-**zoo**-ma   عزومة

invite yi^c-zim   يعزم

Ireland ayr-**lan**-da   ايرلندا

Irish (man) ayr-**lan**-dee
    [ayr-**lan**-dee-ya]   ايرلندي

iron **mak**-wa   مكوة

ironer mak-**wa**-gee   محل كي، مكوجي

ironing kayy   كي

Islam 'is-**lehm**   إسلام

Islamic 'is-**leh**-mee   إسلامي

island gi-**zee**-ra
    (pl.) **gu**-zur   جزيرة / جزر

Israel is-ra-'**eel**   إسرائيل

Israeli is-ra-'**ee**-lee
    [is-ra-'**ee**-lee-ya]   إسرائيلي

Italian i-**Taa**-lee
    [i-**Taa**-lee-ya]   إيطالي

Italy i-**Taal**-ya   إيطاليا

ivory sinn il-**feel**   سن الفيل

J

jack (car) ku-**reek**, jehk   مرفاع السيارة

jacket ja-**kit**-ta   جاكيتة

jail sign   سجن

jam mu-**rab**-ba   مربى

January ya-**neh**-yir   يناير

Japan il-ya-**behn**   اليابان

Japanese ya-beh-nee
    [ya-beh-**nee**-ya]   ياباني

jasmine yas-**meen**   ياسمين

Jerusalem il-**quds**   القدس

jewelry ga-**weh**-hir,
    mu-gaw-ha-**raat**   مجوهرات

jewelry store
    ga-wa-**hir**-gee   جواهرجي

Jewish yu-**hoo**-dee
    [yu-hoo-**dee**-ya]   يهودي

job, post wa-**Zee**-fa   وظيفة

joke **nuk**-ta   نكتة

Jordan il-'**ur**-dun   الأردن

Jordanian '**ur**-du-nee   أردني

journalist **Sa**-Ha-fee   صحفي

juice ^ca-**Seer**   عصير

July **yul**-yoo   يوليو

June **yun**-yoo   يونيو

K

key *mif-tehH* مفتاح
(pl.) ma-fa-teeH مفاتيح

keyboard *loo-Hit* لوحة المفاتيح
il-ma-fa-teeH

kidnap *yikh-Taf* يختطف

kill *yi-maw-wit, yi"-til* يقتل

kilo *kee-loo* كيلو

kind (noun) *Sanf* صنف
(pl.) 'aS-naaf, noh^c
(pl.) 'an-weh^c نوع

kind (adj.) *lu-Teef* لطيف
[la-Tee-fa]
(pl.) lu-**Taaf**

king *ma-lik* (pl.) mu-**look** ملك

kiosk *kushk* كشك
(pl.) kush-**keht** كشكات

kiss (verb) *yi-boos* سوس

kiss (noun) *boh-sa* بوسة

knife *sik-kee-na* سكينة
(pl.) sa-ka-keen سكاكين

knock *yi-khab-baT,* بدق
yi-**du""**

know *yic-raf* يعرف

Koran *'il-qur-'ehn* القرآن

Kuwait *'ik-ku-weyt* الكويت

Kuwaiti *ku-wey-tee* كويتي

L

laboratory *ma^c-mal* معمل

ladder *sil-lim* سلم

lady *sitt* (pl.) sit-**teht** سيدة، سيدات

lake *bu-Hey-ra* بحيرة

lamb *Daa-nee* لحم خروف، ضاني

lamp *lam-ba* لمبة

table lamp
'a-ba-joo-ra مصباح كهربائي

land, earth *'arD* أرض

language *lu-gha* لغة

laptop *lab-tob* كمبيوتر
محمول

large *ki-beer* [ki-bee-ra] كبير

larger, largest *'ak-bar* أكبر

last (adj.) *'a-kheer* أخير

(at) last! *'a-khee-ran!* أخيرا

late *wakh-ree,* متأخر
mut-'akh-khir

later *ba^c-deyn* بعد ذلك

laugh *yiD-Hak* يضحك

laundry *gha-seel* غسيل
(washing place)
magh-sa-la مغسلة

lavatory *twa-litt,* تواليت،
doh-rit il-may-ya دورة مياه

law qa-**noon** قانون

lawyer mu-**Heh**-mee محامي

laxative mu-**lay**-yin ملين

lazy kas-**lehn** كسول

learn yit-**c**al-lim يتعلم

leather gild جلد

leave (tr.) yi-**seeb** يترك

leave (intr.) **yim**-shee يغادر

Lebanon lib-**nehn** لبنان

Lebanese lib-**neh**-nee لبناني

left shi-**mehl**, yi-**saar** يسار

leg rigl رجل

legal qa-**noo**-nee قانوني

lemon la-**moon** ليمون

lend yi-**sal**-lif يسلف

lens **c**a-da-sa عدسة
(pl.) **c**a-da-**seht** عدسات

lentils **c**ads عدس

lesson dars درس
(pl.) du-**roos** دروس

letter ga-**wehb** خطاب
(pl.) ga-weh-**beht**

liar kad-**dehb** كذاب

library mak-**ta**-ba مكتبة

Libya **lib**-ya ليبيا

Libyan **lee**-bee ليبي

license, permit **rukh**-Sa رخصة

lie (noun) **kid**-ba كذبة

lie (verb) yik-**dib** يكذب

light (noun) noor نور

light (verb) yi-**wal**-la**c** يشعل

light (in color) feh-tiH فاتح
[**fat**-Ha]

light (in weight) kha-**feef** فاتح
[kha-**fee**-fa]

lighter (noun) wal-**leh**-**c**a ولاعة

like (verb) yi-**Hibb** يحب

like (prep.) zayy/keyf زاي/مثل

limit (verb) yi-Had-**did** يحدد

line khaTT خط
(pl.) khu-**TooT** خطوط

lip **shif**-fa شفة
(pl.) sha-**feh**-yif شفائف

liquor **kham**-ra خمرة

list "**ay**-ma قائمة

listen yis-ma**c** يستمع

little Su-**ghay**-yar صغير

(a) little shway-ya قليل

live (verb) **yus**-kun, يسكن
yi-**c**eesh يعيش

loaf ri-**gheef** رغيف
(pl.) 'ar-**ghi**-fa أرغفة

local ma-**Hal**-le محلي

long Ta-**weel** طويل

look, appearance *shakl* مظهر، شكل
he (she) looks — مظهره -
shak-loo [shak-la-ha] - شكله

look (at) *yit-far-rag* (*a-la*) ينظر (إلى)

look (for)
yi-daw-war (*a-la*) يبحث (عن)

loose (clothes) *weh-si*^c واسع

lose *yi-Dee*^c يفقد

(get) lost *yi-tuuh* يتيه. يضل الطريق

a lot *ki-teer* كثير

love (noun) *Hubb* حب

love (verb) *yi-Hibb* يحب

low *waa-Tee* منخفض. واطى

luck *bakht, HaZZ* حظ

luggage *shu-naT/*^c*afsh* أمتعة

lunch (noun) *gha-da* غذاء

(verb) *yit-ghad-da* يتغدى

M

machine *ma-ka-na,* آلة
'eh-la

magazine *ma-gal-la* مجلة
(pl.) *ma-gal-leht* مجلات

magnificent ^c*a-Zeem* عظيم

maid *khad-deh-ma* خادمة

mail *ba-reed* بريد

make *yi*^c *mil* يعمل

man *ruu-gil* رجل
(pl.) *rig-geh-la* رجال

manager *mu-deer* مدير

mangoes *man-ga* منجو

manicure *ma-ni-keer* مانيكير

many *ki-teer* كثير

map *kha-ree-Ta* خريطة

March *meh-ris* مارس

market *soo"* سوق

married *mit-gaw-wiz* منزوج
[*mit-gaw-wi-za*]

marry *yit-gaw-wiz* يتزوج

massage *tad-leek* تدليك

(football) match *matsh* مباراة (كرة)
(*koh-ra*)

matches *kab-reet* كبريت

(it doesn't) matter
may-him-mish غير مهم

mattress *mar-ta-ba* فرشة

May *may-yoo* مايو

maybe *yim-kin* يمكن. ربما

meal *'akl* طعام. أكل

measure *yi-"ees* يقيس

meat *laHm* لحم

medicine *da-wa* دواء
(pl.) *'ad-wee-ya*

Mediterranean *il-baHr* البحر
il-'ab-yaD الأبيض

meet	yi-**"eh**-bil	يقابل
meeting	ig-ti-**meh**ᶜ	اجتماع
melon	sham-**mehm**	شمام
member	ᶜu**Dw**	عضو
(pl.)	'aᶜ-**Daa'**	أعضاء
memory card	bi-**Tah**-qit iz-**zeh**-ki-ra	بطاقة الذاكرة
mend	yi-**Sal**-laH	يصلح
menu	**min**-yoo/"**ay**-ma	منيو .قائمة
message	ri-**seh**-la	رسالة
meter (taxi)	ᶜad-**dehd**	عداد
meter (measurement)	mitr	متر
Middle East	ish-**sharq** il-'**aw**-saT	الشرق الأوسط
military	ᶜas-ka-ree	عسكري
milk	**la**-ban/Ha-**leeb**	لبن. حليب
million	mil-**yohn**	مليون
(pl.)	ma-la-**yeen**	ملايين
(never) mind!	ma-ᶜa-**lish**!	معلهش! لا بأس!
mind	ᶜa"l	عقل
mine	bi-**teh**-ᶜee	لي
minister	wa-**zeer**	وزير
ministry	wi-**zaa**-ra	وزارة
mint	niᶜ-**neh**ᶜ	نعناع
minute (time)	da-"**ee**-"a	دقيقة
(pl.)	da-"**eh**-yi"	دقائق
mirror	mi-**reh**-ya	مرايا
Miss —	il-eh-**ni**-sa —	الآنسة -

mistake	**ghal**-Ta	غلطة
mistaken	ghal-**Taan**	غلطان
modern	ᶜa**S**-ree/ Ha-**dees**	عصري. حديث
moment	**laH**-Za	لحظة
monastery	deyr	دير
Monday	(yohm) lit-**neyn**	يوم الأثنين
money	fi-**loos**	فلوس
money exchange	**mak**-tab Sarf	مكتب الصرف
month	shahr	شهر
(pl.)	shu-**hoor**	أشهر
monument	'a-sar	أثر
(pl.)	'a-**saar**	آثار
more	'**ak**-tar	أكثر
morning	Sub**H**/ Sa-**baaH**	صبح. صباح
in the morning	iS-**SubH**	صباحا
mosque	geh-miᶜ	جامع
(pl.)	ga-**weh**-miᶜ	جوامع
mosquitoes	na-**moos**	ناموس
mother	'umm	أم
mountain	ga-**bal**	جبل
(pl.)	gi-**behl**	جبال
mouse	faar	فار
(pl.)	fi-**rehn**	فئران
mouth	bu""/fumm	فم
MP3 player	gi-**hehz** em-bee-sree	جهاز ام بي سري

Mr. — is-**say**-yid — السيد -

Mrs. — is-**say**-yi-da, السيدة،
ma-**dehm** — مدام -

museum **mat**-Haf متحف

music mu-**see**-qa موسيقى

Muslim **mus**-lim مسلم
[**mus**-li-ma] مسلمة
(pl.) mus li **meen**

(I, you, etc.) must يجب أن -
— **leh**-zim —

mustache **sha**-nab شنب،شارب

N

name 'ism اسم
(pl.) 'a-**seh**-mee أسامي

napkin foo-Ta فوطة. منشفة
(pl.) fo-waT

sanitary napkin
foo Ta siH Hee ya فوطة صحية

narrow **day**-ya" ضيق

national, nationalist
qaw-mee قومي

nationality gin-**see**-ya جنسية

natural Ta-**bee**-^cee طبيعي

naughty **sha**-"ee شقي.شرير

near (to) "u-**ray**-yib (min) قريب (من)

nearby "u-**ray**-yib قريبا

nearly ta"-**ree**-ban تقريبا

(it is) necessary **leh**-zim يلزم

(I) need ^c**a**-wiz [^c**aw**-za] أريد. أحتاج

neighbor gaar جار
(pl.) gi-**rehn** جيران

never 'a-ba-dan أبدا

new gi-**deed** جديد

news 'akh **baar** أخبار

newspaper ga-**ree**-da جريدة
(pl.) ga-**raa**-yid جرائد

next gayy قادم

night **ley**-la ليلة

at night bil-**leyl** ليلا

Nile in-**neel** النيل

nine **tis**-^ca تسعة

no la' لا

nobody ma-**Had**-dish لا أحد

noise **daw**-sha دوشة. صخب

noon Duhr ظهر

north sha-**mehl** شمال

nose ma-na-**kheer** أنف

not mish ليس. ما. لا

notebook **noh**-ta دفتر جيب

nothing wa-la **Ha**-ga لا شيء

novel (noun) ri-**weh**-ya رواية

November nu-**vim**-bir نوفمبر

now dil-**wa**"-tee الآن

Nubia in-**noo**-ba — النوبة

Nubian **noo**-bee — نوبي

number **nim**-ra/**ra**-qam — رقم

number (quantity) ^c**a**-dad — عدد

nurse mu-**mar**-ri-Da — ممرضة

O

oasis **weh**-Ha — واحة
   (pl.) wa-**Heht** — واحات

(I've/we've no) objection. — ليس عندي
   ma feesh **meh**-ni^c — مانع

obvious **waa**-DiH — واضح

October ok-**too**-bar — أكتوبر

of course **Tab**-^can — طبعا

offer yi-"**ad**-dim — يقدم

office **mak**-tab — مكتب

office worker mu-**waZ**- — موظف
   Zaf [mu-**waZ**-**Za**-fa]

officer **Zaa**-biT — ضابط
   (pl.) Zub-**baaT** — ضباط

often ki-**teer** — كثيرا

oil zeyt — زيت

   olive oil zeyt zey-**toon** — زيت زيتون

oil (petroleum) bit-**rohl**, — بترول،
   nafT — نفط

okay! **meh**-shee! — لا مانع

old (people) ki-**beer** — كبير
   [ki-**bee**-ra]
   (pl.) ku-**baar** — كبار

old (things) "a-**deem** — قديم
   ["a-**dee**-ma]

I'm — years old. — عمري -
   ^c**an**-dee — **sa**-na — سنة

How old are you? ^c**an**-dak — عمركم
   [^c**an**-dik] kam **sa**-na? — كم سنة؟

olives zey-**toon** — زيتون

on ^c**a**-la — على

on foot — ماشيا، على الأقدام
   ^c**a**-la rig-**ley**-na

on time fil-ma-^c**ehd** — في الميعاد

once **mar**-ra waH-da — مرة واحدة

one **weh**-Hid — واحد
   [**waH**-da] — واحدة

one another ba^cD — بعض

onions **ba**-Sal — بصل

only (just) bass — فقط

only (sole) wa-**Heed** — وحيد

open yif-**taH** — يفتح

open (adj.) **feh**-tiH, — مفتوح
   maf-**tooH**

opportunity **fur**-Sa — فرصة
   (pl.) **fu**-raS — فرص

optician — محل نظارات
   naD-Da-**raa**-tee

or 'aw; **wal**-la — أو؛ لا
   (in questions)

orange *bur-tu-'aan* برتقال

order (verb) *yuT-lub* يطلب

ordinary *ᶜeh-dee* عادي

organize *yi-naZ-Zam* ينظم

organization *mu-naZ-Za-ma* منظمة

origin *'aSl* أصل

other *teh-nee [tan-ya]*, *'eh-khir ['ukh-ra]* آخر

out of order *ᶜaT-laan* معطل

outing, break *fus-Ha* فسحة

outside *bar-ra* في الخارج

oven *furn* فرن

over *foh"* فوق

It's over; that's it! *kha-laaS!* خلاص!

overcoat *bal-Too* بالطو، معطف

(on my) own *li waH-dee* وحدي

(on your) own *li waH-dak [li waH-dak]* وحدك

P

package *Tard* طرد
(pl.) *Tu-rood*

packet *ᶜil-ba* (pl.) *ᶜi-lab*, علبة
beh-koo(pl.) علب
beh-ku-weht

pail *gar-dal* دلو

pain *wa-gaᶜ/'a-lam* وجع. ألم

palace *"aSr* قصر

Palestine *fi-lis-Teen* فلسطين

Palestinian *fi-lis-Tee-nee* فلسطيني

palm trees *nakhl* نخل

panties *kee-lott* سروال داخلي نسائي

pants, trousers بنطلون
ban-Ta-lohn

paper *wa-ra"* ورق
(pl.) *'aw-reh"* أوراق

paper towels *fu-waT* فوط ورق
wa-ra

parcel *Tard* (pl.) *Tu-rood* طرد. طرود

Pardon me, but — *is-maH-lee —,* اسمح لي
law sa-maHt —

park *gi-ney-na* حديقة
(pl.) *ga-neh-yin*

park (verb) *yu-"af* يقف

parking *'in-ti-Zaar* انتظار

party *Haf-la* حفل

passenger *reh-kib* راكب
(pl.) *ruk-kehb* ركاب

passport *bas-boor/* جواز السفر
ga-wehz is-sa-far

password *kil-mit is-sirr* كلمة السر

past (noun) *maa-Dee* ماضي

pasta *ma-ka-roh-na* مكرونة

pastries *Ha-la-wee-yeht* حلويات

pastry shop *Ha-la-weh-nee* حلواني

patience *Sabr*   صبر

pay (verb) **yid-fa**^c   يدفع

peach *khokhh*   خوخ

peanuts *fool su-deh-nee* فول سوداني

peasant *fal-lehH*   فلاح
   (pl.) *fal-la-Heen*

pen, pencil *"a-lam*   قلم

pension *ma-^cehsh*   راتب تقاعدي

people *nehs*   ناس

pepper *fil-fil*   فلفل

percentage *nis-ba*   نسبة
   mi-'a-wee-ya   مئوية

perhaps *yim-kin*   يمكن، ربما

person *na-far*   نفر
   (pl.) *'an-faar*, *shakhS*   أنفار
   (pl.) *'ash-khaaS*   شخص،
    أشخاص

personal *shakh-See*   شخصي

personally *shakh-See-yan*   شخصية

petrol *ban-zeen*   بنزين

Pharaonic *far-^coo-nee*   فرعوني

pharmacy *'ag-za-kheh-na*,   أجزخانة،
   Say-da-lee-ya   صيدلية

photograph, picture
   Soo-ra   صورة
   (pl.) *So-war*   صور

photograph (verb)
   yi-Saw-war   يصور

pickles *Tur-shee/*   طرشي،
   mi-khal-lil   مخلل

pigeon *Ha-mehm*   حمام

pillow *mi-khad-da*   مخدة

pills *Hu-boob*   حبوب

   sleeping pills   حبوب
   Hu-boob   منومة
   mi-naw-wi-ma

(what a) pity! *ya kh-*   يا خسارة
   Saa-ra!

place *ma-kehn*   مكان
   (pl.) *'a-meh-kin*   أماكن

plain *seh-da*   سادة

plants *na-ba-teht*   نباتات

plate *Ta-ba"*   طبق
   (pl.) *'aT-baa"*   أطباق

platform *ra-Seef*   رصيف

play (verb) *yil-^cab*   يلعب

play (theater)   مسرحية
   mas-ra-Hee-ya

pleasant (things) *Za-reef*   ظريف

   (people) *la-Teef*   لطيف
   [*la-Tee-fa*] (pl.)   لطفاء
   lu-Taaf

please — *min faD-lak* - من فضلك -
   — [*min faD-lik*]

pleased, happy *mab-*   سعيد
   SooT, *far-Haan*   فرحان، مبسوط

Pleased to meet you.   تشرفنا،
   it-shar-raf-na,   فرصة
   fur-Sa sa-^cee-da   سعيدة

plumber *sab-behk*   سباك

police *bu-leeS/shur-Ta* بوليس، شرطة

policeman *^cas-ka-ree* شرطي
(pl.) *^ca-seh-kir* شرطي

politics *si-yeh-sa* سياسة

poor *fa-"eer* فقير
(pl.) *fu-"a-ra* فقراء

popcorn *fi-shaar* فشار

popular (of the people) شعبي
sha^c-bee

porter *shay-yehl* شيال.حمال

possible *mum-kin* ممكن

post *ba-reed* بريد

postcard كارت بوستال.
kart bus-tehl بطاقة بريدية

post office *mak tab* مكتب
il-ba-reed البريد

potatoes *ba-Taa-Tis* بطاطس

sweet potatoes بطاطا
ba-Taa-Ta

pottery *fukh-khaar* فخار

pound (currency) *gi-ney* جنيه

pound (weight) *raTl* رطل

pour *yi-Subb* يصب

pray *yi-Sal-lee* يصلي

prefer *yi-faD-Dal* يفضل

pregnant *Heh-mil* حامل

prepare *yi-gah-hiz,* يحضر
yi-HaD-Dar

prescription *ru-shit-ta* روشتة

present (gift) *ha-dee-ya* هدية
(pl.) *ha-deh-ya*

present (adj.) *maw-good* موجود

president *ra-'ees* رئيس

press (noun) *Sa-Haa-fa* صحافة

pretty *Hilw* حلو

prevent *yim na^c* يمنع

price *ta-man, si^cr* ثمن.سعر

print (photo) *nus-kha* نسخة

private *khaaS* خاص

problem *mush-ki-la* مشكلة
(pl.) *ma-sheh-kil* مشاكل

profession *mih-na* مهنة

professor *'us-tehz* أستاذ

promise (verb) *yiw-^cid* بعد

prophet *na-bee* نبي

public *^camm* عام

pull *yi-shidd* يشد

pupil *til-meez* تلميذ
(pl.) *ta-lam-za* تلامذة

purse, wallet *maH-fa-Za* محفظة

purse, bag *shan-Ta* شنطة.
(pl.) *shu-naT* حقيبة

push *yi-zu""* يدفع

put *yi-HuTT* يضع

pyramids *il-ha-ram* أهرام

Q

quantity ^ca-dad, qee-ma عدد، قيمة

quarrel (verb) yi-kheh-ni" يخانق

question (query) su-'ehl سؤال
(pl.) 'as-'i-la أسئلة

queue Ta-boor طابور

quick sa-ree^c سريع

quickly bi-sur-^ca بسرعة

quiet heh-dee هادئ

R

rabbit 'ar-nab أرنب
(pl.) 'a-reh-nib أرانب

race (competition) سباق
si-beh"

radio rad-yoo راديو

railroad is-sik-ka السكة
il-Ha-deed الحديدية

railroad station محطة
ma-HaT-Tit il-"aTr القطار

by rail bil-"aTr بالقطار

rain (noun) ma-Tar مطر

rain (verb) ti-maT-Tar تمطر

rare (unusual) neh-dir نادر

rate of exchange سعر
si^cr it-taH-weel التحويل

rather (somewhat) إلى حد ما،
shway-ya قليلا

raw nayy خام، نيء

razor blades 'am-wehs أمواس
Hi-leh-"a حلاقة

read yi"-ra يقرأ

ready geh-hiz [gah-za] جاهز

really? Sa-HeeH? صحيح!

to the rear wa-ra إلى الوراء

reason sa-bab سبب
(pl.) 'as-behb أسباب

receipt waSl إيصال

reception is-ti"-behl استقبال

recipe waS-fa وصفة

record (verb) yi-sag-gil يسجل

recordable CDs اسطوانات
is-Ti-wa-naht ley-zar فارغة
far-gha lit-tas-geel للتسجيل

recover (health) يشفى
yi-khiff, yish-fee

red 'aH-mar [Ham-ra] أحمر

reduction takh-feeD تخفيض

reef shi^c-ba شعبة

refrigerator tal-leh-ga ثلاجة

region man-Ti-qa منطقة

relation "a-reeb قريب
(pl.) "a-raa-yib أقرباء

remember yif-ti-kir يفتكر، يتذكر

remind yi-fak-kar يذكر

rent (verb) yi-'ag-gar يؤجر، يستأجر

repair (verb) yi-Sal-laH يصلح

(noun) taS-leeH تصليح

repeat yi-kar-rar يكرر

reply (verb) yi-rudd يرد

republic gum-hoo-ree-ya جمهورية

reservation Hagz حجز

reserve yiH-giz يحجز

respect (noun) iH-ti-raam احترام

responsible mas-'ool مسؤول

rest (verb) yis-ta-ray-yaH يستريح

restaurant maT-ʿam مطعم
(pl.) ma-Taa-ʿim مطاعم

restroom twa-litt تواليت، دورة المياه

return (verb) yir-gaʿ يعود، يرجع

rice ruzz أرز

rich gha-nee [gha-nee- غني
ya] (pl.) 'agh-nee-ya

ride (verb) yir-kab يركب

right (correct) صحيح،
maZ-booT مضبوط

right (direction) yi-meen يمين

ring (jewelry) kheh-tim خاتم

rise yi-"oom يقوم

river nahr نهر

road Ta-ree" (pl.) طريق
Tu-ru" طرق

sik-ka (pl.) si-kak سكة، سكك

roast mash-wee مشوي

robe, dressing gown rohb ثوب، روب

rock Sakhr صخر

roof SatH سقف، سطح

room 'oh-Da غرفة، غرف
(pl.) 'o-waD/
ghur-fa (pl.) ghu-raf

roses ward ورد

rug sig-geh-da سجاد، سجاجيد،
(pl.) sa-ga-geed كليم، أكلمة
ki-leem (pl.) 'ak-li-ma

run yig-ree يركض

Russia roos-ya روسيا

Russian roo-see روسي

S

sad Ha-zeen حزين

safe khaz-na خزنة

sailboat yakht, fa-loo-ka يخت، فلوكة

sailor baH-Haar بحار

salad sa-la-Ta سلطة

salary ma-hee-ya, مرتب
mu-rat-tab

sale beeʿ بيع

salt malH ملح

(the same) — nafs il نفس الـ -
— —

sand raml رمل

sandstorm *zaw-ba-*^c*a* عاصفة رملية

sandals **san**-dal صندل
(pl.) sa-na-**deel**

sandwich **sand**-witsh سندويتش
(pl.) sand-wit-**sheht** سندويتشات

sanitary napkins *fo-waT* فوطصحية
SiH-**Hee**-ya

sardines sar-**deen** سردين

Saturday (yohm) is-**sabt** يوم السبت

sauce **Sal**-Sa صلصة

sausages *su-gu" "* سجق

save (time, money) يوفر
*yi-**waf**-far*

say yi-**"ool** يقول

scarf *'i-**sharb**, ku-**fee**-ya* منديل الرأس

scene, view **man**-Zar منظر
(pl.) ma-**naa**-Zir مناظر

schedule **gad**-wal جدول
il-ma-wa-^c**eed** المواعيد

school mad-**ra**-sa مدرسة
(pl.) ma-**deh**-ris مدارس

science ^cilm (pl.) ^cu-**loom** علم، علوم

scientific ^c**il**-mee علمي

scissors ma-**"aSS** مقص

scotch (whiskey) **wis**-kee ويسكي

screen **sheh**-sha شاشة

screwdriver mu-**fakk** مفك
ma-sa-**meer** مسامير

sea baHr بحر

search for yi-**daw**-war يبحث عن
^ca-la

seashore shaTT شاطئ (البحر)

season faSl فصل

second **teh**-nee [**tan**-ya] ثاني

secretary si-kir-**teer** سكرتير
[si-kir-**tee**-ra] [سكرتيرة]

security 'amn أمن

see yi-**shoof** يرى

sell yi-**bee**^c يبيع

send yib-^cat يرسل،يبعث

September sib-**tim**-bir سبتمبر

serious gadd جاد

seriously bi-**gadd** بجد

service **khid**-ma خدمة

seven **sab**-^ca سبعة

sew yi-**khay**-yaT يخيط

shampoo sham-**poo** شامبو

shark "irsh (pl.) "u-**roosh** سمك القرش يحلق

shave yiH-**la"** يحلق

she **hee**-ya هي

sheep (and goats) غنم
gha-nam

shells **Sa**-daf صدف

ship **mar**-kib/sa-**fee**-na مركب،
سفينة

shirt "a-**meeS** قميص
(pl.) "um-**Saan** قمصان

shoemaker *gaz-ma-gee*	جزمجي
shoe polish *war-neesh gaz-ma*	ورنيش جزمة
shoes *gaz-ma*	حذاء جزمة
shop *duk-kehn* (pl.) *da-ka-keen*	محل محلات
ma-Hall (pl.) *ma-Hal-leht*	قصير
short *"u-Say-yar*	قصير
shoulder *kitf*	كتف
show (stage, floor) *carD*	عرض
show (verb) *yi-war-ree*	بري
shower *dush*	دش
shrimp *gam-ba-ree*	جمبري
shy *mak-soof* [*mak soo fa*]	مكسوف
sick *cay-yehn* [*cay-yeh-na*], *ma-reeD* [*ma-ree-Da*]	مريض
sight *man-Zar* (pl.) *ma-naa-Zir*	منظر مناظر
sign (verb) *yim-Dee*	يمضي
silent (of people) *seh-kit* [*sak-ta*]	ساكت
silk *Ha-reer*	حرير
silver *faD-Da*	فضة
Sinai *see-na*	سيناء
sing *yi-ghan-nee*	يغني

singer *mu-ghan-nee* [*mu-ghan-nee-ya*]	مغني [مغني]
sister *'ukht*	أخت
sit *yu"-cud*	يقعد
six *sit-ta*	ستة
size *ma-"ehs*	مقاس
skin *gild/bash-ra*	جلد.بشرة
skirt *gu-nil-la*	جيبة.جونلة
sky *sa-ma*	سماء
slaughter *yid-baH*	يذبح
sleep (verb) *yi nehm* (noun) *nohm*	ينام نوم
sleeping pills *Hu-boob mi-naw-wi-ma*	حبوب منومة
slippers *shib-shib*	شبشب
slow *ba-Tee'*	بطيء
slowly *bir-raa-Ha*	ببطء
Slow down! *ca-la mah-lak!*	قلل السرعة. على مهلك!
SLR digital camera *ka-me-ra ra-ga-mee-ya es-el-ar*	كاميرا رقمية إس إل آر
small *Su-ghay-yar* [*Su-ghay-ya-ra*]	صغر
smell (noun) *ree-Ha*	رائحة
smoke (verb) *yi-dakh-khan*	يدخن
smoking *tad-kheen*	تدخين
snake *ticbehn*	حبة
snow *talg*	ثلج

so, thus **ki**-da	هكذا
soap Sa-**boon**	صابون
soap opera mu-**sal**-sal (pl) mu-sal-sa-**leht**	مسلسل مسلسلات
soccer **koh**-ra	كرة القدم
soccer match matsh **koh**-ra	مباراة في كرة القدم
socialist ish-ti-**raa**-kee	اشتراكي
socks sha-**raab**	شراب
soldier ^cas-ka-ree (pl.) ^ca-**seh**-kir	عسكري
some—— ba^cD —	بعض -
somebody Hadd, **weh**-Hid	واحد
something **Ha**-ga	شيء
sometimes sa-^c**eht**, 'aH-yeh-nan	أحيانا
son 'ibn	ابن
soon "u-**ray**-yib	قريبا
Sorry! '**eh**-sif! ['**as**-fa!]	آسف
sort, kind noh^c (pl.) 'an-**weh**^c	نوع أنواع
sound, voice Soht	صوت
soup **shur**-ba	شربة
south ga-**noob**	جنوب
Spain as-**ban**-ya	إسبانيا
Spanish as-**beh**-nee [as-ba-**nee**-ya]	إسباني

spark plugs boo-jey-**heht**	بوجيهات، شمعة الشرارة
speak yit-**kal**-lim	يتكلم
speak to yi-**kal**-lim	يكلم
speakers sam-ma-**ceht**	سماعات
special makh-**SooS**	مخصوص
spend **yiS**-rif	يصرف
in spite of bir-**raghm** min	بالرغم من
sponge si-**fing**	إسفنج
spoon ma^c-**la**-"a	ملعقة
sports ri-**yaa**-Da	رياضة
spring (season) ra-**bee**^c	ربيع
square (place) mi-**dehn**	ميدان
stairs **sil**-lim	سلم
stamps Ta-**waa**-bi^c	طوابع
stand (up) yi-**"oom**	يقوم
standing **weh**-"if [**wa**"-fa]	واقف [واقفة]
star **nig**-ma (pl.) nu-**goom**	نجمة نجوم
start yib-**ti**-dee	يبدأ
state (noun) **daw**-la (pl.) **du**-wal	دولة دول
station ma-**HaT**-Ta	محطة
stay (in, at) **yin**-zil (fi), yu"-^cud	ينزل، يبقى
steal **yis**-ra"	يسرق

still (adverb) *lis-sa*   لا يزال

stockings *sha-raab*   شرابات. جوارب

stomach *mi^c-da, baTn*   معدة. بطن

stone *Ha-gar*   حجر

stop (noun) *maw-"af*   موقف
(pl.) *ma-weh-"if*

stop (verb) *yu-"af*   يقف

store *duk-kehn*   دكان
(pl.) *da ka keen*   دكاكين

ma-Hall   محل
(pl.) *ma-Hal-leht*   محلات

story *Hi-keh-ya*   قصة. حكاية

straight (on) *dugh-ree*   إلى الأمام. دغري

strange *gha-reeb*   غريب

strawberries *fa-raw-la*   فراولة

street *sheh-ri^c*   شارع
(pl.) *sha-weh-ri^c*   شوارع

strong *qa-wee*   قوي
[*qa-wee-ya*]

student *Taa-lib* [*Taa-li-*   طالب
ba] (pl.) *Ta-la-ba*   طلبة

study *yid-ris*   يدرس

stupid *gha-bee* [*gha-*   غبي
bee-ya]

style *'us-loob*   أسلوب

subway *mit-roo*   مترو

suddenly *biS-Sud-fa*   بالصدفة

sugar *suk-kar*   سكر

sugarcane *"a-Sab*   قصب

suit *bad-la, kis-wa*   كسوة. بدلة

suitable *mu-neh-sib*   مناسب

summer *Seyf*   صيف

sun *shams*   شمس

Sunday (yohm) *il-Hadd*   يوم الأحد

sunglasses *naD-Daa-rit*   نظارة
ish-shams   الشمس

suntan lotion *kreym*   كريم
li Hi-meh-yit   لحماية
il-bash-ra   البشرة

sweater *bu-loh-var*   بلوفر

sweet *Hilw*   حلو

swim *yis-ta Ham-ma,*   يستحم.
yi-^coom   يسبح

swimming pool *Ham-*   حمام
mehm si-beh-Ha   سباحة

system *ni-Zaam*   نظام

T

table *Ta-ra-bey-za*   طاولة. طربيزة

tailor *tar-zee, khay-yaaT*   ترزي. خياط

take *yeh-khud*   يأخذ

take off (plane) *yiT-la^c*   يقوم

take off (clothes)   يقلع. يخلع
yi"-la^c, yikh-la^c

take a picture *yi-Saw-war*   يصور

talk (noun) *ka-lehm* كلام

tapes *sha-raa-yiT* شرائط

taste (noun) *Ta^cm* طعم

tax *Da-ree-ba* ضريبة
(pl.) *Da-raa-yib* ضرائب

taxi *tak-see* تاكسي

taxi stand *maw-"af* موقف
tak-see تاكسي

tea *shayy* شاي

teach *yi-dar-ris* يدرس

teacher *mu-dar-ris* مدرس،
(mu-dar-ri-sa] معلم

team *fa-ree"* فريق

T-shirt *fa-nil-la* فانلة.قميص نصف كم

telephone *ti-li-fohn* تليفون

telephone call *mu-kal-ma* مكالمة

telephone number *nim-* رقم تليفون
rit/ra-qam ti-li-fohn

television *ti-li-viz-yohn* تليفزيون

tell *yi"-ool* يقول

tell me... *"ul-lee...* قل لي ...

temperature *Ha-raa-ra* حرارة

temple *ma^c-bad* معبد
(pl.) *ma-^ceh-bid* معابد

ten *^ca-sha-ra* عشرة

tent *khey-ma* خيمة

terrible *ra-heeb* رهيب

terrorism *'ir-hehb* إرهاب

terrorist *'ir-heh-bee* إرهابي

thank you *shuk-ran* شكرا

the — *il —* الـ —

theater *mas-raH* مسرح

there *hi-nehk* هناك

there is/are — *fee –is/* يوجد/توجد.
are there? *fee?* هل يوجد/توجد؟

there isn't/aren't لا يوجد
ma feesh

thief *Ha-raa-mee* حرامي

thin *ru-fay-ya^c* رفيع

thing *Ha-ga* شيء
(pl.) *Ha-geht* أشياء

think *yi-Zunn* يظن

thirsty *^caT-shaan* عطشان

thousand *'alf* ألف
(pl.) *'a-lehf* آلاف

three *ta-leh-ta* ثلاثة

throat *zohr* حنجرة

Thursday *yohm* يوم
il-kha-mees الخميس

thus *ki-da* هكذا

ticket *taz-ka-ra* تذكرة
(pl.) *ta-zeh-kir* تذاكر

tidy (adj.) *mu-rat-tab* مرتب

tight *day-ya"* ضيق

time *wa"t*, *za-man* وقت، زمن

What time is it? كم
is-seh-Ca kam? الساعة؟

tip (gratuity) *ba"-sheesh* بقشيش

tired *taC-behn* متعب

tiring *mut-Cib* متعب

to *li* إلى

today *in-na-haar-da/* اليوم
il-yohm

together *sa-wa* سويا

tomb *ma"-ba-ra*, مقبرة
(pl.) *ma-"eh-bir* مقابر

tomorrow *buk-ra* غدا

too, also *ka-mehn* أيضا

(on) top *foh"* فوق

tooth *sinn* سن
(pl.) *'as-nehn* أسنان

tourist *saw-wehH* سائح
[*saw-weh-Ha*] سواح
(pl.) *suw-wehH*

towel *foo-Ta* (pl.) منشفة، مناشف
fo-waT فوطة، فوط

traditions *ta-qa-leed* تقاليد

traffic *mu-roor* مرور

train (noun) *"aTr* قطار
(pl.) *"u-Tu-raat*

translate *yi-tar-gim* يترجم

travel (verb) *yi-seh-fir* يسافر

tree *sha-ga-ra* شجرة
(pl.) *sha-gar* شجر

trip *riH-la* رحلة

true *Sa-HeeH* صحيح

Tuesday (yohm) *it-ta-leht* يوم الثلاثاء

two *it-neyn* اثنان

typewriter *'eh-la kat-ba* آلة كاتبة

U

ugly *wi-Hish* [*wiH-sha*] قبيح

uncle (paternal) *Camm* عم

(maternal) *khchl* خال

under *taHt* تحت

undershirt فانلة،
fa-nil-la قميص تحتاني

understand *yif-ham* يفهم

undo *yi-fukk* يفك

unemployed *Caa-Til* عاطل

unfortunately *ma-Cal-* مع الأسف
'a-saf

United States *il-wi-la-* الولايات
yeht il-mut-ta-Hi-da المتحدة

university *gam-Ca* جامعة

unlikely *mish min* بعيد
il-muHta-mal الاحتمال

until *li gheh-yit* إلى

up *foh"* — إلى فوق

   get up *yi-"oom* — يقوم

Upper Egypt *iS-Si-ceed* — الصعيد

use (verb) *yis-tac-mil* — يستعمل

useful *mu-feed* — مفيد

user name *ism taw-qeec* — اسم توقيع

usually *ca-da-tan* — عادة

V

vacation *'a-geh-za* — عطلة، إجازة

valley *weh-dee* — وادي

vegetables *khu-Daar* — خضر

vegetarian *na-beh-tee* — نباتي

veil *Hi-gehb* — حجاب

very *"a-wee, gid-dan* — جدا

video *vid-yo* — فيديو

view *man-Zar* — منظر
   (pl.) *ma-naa-Zir* — مناظر

village *qar-ya* — قرية
   (pl.) *qu-ra* — قرى

villager *fal-lehH* — فلاح
   (pl.) *fal-la-Heen* — فلاحون

visa *vee-za* — تأشيرة

visit (verb) *yi-Zoor* — يزور

voice, vote *Soht* — صوت
   (pl.) *'aS-waat* — أصوات

voltage *volt* — فولت

W

wages *ma-hee-ya* — ماهية

wait *yis-tan-na/yin-ti-Zir* — ينتظر

wake up (trans.)
   yi-SaH-Hee — يصحى

walk *yim-shee,*
   yit-mash-sha — يمشي يتمشى

wallet *maH-fa-Za* — محفظة

want *ca-wiz [caw-za]* — بريد

war *Harb* — حرب

warm *deh-fee* — دافئ

wash (verb) *yigh-sil* — يغسل
   (noun) *gha-seel* — غسيل

waste *yi-Day-yac* — يضيع

watch (verb) *yit-far-rag* — ينظر إلى
   (ca-la)

watch (noun) *seh-ca* — ساعة

water *may-ya* — ماء، مياه

   hot water *may-ya* — مياه
   sukh-na — ساخنة

watermelon *baT-Teekh* — بطيخ

waves (water, air) — أمواج
   'am-wehg

way *Ta-ree"* — طريق

we *iH-na* — نحن

weak *Da-ceef* — ضعيف

wear **yil**-bis — يلبس

weather gaww, Ta"S — جو. طقس

wedding **fa**-raH — عرس

Wednesday (yohm) **lar**-ba^c — يوم الأربعاء

week 'is-**boo**^{c} (pl.) 'a-sa-**bee**^{c} — أسبوع أسابيع

welcome! **mar**-Ha-ba! You're welcome, don't mention it. ^{c}af-wan — مرحبا / عفوا

wcll **kway**-yis — كويس

well done (meat) mis-**ti**-wee — تام النضج

West (Occident) gharb — غرب

Western **ghar**-bee [ghar-**bee**-ya] — غربي

wct mab-**lool** — مبلول

What? 'eyh? — ما ؟

What!! (surprise) ya sa-**lehm**!! — يا سلام!

What time? is-**seh**-^{c}a kam? — كم الساعة؟

wheel ^{c}**a**-ga-la — عجلة

When? 'im-ta? — متى؟

when **lam**-ma — لما

Where? feyn? — أين؟

Where from? mi-**neyn**? — من أين؟

Which? 'an-hee? — أي؟

which (relative) **il**-lee — الذي

whiskey **wis**-kee — ويسكي

white 'ab-yaD — أبيض

Who? meen? — مَن؟

Why? leyh? — لماذا؟

wide **weh**-si^c [was-^{c}a] — واسع

wife **ma**-ra, sitt/**zoh**-ga — زوجة

win **yik**-sab — يكسب

window shib-**behk** (pl.) sha-ba-**beek** — شباك شبابيك

wine ni-**beet** — نبيذ

winter **shi**-ta — شتاء

wish (verb) yit-**man**-na — يتمنى

with ma ^{c}a, bi — مع. بـ

without min-**gheyr**. bi-**doon** — بدون

woman **ma**-ra (pl.) ni-**seh**', sitt (pl.) sit-**teht** — امرأة، سيدة

wonderful mum-**tehz**, ^{c}u-**Zeem** — ممتاز عظيم

wood **kha**-shab — خشب

wool Soof — صوف

word **kil**-ma — كلمة

work (verb) yish-**ta**-ghal — يعمل يشتغل

work (noun) shughl — عمل. شغل

world 'il-^{c}**eh**-lam, **dun**-ya — عالم

worried "al-"ehn — قلق. قلقان

worse **'aw**-Hash أسوأ

wrap yi-**liff** يلف

write yik-**tib** يكتب

writer keh-tib, mu-**'al**-lif كاتب مؤلف

writing pad دفتر، كراسة
blok noht للكتابة

wrong **gha**-laT خطأ غلط

X

X rays 'a-**shi**c-ca أشعة

Y

year **sa**-na سنة.
(pl.) si-**neem** سنوات

this year is-sa-**neh** هذه السنة
dee

last year is-**sa**-na السنة التي
il-lee-**feh**-tit فاتت

yellow **'aS**-far [Saf- أصفر
ra]

yes **'ay**-wa, na-cam نعم

yesterday im-beh- أمس
riH/'ams

(not) yet **lis**-sa حتى الآن

you (sing.) in-ta أنت
[in-tee]

you (pl.) in-**tum**-ma أنتم

You're welcome, don't عفوا
mention it. caf-wan

young Su-**ghay**-yar صغير
[Su-ghay-**ya**-ra]

younger, youngest أصغر
'aS-ghar

young man shabb شاب
(pl.) sha-**behb** شابة

yours bi-**teh**-cak لك

Z

zipper **sus**-ta سوستة

zone man-**Ti**-qa منطقة

zoo gi-**ney**-nit il-Ha-ya- حديقة
wa-**neht** الحيوان

zoom lens **ca**-da-sit عدسة زوم
zoom

ARABIC-ENGLISH

DICTIONARY

The verbs are given in the third person singular present form ("he goes," etc.), beginning with *yi-*. For other forms of the verb see Grammar Notes on page 215.

As in the text, feminine forms are given in square brackets.

The following alphabetical order is used:

" or *'*, a, b, d, D, e, f, g, h, H, i, j, k, kh, 1, m, n, p, q, r, s, S, sh, t, T, u, v, w, y, z, Z, ^c

" or *'*

'u-ba-dan never

'abb father

"abl before (prep.)

"ab-li ki-da before (now)

'a-boo ga-lam-boo crab

'a-boo-ya my father

'ab-yaD [bey-Da] white

"a-deem ["a-dee-ma] old

'a-gaa-za holiday, vacation

'ag-na-bee ['ag-na-bee-ya] foreign

'ag-za-kheh-na pharmacy (chemist's)

'ah-lan! Hi!

'ah-raam pyramids

"ah-wa coffee, café

'aH-mar [Ham-ra] red

'aH-san better

'ak-bar bigger

'akl food

'akh-baar news

'akh-Dar [khaD-ra] green

'a-kheer last

'a-khee-ran! at last!

'al-maaz diamonds

'a-lam pain

"al-"ehn worried

"a-lam pen, pencil

"a-lam gaff ballpoint pen

"alb heart

'alf (pl.) 'a-lehf thousand

"a-meeS (pl.) "um-Saan shirt

'amn security

'am-wehg waves

'am-wehs Hi-leh-"a   razor blades

'an-hee?   which?

'arD   land, earth

'ar-khaS   cheaper

'ar-nab (pl.) 'a-reh-nib   rabbit

'a-san-Seer   elevator, lift

'a-sar (pl.) 'a-saar   monument, ruin

'as-mar [sam-ra]   brown-skinned

'a-shi^c-^c-a   X rays

"a-Sab   sugar cane

'aS-far [Saf-ra]   yellow

'aS-ghar   smaller, younger

'aSl   origin

"aSr   palace

'aS-waan   Aswan

"aTr   train

'aT-rash [Tar-sha]   deaf

'aw   or

'aw-Hash   worse

'aw-reh"   papers, documents, bills

'aw-reh" na"d   paper money

'aw-wil ['oo-la]   first

"ay-ma   list, menu

'ay-wa   yes

'ayy   any

'az-ma   crisis

'az-ma qal-bee-ya   heart attack

'az-ra" [zar-"a]   blue

'a^c-ma [^c-am-ya]   blind

'eed (pl.) 'a-yeh-dee   hand

"eh-dir ["ad-ra]   able

'eh-khir ['ukh-ra]   other

'eh-la   machine

'eh-la kat-ba   typewriter

'eh-sif! ['as-fa!]   sorry!

'eyh?   What?

"ib-Tee   Coptic

'ibn   son

'i-dàa-ra   administration

'il-la   except

'il-ti-hehb   infection, inflammation

'im-sehk   constipation

'im-ta?   when?

'in shaa' al-laah   God willing (I hope so).

'in-ti-Zaar   waiting, parking

'iq-ti-Saad   economics

"irsh (pl.) "u-roosh   piastre

"irsh (pl.) "u-roosh   shark

'is-boo^c (pl.) 'a-sa-bee^c   week

'is-hehl   diarrhea

'is-kin-di-ree-ya   Alexandria

'is-lehm   Islam

a

'ism (pl.) 'a sch mee name

'is-wid [soh-da] black

'is-^cehf ambulance service

'i-sharb scarf

"ish-Ta cream

"i-zehz glass

"i-zeh-za (pl.) "a-zeh-yiz bottle

'i^c-lehn advertisement

'oh-Da (pl.) 'o-waD room

"ud-dehm in front (of)

"uf-Taan (pl.) "a-fa-Teen caftan

'ug-ra fee, rent

"ul-lee ["u-lee-lee] tell me-.-.-.

"u-mehsh cloth, material

'umm mother

"u-ray-yib soon

"u-ray-yib (min) near (to)

'ur-du-nee Jordanian

'us-loob style

'us-tehz professor

"u-Say-yar short

'u-teel hotel

'u-tu-bees (pl.) 'u-tu-bee-seht bus

"uTn cotton

a-loh hello

af-lehm dee-vee-dee DVD

a-na I

af-reeq-ya Africa

a-ghuS-Tus August

ak-tar more

al-man-ya Germany

al-meh-nee [al-ma-nee-ya] German

am-ree-ka America

am-ree-keh-nee [am-ree-ka-nee-ya] American

ar-ba-^ca four

as-ban-ya Spain

as-bee-reen aspirin

as-beh-nee [as-ba-nee-ya] Spanish

ayr-lan-da Ireland

ayr-lan-dee [ayr-lan-dee-ya] Irish

ays kreem ice cream

b

ba"-"ehl grocery store

ba-"ar cows

ba"-sheesh tip, gratuity

baar bar

ba-**dal** instead of

bad-la suit

bad-ree early, sooner

baH-**Haar** sailor

baHr sea

ba-laH dates

ba-lad town, country

bal-**Too** overcoat

ban-Ta-**lohn** pants, trousers

ban-yoo bathtub

ban-**zeen** gasoline

bank (pl.) bu-**nook** bank

ba-ra-**zeel** Brazil

ba-ra-**zee**-lee [ba-ra-zee-lee-ya] Brazilian

bard cold (noun)

bar-**dehn** [bar-**deh**-na] cold

bar-Doo also

ba-**reed** post, mail

bar-ra outside

bas-**boor** passport

bas-ka-**weet** biscuits, cookies

bass only, just

bash-ra skin

ba-**Sal** onions

ba-**Taa**-Ta sweet potatoes

ba-**Taa**-Tis potatoes

ba-**Tee'** slow

baT-Ta-**nee**-ya blanket

baT-Ta-**ree**-ya battery

baT-**Teekh** watermelon

ba-**weh**-ba gate

*ba*ᶜ*d* after

*ba*ᶜ-**deyn** afterwards, later

*ba*ᶜ-di **buk**-ra the day after tomorrow

*ba*ᶜ*d iD*-**Duhr** in the afternoon

*ba*ᶜ*D* one another

*ba*ᶜ*D* — some of —

bee-ra beer

*bee*ᶜ sale

beh-"ee remainder, change

behb door

beh-rid [**bar**-da] cold

beyD eggs

beyn between

beyt (pl.) bu-**yoot** house

bi ba-**lehsh** free, for nothing

bi-din-**gehn** eggplant (aubergine)

bi-**doon** without

bil-"**aTr** by train

bil-ba-**reed** ig-**gaw**-wee by airmail

bi-**lehj**, plehj beach

bi-nas hairpins

bing anesthetic

*bint (pl.) ba-**neht*** girl, daughter

*bi-**sur**-^ca* fast

*bi-**Tah**-qit iz-**zeh**-ki-ra* memory card

bi-teh^c — belonging to —

*biS-**Sud**-fa* suddenly

*bi-**Taa**-qa (pl.) bi-Taa-qaat* card

bi-^ceed far

***boh**-sa* kiss

***bloo**-za* blouse

*bon-bo-**neht*** candy

*boo-jey-**heht*** spark plugs

*bri-**Taa**-nee [bri-Taa-**nee**-ya]* British

*bri-**Tan**-ya* Britain

bu" " " mouth

*bu-**feyh*** dining car

*bu-**Hey**-ra* lake

*bu-**khoor*** incense

*bu-**leeS*** police

*bu-**loh**-var* sweater

bunn (ground) coffee

***bun**-nee* brown

*bur-**ney**-Ta* hat

*bur-tu-"**aan*** oranges

d

da"n chin, beard

dafn burial

***da**-hab* gold

*da-**jehj*** chicken

*da-**leel*** guide, guidebook

*da-**leel** 'al-**wehn*** color chart

damm blood

***da**-ra-ga* class

*dars (pl.) du-**roos*** lesson

***da**-wa (pl.) 'ad-**wee**-ya* medicine

***daw**-la (pl.) du-wal* state

***daw**-lee* international

***daw**-sha* noise

***day**-man* always

***day**-ya"* tight, narrow

***dee**-zil* diesel fuel

***deh**-fee* warm

deyr monastery

*di- "**ee**"* flour

*dib-**behn*** flies

*dil-**wa**"-tee* now

*di-**reh**^c* arm

*di-**sim**-bir* December

*dohr (pl.) 'ad-**waar*** floor

*do-**laar** (pl.) do-la-**raat*** dollar

***dugh**-ree* straight on

duk-kehn (pl.) da-ka-keen shop, store

duk-toor [duk-too-ra] doctor

du-khool entry

'dun-ya world

dush shower

D

Daa-nee mutton, lamb

Dahr back

DakhT id-damm blood pressure

Da-ree-ba (pl.) Da-raa-yib tax

Deyf (pl.) Du-yoof guest

Didd against

Duhr noon

f

fa-"eer (pl.) fu-"a-ra poor

faa-Dee [faD-ya] free, unoccupied

faar (pl.) fi-rehn mouse, rat

faD-Da silver

fak-ha fruit

fak-ka small change

fal'-lehH (pl.) fal-la-Heen villager, farmer

fukh-khaar pottery, ceramics

fal-lehH (pl.) fal-la-Heen peasant farmer

fa-loo-ka sailboat

fa-nil-la T-shirt, undershirt

fann (pl.) fu-noon art

fan-nehn artist

fa-raa-mil brakes

fa-raH wedding

fa-ran-sa France

fa-ran-seh-wee [fa-ran-sa-wee-ya] French

fa-raw-la strawberries

far" difference

fa-ree" team

farsh furniture

far^c branch

far-^coo-nee Pharaonic

fa-sehd corruption

faSl season, class, classroom

fa-Sul-ya beans

fa-Zee^c dreadful

fee there is/are

feh-righ [far-gha] empty

feh-tiH [fat-Ha] light (colored)

feyn? where?

fi in, at

fib-**reh**-*yir* February

fik-*ra (pl.)* '*af*-**kaar** idea

fil-**fil** pepper

fi-lis-**Teen** Palestine

fi-liS-**Tee**-*nee* Palestinian

fil-*ma*-^c***ehd*** on time, punctually

film (pl.) '*af*-**lehm** film

fi-**loos** money

fi-**rehkh** chicken

fis-*seh*-^c*a* per hour

fi-**saal** bargaining

fi-**shaar** popcorn

fi-**Taar** breakfast

Fi^c-*lan* indeed

foh" above, on top

foo-*Ta (pl.)* *fo*-*waT* towel

foo-*Ta SiH*-**Hee**-*ya* sanitary napkin

fool pureed beans

fool su-**deh**-*nee* peanuts

fumm mouth

fun-*du"* hotel

furn oven, bakery

fur-*Sa* chance, opportunity

fur-*sha* brush

fus-*Ha* outing, break

fus-**tehn** dress

fu-*wat wa*-*ra* paper towels

g

gaar (pl.) *gi*-**rehn** neighbor

ga-*bal (pl.)* *gi*-**behl** mountain

gad-*wal il*-*ma*-*wa*-^c***eed*** timetable

gadd serious

  bi **gadd** seriously

gal-*la*-**bee**-*ya* galabiyya

ga-*mal* camel

gam-*ba*-**ree** shrimps, prawns

gam-^c*a* university

ga-**noob** south

gar-*dal* pail, bucket

ga-**ree**-*da (pl.)* *ga*-**reh**-*yid* newspaper

ga-**toh** *(pl.)* *ga*-*to*-**heht** cake

ga-*wa*-**hir**-*gee* jeweler's

ga-**weh**-*hir* jewelry

ga-**wehb** *[ga*-*weh*-**beht**]* letter

ga-**wehz** *is*-*sa*-**far** passport

gaww weather, atmosphere

gayy coming, next

gaz-**zaar** butcher's

gaz-*ma* shoes

gaz-*ma*-**gee** shoemaker

ga-^c***ehn*** hungry

geh-*hiz [**gah**-*za]* ready

geh-*mi*^c *(pl.)* *ga*-**weh**-*mi*^c mosque *gib-na*   cheese

gidd   grandfather

gid-da   grandmother

gi-deed   new

gi-hehz dee-vee-dee
  DVD player

gi-hehz em-bee-sree
  MP3 player

gi-hehz ka-sitt   cassette player

*gi-hehz li tag-ceed ish
  shacr*   curling iron

gild   leather

gi-ney   pound (currency)

*gi-ney-na (pl.) ga-neh-
  yin*   garden, park

*gi-neyn-t il-Ha-ya-wa-
  neht*   zoo

gin-see-ya   nationality

gism   body

gi-zee-ra (pl.) gu-zur   island

gohz   husband

gow-wa   inside

gum-hoo-ree-ya   republic

gum-ruk   customs

gu-nil-la   skirt

gh

gha-bee [gha-bee-ya]   stupid

gha-da   lunch

gha-laT   wrong

ghal-Ta   mistake

ghal-Taan   mistaken

gha-nam   sheep (and goats)

gharb   west

*ghar-bee [ghar-bee-
  ya]*   Western

gha-seel   laundry

gheh-lee [ghal-ya]   expensive

gheh-yib [ghay-ba]   absent

ghi-wey-sha   bracelet

ghur-fa (pl.) ghu-raf   room

h

ha-dee-ya (pl.) ha-deh-ya   gift

han-da-sa   engineering

hee-ya   she

heh-dee [had-ya]   quiet, calm

hi-na   here

hin-dee [hin-dee-ya]   Indian

hi-nehk   there

hi-weh-ya   hobby

ho-lan-da   Holland

ho-lan-dee   Dutch

hu-doom   clothes

huw-wa   he

H

Ha"l *(pl.)* **Hu-"ool** field

Haa-*Dir* certainly

Ha-*beeb* beloved

Heh-*lan* immediately

Hadd someone

Had-*sa* accident

Haf-*la* party, concert

Haf-*la mu-si-qee-ya* concert

Ha-*ga* thing, something

Ha-*gar* stone

Hagz reservation

*Ha-la-wee-***yeht** dcsscrts

*Ha-la-***weh**-*nee* confectioner's

Ha-**leeb** milk

Hal-**leh"** barber's

Ha-**mehm** pigeons

Ham-**mehm** bathroom

Ham-**mehm** *si-***beh**-
Ha swimming pool

*Ha-na-***fee**-*ya* faucet, tap

Han-**Toor** horsedrawn
carriage

*Ha-***raa**-*mee (pl.) Ha-ra-***mee**-
ya thief

*Ha-***raa**-*ra* temperature

Ha-**reer** silk

*Har-***raan** hot (people)

Harr hot

*Ha-sa-***see**-*ya* allergy

*Ha-sha-***raat** insects

*Ha-***sheesh** hashish

Hashw filling

*Ha-***weh**-*lee* about

Hat-*ta* even

*Ha-ya-***wehn** animal

*Ha-***zeen** sad

Heh-*mee* hot, spicy

Heh-*mil* pregnant

Heh-*ris* guard

*Hi-***gehb** veil

*Hi-***keh**-*ya* story

Hilw sweet, lovely

*Hi-***sehb** bill, check

Hi sch **beht** accounts

*Hi-***zehm** belt

Hu"-*na* injection

Hubb love

*Hu-***boob** pills

*Hu-***boob** *mi-naw-***wi**-
ma sleeping pills

*Hu-***koo**-*ma* government

*Hu-***maar** donkey

Hum-*mus* chickpeas

*Hu-***moo**-*Da* acidity,
indigestion

*Hur-***ree**-*ya* freedom

i

ig-ti-meh[c] meeting

iH-na we

ik-ku-weyt Kuwait

il — the —

il-'eh-ni-sa — Miss —

il-faar mouse

il-'ur-dun Jordan

il-hind India

il-lee who, which

il-qaa-hi-ra Cairo

il-quds Jerusalem

il-qur-'aan the Koran

il-wi-la-yeht il-mut-ta-Hi-da the United States

il-ya-behn Japan

il-yohm today

il-yu-nehn Greece

im-beh-riH yesterday

im-ti-Hehn (pl.) im-ti-Heh-neht exam

in-floo-in-za influenza

in-gi-lee-zee [in-gi-lee-zee-ya] English

in-gil-ti-ra England

in-na-haar-da today

in-nim-ra il-ma-Hal-lee-ya area code

in-noo-ba Nubia

in-ta [in-tee] you (sing.)

in-tum-ma you (pl.)

ir-ri-yaa-Da sport

is-maH-lee pardon me

ism taw-qee[c] user name

is-ra-'eel Israel

is-ra-'ee-lee [is-ra-'ee-lee-ya] Israeli

is-say-yid — Mr. —

is-say-yi-da — Mrs. —

is-ti"-behl reception

is-ti-raad import

is-tiq-lehl independence

is-ti[c]*-la-meht* information

is-Ti-waa-na disc, record

is-Ti-wa-naht ley-zar far-gha lit-tas-geel recordable CDs

iS-Seen China

iS-SubH (in the) morning

ish-sharq il-'aw-saT the Middle East

ish-ti-raa-kee socialist

it-neyn two, both

it-shar-raf-na Pleased to meet you.

i-Taa-lee [i-Taa-lee-ya] Italian

i-Taal-ya Italy

iz-zayy? how?

is-zay-yak? [iz-zay-yik?] How are you?

j

ja-**kit**-ta jacket

jehk jack (mechanical)

k

ka-*ba*-**rey** floor show

kab-**reet** matches

kad-**dehb** liar

kah-**ra**-ba electricity

kalb (pl.) ki-**lehb** dog

ka-**lehm** talk

kam?, bi kam? How much/ many?

ka-**mehn** also

ka-me-ra camera

ka-me-ra ra-qa-**mee**-ya digital camera

ka-me-ra ra-qa-**mee**-ya es-el-ar SLR digital camera

ka-me-ra tir-**mee**-ha ba^cd il-is-ti^c-**mehl** disposable camera

ka-**na**-da Canada

ka-na-**dee** [ka-na-**dee**-ya] Canadian

kart (pl.) ku-**root** card

kart bus-**tehl** postcard

ka-**sitt** (pl.) ka-sit-**teht** cassette

kash-**shehf** headlight, flashlight

ka^cb heel, ankle

kee-loo kilo

kee-lott briefs, panties

keh-mil complete

keh-tib clerk

keyf how, like

keyf il-**Hehl**? How are you?

ki-**beer** [ki-**bee**-ra] (pl.) ku-**baar** big, old

ki-da thus, so

kid-ba lie (noun)

ki-**feh**-ya enough

ki-**leem** (pl.) 'ak-**li**-ma woven rug

kil-mit is-**sirr** password

ki-**nee**-sa church

kis-wa suit

ki-**teer** much, many, often

ki-**tehb** (pl.) ku-**tub** book

kitf shoulder

koh-ra ball, football

ko-**lon**-ya cologne

kom-**byoo**-tar computer

kreym (cosmetic) cream

kreym li 'i-**zeh**-lit il-mak-**yaj** cold cream

kreym li Hi-**meh**-yit il-**bash**-ra suntan cream

kri-dit kard   credit card

kub-beh-ya   glass

kub-ree (pl.) ka-beh-ree   bridge

ku-fee-ya   headscarf

kuH-Ha   cough

kull   each, every

kul-lee-ya   college

kul-li Ha-ga   everything

ku-reek   jack (mechanical)

ku-rumb   cabbage

kushk (pl.) 'ik-shehk   kiosk

kwa-feer   hairdresser

kway-yis [kway-yi-sa]   good, well

kh

khaa-lis   (not) at all

khaaS   private

khadd (pl.) khu-dood   cheek

khad-deh-ma   servant (fem.)

kha-feef [kha-fee-fa]   light (in weight)

khal-laaS!   That's enough! I've finished.

khal-laaT   blender

kham-ra   liquor

kham-sa   five

kha-reef   autumn

kha-ree-Ta   map

khass   lettuce

kha-shab   wood

kha-Tar   danger

kha-Teer   dangerous

khaTT (pl.) khu-TooT   line

khay-yaaT [khay-yaa-Ta]   tailor, dressmaker

khaz-na   safe (noun)

khehl   (maternal) uncle

kheh-la   (maternal) aunt

kheh-tim   ring

kheh-yif [khay-fa]   afraid

khey-ma   tent

khib-ra   experience

khid-ma   service

khi-yaar   cucumber

khohkh   peaches

kubz   bread

khu-Daar   vegetables

khu-roog   exit

khu-Saa-ra   pity

khu-Soo-san   especially

l

la'   no

la-ban   milk

lab-tob   laptop

lag-*na*   committee

laHm, laH-*ma*   meat

laH-*ma ba*-"*a*-*ree*   beef

laH-*Za*   moment

lam-*ba*   lamp, lightbulb

lam-*ma*   when

la-*moon*   lemon

la-*Teef* [*la*-*Tee*-*fa*] (*pl.*) *lu*-*Taaf*   kind, nice

law sa-*maHt* ...   Excuse me ...

la-*zeez*   delicious

lee-*bee*   Libyan

leh-*zim* —   it is necessary, must —

leyh?   why?

ley-*la*   night

li   to, for

lib-*nehn*   Lebanon

lib-*neh*-*nee*   Lebanese

lib-*ya*   Libya

lit-*neyn*   both

lis-*sa*   still, (not) yet

li waH-*dee*   on my own

lohn (*pl.*) *'al*-*wehn*   color

lohz   almonds

loo-*Hit il*-*ma*-*fa*-*teeH*   keyboard

los-*yohn*   lotion

m

maa-*Dee*   past (noun)

ma-"*aSS*   scissors

ma-"*ehs*   size, mesurement

ma"-*ba*-*ra* (*pl.*) *ma*-"*eh*-*bir*   tomb, grave

ma"-*fool*   closed

ma"-*lee*   fried

mab-*lool*   wet

mab-*rook!*   Congratulations!

ma-*dee*-*na*   city, town

ma-*dehm* —   Mrs. —, madame

mad-*fan*   cemetery

mad ra sa (*pl.*) *ma deh ris*   school

ma feesh   there isn't/aren't (any)

maf-*tooH*   open

ma-*gal*-*la* (*pl.*) *ma*-*gal*-*leht*   magazine

mag-*geh*=*nan*   free, for nothing

mag-*lis*   council

mag-*noon*   crazy

magh-*sa*-*la*   laundry, launderette

ma-*hee*-*ya*   salary

ma-*HaT*-*Ta*   station, stop

ma-HaT-Tit 'u-tu-bees bus stop

ma-HaT-Tit ban-zeen gas station

ma-Hat-Tit il-"aTr railway station

ma-Hall (pl.) ma-Hal-leht shop

ma-Hall zu-hoor flower shop

maH-fa-Za wallet, pocketbook

maH-roo" burned

ma-ka-na machine

ma-ka-roh-na pasta

ma-kehn place

mak-soor [mak-soo-ra] broken

mak-tab office, desk

mak-tab il-ba-reed post office

mak-tab Sarf money exchange

mak-ta-ba bookshop, library

mak-wa iron

mak-wa-gee ironer

mak-yaj makeup

ma-khad-da cushion

makh-baz bakery

makh-SooS special

ma-leh-hee entertainment

malH salt

ma-lik (pl.) mu-look king

mal-yehn [mal-yeh-na] full

mam-noon grateful

mam-noo^c forbidden

ma-na-kheer nose

man-ga mangoes

ma-ni-keer manicure, nail polish

man-Ti-qa area

man-Zar (pl.) ma-naa-Zir view

ma-ra (pl.) ni-seh' woman

ma-raD (pl.) 'am-raaD disease, illness

ma-reeD (pl.) [ma-ree-Da] ill

mar-Ha-ba! welcome

mar-ka brand

mar-kaz center (institution)

mar-kib (pl.) ma-reh-kib boat

mar-ra waH-da once

mar-ta-ba mattress

mar-wa-Ha fan

ma-sa-lan for example

mas-'ool responsible

mas-dood blocked

ma-see-Hee Christian

ma-seh-fa distance

mas-loo" boiled

mas-raH theater

mas-ra-Hee-ya play

maS-na^c (pl.) ma-Saa-ni^e factory

maSr Egypt, Cairo

maS-ree [maS-ree-ya] Egyptian

mash-ghool busy

mash-hoor [mash-hoo-ra] famous

mash-roo-beht drinks

mash-wee grilled

mat-Haf museum

matsh (koh-ra) (football) match

ma-Taar airport

ma-Tar rain

maT-^cam (pl.) ma-Taa-^cim restaurant

maw-"af (pl.) ma-weh-"if stop

maw-"af tak-see taxi stand

maw-good present (adj.)

may-ya water

maz-za "mezza," appetizers

maZ booT exact, precise

ma-^ca with

ma-^ca 'inn although

ma-^ca l-'a-saf unfortunately

ma-^ca-lish! Never mind!

ma-^ca s-sa-leh-ma Good-bye.

ma^c-bad (pl.) ma ^ceh-bid temple

ma-^cehd appointment

ma-^cehsh pension

ma^c-mal laboratory

ma^c-raD exhibition

meen? who?

mee-na port, harbor

mee-ya (pl.) mee-yeht hundred

meh-ris March

meh-shee! okay

meh-yit [may-ta] dead

mi-dehn square (place)

mi-fal-lis bankrupt, broke

mif-tehH (pl.) ma-fa-teeH key

mih-na profession

mi-khad-da pillow, cushion

mi-khal-lil pickles

min from

min faD-lak [min faD-lik] please

mi-nab-bih alarm clock

mi-neyn? Where from?

min-yoo menu

mi-reh-ya mirror

mi-seh' evening

mi-seh' il-kheyr Good evening.

mis-ta^c-gil [mis-ta^c-gi-la] in a hurry

mis-ti-wee ripe, cooked

mish not

*mish baT-***Taal**   not bad

mish-*mish*   apricot

mishT   comb

*mit-'***ak**-*kid*   certain, sure

*mit-***gaw**-*wiz [mit-gaw-***wi**-*za]*   married

mitr   headwaiter

mitr   meter

*mi-^c ad-***dee**-*ya*   ferry

mi^c-*da*   stomach

moht   death

mohz   bananas

*mo-***toor**   engine

*mu-"***ab**-*la*   interview, encounter

*mu-'***al**-*lif*   writer, composer

*mu-***beh**-*shir*   direct

*mu-***dar**-*ris [mu-dar-***ri**-*sa]*   teacher

*mu-***deer**   manager, director

***mud**-*min (bi)*   addicted to

*mu-***fakk** *ma-sa-***meer**   screwdriver

*mu-***feed**   useful

*mu-***ghan**-*nee [mu-ghan-***nee**-*ya]*   singer

*mu-***han**-*dis*   engineer

*mu-***himm**   important, interesting

*mu-***Haw**-*wil*   adapter plug

*mu-***Heh**-*mee*   lawyer

*mu-***Heh**-*sib*   accountant

***muH**-*tamm (bi —)*   interested (in —)

*mu-***kal**-*ma*   phone call

*mu-***khad**-*da-***raat**   drugs

*mu-***khal**-*fa*   fine

*mu-***khay**-*yam si-***yeh**-*Hee*   campsite

mukhkh   brain

*mukh-***ta**-*lif [mukh-***ta**-*li-fa]*   different

*mu-***lay**-*yin*   laxative

*mu-mar-***ri**-*Da*   nurse

*mu-***mas** *sil*   actor

*mu-***mill**   boring

*mum-***tehz**   excellent

*mi-***nab**-*bih*   alarm clock

*mu-***naZ**-*Zam*   organized

*mu-***naZ**-*Za-ma*   organization

*mu-***neh**-*sib*   suitable

*mu-***rab**-*ba*   jam

*mu-***rat**-*tab*   tidy

*mur-***gehn**   coral

*mu-***sal**-*sal (pl.) mu-sal-sa-***leht**   soap opera

*mu-***saq**-*qaf*   cultured

*mu-***see**-*qa*   music

mus**-*lim [mus-li**-*ma] (pl.) mus-li-***meen**   Muslim

*mus-***tash**-*fa*   hospital

*mu-***See**-*ba*   disaster

*mush-***ki**-*la (pl.) ma-***sheh**-*kil*   problem

mu-ta-was-siT average

mu-Tah-hir antiseptic

mu-waS-laat communications

mu-waZ-Zaf [mu-waZ-Za-fa] employee, official

mu-weh-fi" agreed

muz-*nib* guilty

mu-Zah-ra demonstration

n

na"d cash

na"-leht gears

naar fire

na-ba-teht plants

na-*bee* prophet

naD-Daa-ra eyeglasses

naD-Da-raa-tee optician

naD-Daa-rit shams sunglasses

na-*far (pl.) 'an-faar* person, individual

nafs il — the same —

nag-gaar carpenter

nahr river

na-Hehs copper

nakhl palm trees

na-moos mosquitoes

na-See-Ha advice

naS-*ya* (street) corner

na-sheeT energetic

nayy raw

na-*c-am* yes

neh-dir rare

neh-yim asleep

neh-*shif [nash-fa]* dry

ni-beet wine

ni-Deef [ni-Dee-fa] clean

nig-*ma (pl.) nu-goom* star

nim-*ra* number

nim-*rit il-ba-lad* country code

nim-*rit ti-li-fohn* telephone number

nis-ba mi-'a-wee-ya percentage

ni-Zaam system

ni^c-neh^c mint

nohm sleep

noh-*ta* notebook

noo-*bee* Nubian

noor light

nuk-*ta* joke

nus-*kha* copy

nuSS half

nu-vim-bir November

o

ok-too-bar October

os-tral-ya Australia

q

*qa-**moos***   dictionary

*qa-**naah***   canal, channel

*qa-**noon***   law

*qa-**noo**-nee*   legal

qar-ya   village

qa-wee [qa-**wee**-ya]   strong

qaw-mee   national, nationalist

*qum-**bi**-la (pl.) qa-**neh**-bil*   bomb

*qun-Su-**lee**-ya*   consulate

r

ra-'ees   president

ra's mehl   capital (finance)

ra"S   dance, dancing

*ra"S **ba**-la-dee*   belly dancing

raa-gil (pl.) rig-**geh**-la   man

*raa-gil 'a^c-**mehl***   businessman

raas   head

*ra-**bee^c***   spring

radd   reply (noun)

rad-yoo   radio

*ra-**hee**-na (pl.) ra-**haa**-yin*   hostage

*ra-**maa**-Dee*   gray

ra-qam   number

*ra-**Seef***   pavement, platform

rash-wa   bribe

raTl   pound (weight)

ray-yis   boss

reef (pl.) 'ar-yehf   countryside

ree-Ha   smell

reh-kib (pl.) ruk-**kehb**   passenger

rigl   leg

*ri-**gheef** (pl.) 'ar-**ghi**-fa*   loaf

riH-la   trip

*ri-**jeem***   diet

*ri-**kheeS** [ri-**khee**-Sa]*   cheap

*ri-**seh**-la*   message

*ri-**weh**-ya*   novel

rohb   robe, dressing gown

roo-see   Russian

roos-ya   Russia

*ru-**baaT***   bandages

*ru-**Fay**-ya^c*   thin, slim

rukh-Sa   license, permit

*ru-**shit**-ta*   prescription

*ru-**Too**-ba*   humidity

ruzz   rice

s

*sa-bab (pl.) 'as-**behb***   reason, cause

sa-bat   basket

*sab-**behk***   plumber

sab-*c a*   seven

sadd   dam

*sa-**faa**-ra*   embassy

*sa-**feer***   ambassador

*sa-**fee**-na*   ship

sahl   easy

sak-raan *[sak-**raa**-na]*   drunk

sa-*la-Ta*   salad

sa-*mak*   fish

*sam-ma-c **eht***   speakers

*sam-ma-c **eht** ir-ra's*   headphones

sam *na*   ghee

sa-*na*   year

sa na wee   annual

san-*dal (pl.) sa-na-**deel***   sandals

*san-**doo"***   box, chest

sund-*witsh (pl.) sand-wit-**sheht***   sandwich

*sar-**deen***   sardines

*sa-**ree**c*   quick

sa-*wa*   together

*saw-**weh"***   driver

*say-**yaa**-ra*   car

see-*na*   Sinai

seh-*da*   plain

seh-*Hil*   coast

seh-*kit [**sak**-ta]*   silent (of people)

seh-*c a (pl.) sa-c **eht***   hour, time

*sesh-**waar***   hairdryer

*si-**beh"***   race, competition

*sib-**tim**-bir*   September

siDr   chest

*si-**fing***   sponges

*si-**gaa**-ra (pl.) sa-**geh**-yir*   cigarette

*sig-**geh**-da (pl.) sa-ga-**geed***   carpet

sign   jail

*si-kir-**teer** [si-kir-**tee**-ra]*   secretary

sik-*ka (pl.)* **si**-*kak*   road, way

sik-*ka Ha-deed*   railway

*sik-**kee**-na*   knife

sil-*lim*   ladder, stairs

*sil-**si**-la*   chain

si-*ni-ma*   cinema

*sinn il-**feel***   ivory

*si-**reer** (pl.) sa-**reh**-yir*   bed

*sitt (pl.) sit **teht***   lady

sit-*ta*   six

sit-*ti beyt*   housewife

*si-**yeh**-sa*   politics

*si*c*r*   price

soo"   market, bazaar

soor   fence

*soo-**tyehn***   bra

*su-'**ehl** (pl.) 'as-'i-la*   question

su-gu" " sausage

suk-*kar* sugar

sukhn hot

*su-khu-**nee**-ya* fever

sur-*^ca* speed

sus-*ta* zip fastener

S

Saa-*Hee* awake

Saa-*Hib (pl.) 'aS-**Haab*** friend

Sa"f ceiling

*Sa-**baaH*** morning

*Sa-**baH** il-**kheyr*** Good morning.

*Sa-**boon*** soap

Sabr patience

*Sa-**daa**-qa* friendship

Sa-*daf* shells

*Sa-**Haa**-fa* press (noun)

Sa-*Ha-fee* journalist

*sa-**HeeH?*** Really?

SaH-*ra* desert

Sakhr rock

*Sa-**lohn** tag-**meel*** beauty parlor

Sal-*sa* sauce

*Sanf (pl.) 'aS-**naaf*** kind, sort

*Sar-**raaf*** cashier

SatH surface, roof

*Say-da-**lee**-ya* pharmacy

Sa^cb difficult

See-*nee [**See**-nee-ya]* Chinese

Seyf summer

SiH-*Ha* health

*Si-**naa**-^ca* industry

Si-*^cee-dee* from upper Egypt

Soof wool

Soo-*ra (pl.) **So**-war* picture, photo

*Soht (pl.) 'aS-**waat*** voice, sound

*Su-**baa**^c (pl.) Sa-**waa**-bi^c* finger

SubH morning

*Su-**daa**^c* headache

Sud-*fa* accidentally

*Su-**ghay**-yar [Su-ghay-**ya**-ra]* small, young

*Su-^c**oo**-ba* difficulty

sh

sha"-"a (pl.) shu-'"a apartment

sha-"ee naughty

*shaa-Tir [**shaT**-ra]* clever

*shabb (pl.) sha-**behb*** young man

sha-ga-ra (pl.) *sha*-gar tree

shagh-**ghehl** [*shagh*-**geh**-la] worker, servant

shahr (pl.) *shu*-**hoor** month

shakl appearance, look

shak-loo [*shak*-**la**-ha] — he (she) looks —

shakhS (pl.) '*ash*-**khaaS** person

shakh-*See* personal

sha-**mehl** north

sham-**meh**-*ca* hanger

sham^c candles

sham poo shampoo

shams sun

sham-*see*-*ya* sunshade, umbrella

sha-**nab** mustache

shan-*Ta* (pl.) *shu*-**naT** bag, suitcase

sha-**raab** socks, stockings

sha-**raa**-*yiT* tapes

shar" cast

shar-"*ee* Eastern, Oriental

sha-*Ta*-**rang** chess

shaTT beach, shore

shayy tea

shay-**yehl** porter

sha^c-*bee* popular

sha^c*r* hair

sheek [*shee*-**keht**] check

shee-**keht** *si*-*ya*-**Hee**-ya** traveler's checks

shee-*sha* nargile, hubble bubble (water pipe)

sheh-*ri*^c (pl.) *sha*-**weh**-*ri*^c street

shib-**behk** (pl.) *sha*-*ba*-**beek** window

shib-*shib* slippers

shif-*fa* (pl.) *sha*-**feh**-*yif* lip

shi-**mehl** left

shir-*ka* (pl.) *sha*-*ri*-**keht** company

shir-*kit Tay*-*ya*-**raan** airline

shi-*ta* winter

shi^c-*ba* reef

sho-*ko*-**laa**-*ta* chocolate

shoh-*ka* fork

shuk-*ran* thank you

shu-*naT* bags, luggage

shur-*ba* soup

shur-*Ta* police

shway-*ya* a little, rather

shway-*yit* — a bit of

t

ta'-**meen** insurance

ta-"*ree*-*ban* nearly, roughly

tad-**kheen** smoking

tad-**leek** massage

taH-leel analysis

taHt under, below

taH-weel exchange (finance)

taH-wee-la detour

tak-see taxi

tak-yeef ha-wa air conditioning

takh-feeD reduction

ta-leh-ta three

talg ice, snow

ta-mal-lee always

ta-man price

ta-man-ya eight

tan-Deef cleaning

ta-qa-leed traditions

ta-reekh date, history

ta-ree-khee historical

tar-zee tailor

taS-leeH repair, mending

ta-Taw-wur development

taw-zee^c distribution

taz-ka-ra (pl.) ta-zeh-hir ticket

ta-^ceh-la! [ta-^ceh-lee!] Come on!

ta^c-leem education

teh-gir merchant, businessman

teh-nee again

teh-nee [tan-ya] another, second

ti-"eel heavy

ti-gaa-ra commerce, business

ti-kheen fat

ti-li-fohn telephone

til-li-ghrehf telegram

ti-li-viz-yohn television

til-meez (pl.) ta-lam-za pupil

tis-^ca nine

tiS-baH ^ca-la kheyr Good night.

ti^c-behn snake

tohm garlic

tuf-fehH apples

twa-litt lavatory

T

Ta"s weather

Ta"-Too-"a ashtray

Taa-lib [Taa-li-ba] (pl.) Ta-la-ba student

Taa-za fresh

Ta-ba" (pl.) 'aT-baa" dish, plate

Tab-baakh cook

Ta-beeb [Ta-bee-ba] doctor

Ta-beeb 'as-nehn dentist

Ta-bee-^cee natural

Ta-boor queue

Tab-^can of course

Ta-ra-bey-za table

Tard (pl.) Tu-rood parcel

Ta-ree" (pl.) Tu-ru" way, road

Ta-ree" ra-'ee-see highway

Ta-waa-bi^c stamps

Ta-waa-ri' emergency

Ta-weel long, tall

Tay-yaa-ra airplane

Tay-yib [Tay-yi-ba] good

Ta^cm taste

Tifl (pl.) 'aT-faal child

Tur-shee pickles

u

u-rub-ba Europe

u-rub-bee European

v

vee-za visa

vid-yo video

volt volt

w

waa-DiH obvious

waa-Tee [waT-ya] low

wa-ga^c pain

wa-Heed sole, only

wa-keel agent

wakh-ree late

wa-la Ha-ga nothing

wa-lad (pl.) 'aw-lehd boy

wal-la (in question) or?

wa-leh-kin but

wal-leh-^ca lighter

wa-ra behind

wa-ra" (pl.) 'aw-reh" leaf, paper

ward roses, flowers

war-neesh gaz-ma shoe polish

war-raa-nee back (adj.)

war-sha repair shop

waS-fa recipe

waSl receipt

wa-zeer minister

wa-Zee-fa job, post

weh-"if [wa"fa] standing

weh-Ha (pl.) wa-Heht oasis

weh-Hid [waH-da] one

weh-si^c [was-^ca] wide, loose

wi and

widn ear

wi-Hish [wiH-sha] bad, ugly

wi-sikh [wis-kha] dirty

wis-kee whiskey

wiST, wuST center

wishsh   face

wi-zaa-ra   ministry

wu-Sool   arrival

y

ya-beh-nee [ya-ba-nee-ya]   Japanese

yakht   yacht

yal-la!   Let's go!

ya-neh-yir   January

yas-meen   jasmine

yee-gee   to come

yeh-kul   to eat

yeh-khud   to take

yi-"ad-dim X li Y   to introduce, offer X to Y

yi-'ag-gar   to hire, rent

yi-'ak-kid   to confirm

yi-"dar   to be able

yi-"ees   to measure

yi-"eh-bil   to meet

yi"-fil   to close

yi"-lee   to fry

yi-"ool   to say, tell

yi-"oom   to get up

yi"-ra   to read

yi"-til   to kill

yib-"a   to become

yi-bee^c   to sell

yi-boos   to kiss

yib-ti-dee   to begin

yib-^cat   to send

yi-dakh-khan   to smoke

yi-dam-mar   to destroy

yi-dar-dish   to chat

yi-dar-ris   to teach

yi-daw-war ^ca-la   to look for

yid-baH   to slaughter, sacrifice

yid-fa^c   to pay

yid-ris   to study

yi-Day-ya^c   to waste

yi-Dee^c   to be lost (objects)

yiD-rab   to hit

yi-faa-sil   to bargain

yi-faD-Dal   to prefer

yi-fah-him   to explain

yi-fak-kar   to remind

yif-Dal   to remain

yif-ham   to understand

yif-taH   to open

yif-ti-kir   to think, remember

yif-Tar   to have breakfast

yi-fukk   to undo

yi-gah-hiz   to prepare

yig-ree   to run

yi-ghan-nee   to sing

yi-ghay-yar   to change (trans.)

yigh-sil to wash

yi-Had-did to limit

yi-Had-Dar to prepare

yi-Hal-lil to analyze

yi-Ham-maD to develop

yi-Has-sin to improve

yi-Haw-wil to exchange (money)

yiH-giz to book

yi-Hibb to like, love

yiH-la" to shave

yiH-ra" to burn

yiH-Sal to happen

yi-kal-lif to cost

yi-kal-lim to speak to

yi-kam-mil to continue

yi-kar-rar to repeat

yik-dib to lie

yik-sar to break

yik-sab to earn, win

yik-tib to write

yi-kuHH to cough

yi-khab-bee to hide (trans.)

yi-khal-laS to finish

yi-khaw-wif to frighten

yi-khay-yaT to sew

yi-knehf to be afraid

yi-kheh-ni" to quarrel with

yi-khiff to get better, recover

yikh-laS to finish (intrans.)

yikh-laᶜ to undress

yikh-taar to choose

yikh-Taf to kidnap

yil-bis to dress

yi-leh-"ee to find

yil-ghee to cancel

yi-liff to wrap

yil-ᶜab to play

yi-maw-wit to kill

yim-Dee to sign

yi-meen right (direction)

yim-kin perhaps

yim-la to fill

yim-naᶜ to forbid, prevent

yim-shee to walk, go away

yim-sik to hold, grasp

yi-naD-Daf to clean

yi-naZ-Zam to organize

yi-nehm to sleep

yin-saH to advise

yin-ti-Zir to wait

yin-zil (fi) to get off, stay (at)

yi-qar-rar to decide

yi-raa-hin to bet

yir-fid to fire, sack

yir-gaᶜ to return

yir-kab to get on, ride

yi-rooH to go

yi-rudd   to reply

yis-'al   to ask

yi-sag-gil   to record, check

yi-sakh-khan   to heat

yi-sal-lif   to lend

yi-sal-lim   to greet

yi-seeb   to leave (fr.)

yi-seh-fir   to travel, leave

yi-seh-miH   forgive

yi-seh-ʿid   to help

yis-maʿ   to hear, listen to

yi-soo"   to drive

yis-ra"   to steal

yis-ta-Ham-ma   to bathe

yis-tan-na   to wait

yis-ta-ray-yaH   to rest

yis-taʿ-mil   to use

yis-ti-lif   to borrow

yi-Sal-laH   to repair

yi-Sal-lee   to pray

yi-Saw-war   to photograph

yiS-raf   to spend, change (money)

yi-Subb   to pour

yi-shag-gaʿ   to support, encourage

yish-fee   to get better

yi-shidd   to pull

yi-shoof   to see

yish-rab   to drink

yish-raH   to explain

yish-tim   to insult

yish-ti-ree   to buy

yit-far-rag (ʿa-la)   to watch, look (at)

yit-gaw-wiz   to get married

yit-ghad-da   to have lunch

yit-ghay-yar   to change (intrans.)

yit-kal-lim   to speak, talk

yit-kheh-ni" (ma-ʿa)   to quarrel, fight (with)

yit-man-na   to hope

yit-mash-sha   to take a walk

yit-mat-taʿ (bi —)   to enjoy

yit-naf-fis   to breathe

yi-tar-gim   to translate

yit-ʿash-sha   to have dinner

yiT-Ti-Sil (bi —)   to contact

yi-waf-far   to save

yi-war-ree   to show

yi-waS-Sal   to accompany

yiw-gaʿ   to hurt

yiw-Sal   to arrive

yiw-ʿid   to promise

yi-zu" "   to push

yi-Zoor   to visit

yi-Zunn   to think

yi-ʿeesh   to live

yiʿ-mil   to do, make

yi-^coom to swim

yi^c-ti-mid (^ca-la) to depend (on)

yi^c-zim to invite

yohm (pl.) 'ay-yehm day

yoh-meyn two days

(yohm) ig-gum-^ca Friday

(yohm) il-Hadd Sunday

(yohm) il-kha-mees Thursday

(yohm) is-sabt Saturday

(yohm) it-ta-leht Tuesday

(yohm) lar-ba^c Wednesday

(yohm) li-neyn Monday

yu-"af to stop

yu-"a^c to fall

yu"-^cud to sit down

yud-khul to enter

yuH-fur to dig

yul-yoo July

yu-neh-nee [yu-neh-nee-ya] Greek

yun-yoo June

yur "uS to dance

yus-kun to live

yuT-bukh to cook

yuT-lub to ask for, order

Z

za-kee [za-kee-ya] intelligent

zab-behl garbage collector

zaw-ba-^ca sandstorm

za^c-lehn angry

zeyt oil

zeyt zay-toon olive oil

zi-beh-la garbage

zib-da butter

zi-meel (pl.) zu-ma-la colleague

zohg husband

zoh-ga wife

zohr throat

zu-hoor flowers

zu-kehm cold (noun)

Z

Zaa-biT (pl.) Zub-baaT (army) officer

Za-reef pleasant

Zarf (pl.) Zu-roof envelope

Zu-raar (pl.) Za-raa-vir button

c

^ca"l mind

^caa-Si-ma capital (city)

^caa-Til unemployed

^ca-dad number, quantity

ᶜa-dam in-nohm insomnia

ᶜa-da-sa (pl.) ᶜa-da-seht lens

ᶜa-da-sit zoom zoom lens

ᶜad-dehd meter

ᶜads lentils

ᶜaDm bone

ᶜafsh luggage, furniture

ᶜaf-wan Not at all, don't mention it.

ᶜa-ga-la wheel, bicycle

ᶜa-la on

ᶜa-la fik-ra . . . by the way . . .

ᶜa-la mah-lak! slow down!

ᶜamm (paternal) uncle

ᶜam-ma (paternal) aunt

ᶜan about (concerning)

ᶜand with (= have)

ᶜa-ra-bee [ᶜa-ra-bee-ya] Arab, Arabic

ᶜa-ra-bee-ya car

ᶜarD show (noun)

ᶜa-rees bridegroom

ᶜa-roo-sa bride

ᶜas-ka-ree (pl.) ᶜa-seh-kir soldier

ᶜa-Seer juice

ᶜaS-foor (pl.) ᶜa-Sa-feer bird

ᶜaS-ree modern

ᶜa-sha dinner

ᶜa-shehn, li-ann because

ᶜaT-laan [ᶜaT-laa-na] broken down, out of order

ᶜaT-shaan thirsty

ᶜa-wiz [ᶜaw-za] (pl.) ᶜaw-zeen want

ᶜay-yehn [ᶜay-yeh-na] ill

ᶜa-Zeem marvelous, magnificent

ᶜeed feast, festival

ᶜeed il-mi-lehd Christmas

ᶜeed mi-lehd birthday

ᶜeh-dee ordinary

ᶜeh-lam world

ᶜeh-lee high

ᶜey-la family

ᶜeyn eye

ᶜil-ba (pl.) ᶜi-lab packet, can

ᶜilm (pl.) ᶜu-loom science

ᶜil-mee scientific

ᶜi-maa-ra (pl.) ᶜi-maa-raat building, block

ᶜi-nab grapes

ᶜin-wehn address

ᶜuDw (pl.) 'aᶜ-Daa' member, organ

ᶜum-la currency

ᶜum-la Saᶜ-ba hard currency

ᶜu-zoo-ma invitation

ᶜuzr excuse (noun)

INDEX

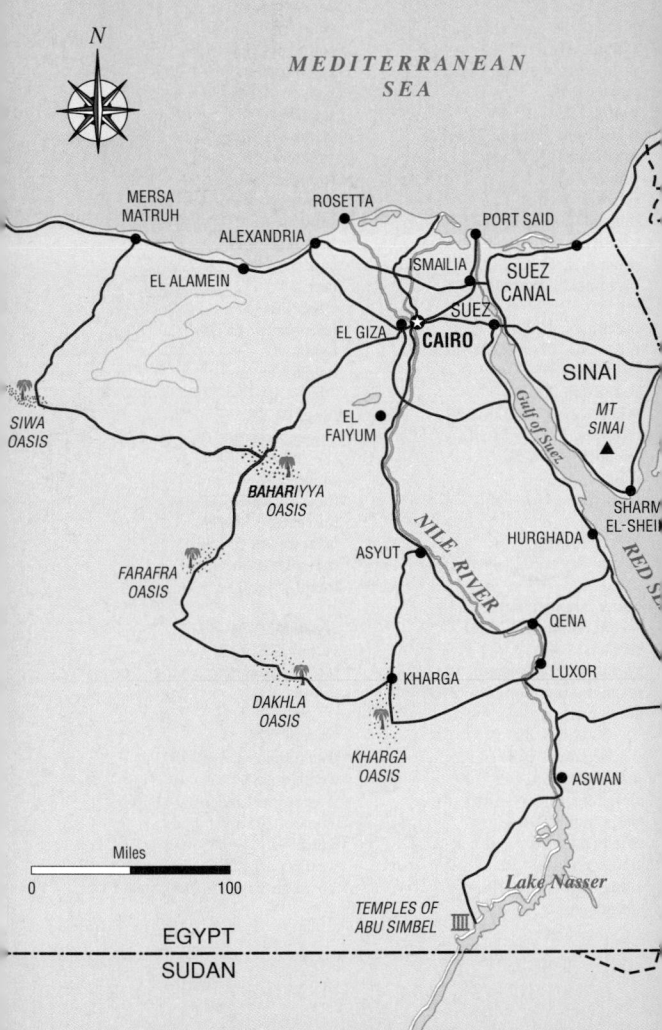